W9-CCP-345

Best Food Writing

2000

Best Food Writing 2000

EDITED BY

Holly Hughes

FOREWORD BY

Alice Waters

Marlowe & Company and
Balliett & Fitzgerald Inc.

Best Food Writing 2000

Compilation and introductions copyright © 2000 by Holly Hughes and Balliett & Fitzgerald Inc.
Foreword copyright © 2000 by Alice Waters

All rights reserved. No part of this book may be reproduced in any form without prior written permission from the publishers and the copyright owner, except by reviewers who wish to quote brief passages.

Published by
Marlowe & Company
A Division of Avalon Publishing Group Incorporated
841 Broadway
New York, NY 10003

and

Balliett & Fitzgerald Inc.
66 West Broadway, Suite 602
New York, NY 1007

Book Design: Susan Canavan
Photography: Tessa Traeger

ISBN: 1-56924-616-5

Library of Congress Card Number: 00-108323

Distributed by Publishers Group West

Printed in the United States of America

10 9 8 7 6 5 4 3 2 1

Contents

Home Cooking

Someone's in the Kitchen

Dining Around

Personal Tastes

Foreword

by Alice Waters

Eating is an art—the only art everyone can participate in. Eating educates our senses by sharpening our sensual awareness of everyday reality; it opens us up daily to the world around us. Yet of all human endeavors, the preparation, service, and consumption of food and drink may be the most difficult to write about. Only when we write about eating must we describe the *simultaneous* exercise of all five senses, finding words not just for tastes and smells, but also for such sensations as the visual ravishment of the blush on a peach, the aural thrill of a crackling fire behind a turning spit, and the tactile shock in the mouth when the delicate crunch of a deep-fried zucchini flower gives way to the creamy melting cheese inside. Only food blazes so many trails into our minds at the same time.

The writer's task is made even more difficult by food's sheer ephemerality, compared to the other performing arts (and cooking is nothing if not a performing art). Take music, for example: Recording technology allows actual performances to be faithfully reproduced, and musical notation and an established technical vocabulary permit us to study music, perform it, and talk about it with an exactitude that even the best-written food writing simply cannot provide. Nothing in any recipe approaches the precision of the statement that a piece of music is in, say, C major.

Nor does a fine meal closely resemble a work of visual art. An actual masterwork, once painted, can hang on a wall and be apprehended again and again; a *chef d'oeuvre* of culinary art, on the other hand, is irreplaceable—once consumed, it is gone forever. No mere description can bring it back, nor can any recipe fully reconstruct the complex circumstances of its invention. Timing, technique, and tools vary greatly every time that recipe is executed; raw materials, even more. No dish worth the making will ever taste exactly the same twice.

And yet we need to write about food and talk about it precisely *because* food is never the same. The world is neither permanent nor predictable: There's no better place to learn such a hard lesson than in the kitchen, where we must reevaluate our behavior every single day. We head down this path as best we can, and we need other people's perceptions to help us get to where we're going. This is the never-ending process we go through at my restaurant, where we never repeat a menu; We are constantly fine-tuning our senses, experiencing the food for what it is *right now,* and making the best meal from it that we can.

We will always need good food writing to feed this process, because knowledge is always preferable to ignorance, and there is much to learn. An unexamined life is no more worth living in the kitchen than anywhere else, so it is good to know that philosophical consolations can be found in cookbooks as well as in Camus.

When we write about food, we attempt to describe the indescribable and slow the passage of time by fixing in memory our most elusive experiences. We may try to write about food the way M.F.K. Fisher did, as another way of writing about love; or we may try to write as Richard Olney did, to give voice to our conscience, which will tell us that the way we eat is inseparable from the way we live—and how wisely and well he ate! We may be driven to share recipes, to research their history, or to push them in what we imagine to be a new direction. And in the writing, we may also manage not only to be didactic, but to amuse as well, as Elizabeth David did. The food-obsessed often seem to understand intuitively, as she did, that knowledge is not only power, it is also *fun*.

It was Elizabeth David's food writing, in fact, that changed my own life forever. I was introduced to her books not long after I returned from the college year in France that had first opened up my senses to the pleasures of the table. Good writing floods the world with possibility, and as I read her fresh and pure prose, I began to see before me a lifetime of sharing these pleasures with others. The recipes were the least of it, although they, too, are lodged in my memory as lucid models of the genre. (Today no American cookbook editor would allow them to stand as written. Unmeasured quantities? Out of the question! Yet we cook best when we cook the least slavishly.) On the blank canvas of my hungry imagination, primed in France, she painted unforgettable scenes: the spectacular market near the Rialto in Venice, the fish market in Genoa, the great covered marketplace of Nancy, the airy dining room of the Hotel de la Poste at Duclair, a *café routier* outside Bourg-en-Bresse. . . . These visions have molded my life and my career for the better, as I have strived to cook and eat and live in their spirit. And that is what the best food writing is for.

Introduction

by Holly Hughes

This first volume of *Best Food Writing* is a book for readers who love to eat, for cooks who love to read, and for diners who love to cook and read and shop and think about food. There's no need to keep it in the kitchen—if anything, I imagine readers curling up with it in bed at night, when the dishes are done, the grocery stores closed, the restaurants shuttered and dark.

A really great piece of food writing can make you crave the food you're reading about—or, even better, can make you feel as satisfied as if you've just eaten, and eaten well. That's what I've searched for, in countless cookbooks and magazines and newspapers and websites and newsletters. The style may be irreverent, rapturous, thoughtful, funny, opinionated, or finely-wrought, but the bottom line is the quality of the writing—it has to work as great prose.

In the process of combing through all this material, I realized that two of the most common types of food writing—the recipe piece and the restaurant review—would end up being underrepresented in this collection. Many perfectly interesting recipes are so focused on the technical cooking information that elegant prose style is almost beside the point; the recipes you'll find here were either essential to the point of the accompanying story, or were themselves written with some sort of extra pizzazz. (Often I've also chosen to reprint a magazine or newspaper piece and not include companion recipes.) As for restaurant reviews, I found surprisingly few which could survive divorced from context. Not knowing the writers' neighborhoods, their communities' dining scene and locally famous chefs, and having no expectation of ever needing to know whether or not to eat there, for me robbed most reviews of their power. The few reviews you'll find here achieved something more than a yea-or-nay recommendation, and gave some insight into why people choose to eat out—and where they like to eat when they do. These reviews deliver their own intrinsic pleasure, and for that I happily included them.

What is left? Profiles of people who cook, be they four-star chefs or humble home cooks; culinary memoirs; essays on trends and techniques; insightful reportage; first-person opinion pieces; travel essays; and social history. As it turned out, I had more to choose from than I expected when I first started.

Some of the authors are names you already know; others are newer voices who deserve to be more widely known. Some are master technicians, who transmit a precise special knowledge about cooking; others share their sensual experience of food— the taste, the smell, the texture, the look of a dish or a whole meal. Others are philosophers, musing over what food means to them, and why. After reading all this great writing from all these different writers, I found myself approaching food differently. I suddenly took more pleasure in cooking; I had new perceptions about the restaurants I ate in; I browsed more avidly through food shops. I started to pay more attention to sharpening my knives, to throwing out jars of stale herbs, to tempting my children to try new foods. I stopped ordering take-out. I asked my mother to write down some family recipes I remembered from my childhood. I sincerely hope that reading this volume will reawaken the pleasure you take from food, too.

Many people helped me navigate this vast and bewildering territory. I'd like to thank Nach Waxman, proprietor of the wonderful Manhattan cooks' bookstore, Kitchen Arts and Letters; thanks are also due to Pam Kaufman at *Food & Wine,* Shoshanna Goldberg at *Saveur,* Laura Dyer at *Bon Appetit,* and most especially Kemp Minifie at *Gourmet.* And apologies in advance to those wonderful food writers whose work somehow escaped me. Send me your best new pieces for the 2001 edition; I'm already hungry to read them.

—Holly Hughes

Stocking
the
Larder

The Cook and the Gardener

by Amanda Hesser

from *The Cook and the Gardener*

During a year in Burgundy as in-house cook at Anne Willan's famous cooking school, École de Cuisine La Varenne, Amanda Hesser forged a delicate relationship with M. Milbert, the château gardener. In her captivating cookbook/memoir, she delineates the often roundabout routes by which the fruits of the garden made their way to the kitchen.

When I reached the garden gate, I could see him bent over the rows of radishes he told me weren't yet ready. He seemed to be poking at them. I figured he was digging at the soil around them to give them more room to grow (a technique he had shown me earlier). He was apparently very involved in what he was doing, because he didn't notice me. As I got closer I could see he wasn't poking at all. He was picking the radishes and putting them right into his pockets—for lunch, of course. I was very close when he noticed me, and he jumped to attention like a kid caught with his hand in the cookie jar. I jumped back, too. But I didn't want to anger him by having him think I was snooping on him, so I immediately presented him with the gourd. He slyly dropped the radishes from behind his back onto the soil while we talked, and he pretended to be very interested in the splintery mess of gourd I held in my hand. I didn't want to torment him too long, so we discussed, superficially, plot selection for the gourds. Then I left, briskly. (In the kitchen we didn't see that first crop of radishes for another week, after they had lost their sweetness and had turned spicy from the summer heat. Thankfully, he was more generous with the next crop.)

Throughout the month Monsieur Milbert was busy both in the garden and on the château grounds, cutting the grass with his tractor and spending a lot of time tilling the unplanted plots of soil—working up an appetite for those radishes, I suppose. Again and again he went over the soil. He used two tillers, so I assumed they did different jobs. I tried to sound thoughtfully inquisitive one day when I asked him the difference between them. And he tried to conceal his grin, dragging out his answer: "Well . . . one is big . . . and the other one is smaller."

Lessons like that steered me toward the kitchen. My realm. And the kitchen was a comfortable place to be in June. The stone floor kept it cool, as did the presence of fresh fruits and vegetables. I was amazed by how little you needed to work on summer produce to reveal its freshness and make beautiful, satisfying meals. The labor lay in the washing and trimming. The hearts of the Bibb lettuces Monsieur Milbert brought every morning were so silky and sweet, all I had to do was wash them and dress them lightly with a little olive or walnut oil and salt. In fact, all the lettuces were so outrageously good—sweet and soft—that they rarely escaped our table. I often combined the mix of lettuces we had with chive flowers. I would pinch the lavender-colored flower buds between my fingers to separate them into cylindrical petals, which scattered an oniony scent through the salad.

Peas and carrots I dipped in boiling water, then rolled in butter in a warm pan. I boiled artichokes and made simple dipping sauces for them, I made sweet-pastry tart shells and filled them with fresh berries and cream.

The first cherries I picked were bland and watery, like the weather under which they had developed that spring. Just a week passed, though, and they, too, joined the ranks of gorgeous produce passing through the kitchen. I used bowls of loose raspberries, cherries, and even radishes to keep hungry diners amused and stimulated. People will linger at a table when bowls of fruit are passed around at the end of a meal. I think there is an instinctive need to finish the fruit before getting up and moving on. Of course, it's a good excuse to put off washing dishes, too.

Until this month I had spent a lot of time observing the garden, getting to know Monsieur Milbert but making sure I didn't interfere. I watched how he worked, occasionally giving a hand with projects. This month was marked almost as much by growth in the garden as by growth in our friendship. Monsieur Milbert was no longer just tolerating me. I learned I could talk to him when he was planting or picking or trimming—just not when he was hoeing. When Madame was very sick over the winter, he spent hours hoeing, bent over and clawing at the hard ground beneath him like the pain that was clawing at him. When his hoe was in hand, it was his time, his space, his solace.

He began asking me when his *"petite jardinière"* was going to pick those raspberries that were weighing down the bushes. The first time he asked, I failed terribly. I told him I would get up early the next day so I could pick them while it was cool. But I woke up late the next day—8:00—and was greeted by pans full of raspberries on the counter. I went to the garden and sheepishly apologized. Monsieur Milbert was well into his watering of the tomatoes, zucchini, and peas. He smiled and tapped me on the head. "What were you doing? I had to do your job! Those things are small, eh? A pain to pick. *Insupportable!"* (He never let me forget it. From time to time, he would refer to me as *"la jardinière qui dort,"* the gardener who sleeps.)

From then on, I harvested raspberries often and in large amounts. There were about 40 canes, maybe more. Harvesting them was a science. The berries on the tip of a branch always ripen first, and the others ripen in alternating order, receding on the cane. Perhaps due to their exposure to the sun. Raspberries also feel the effects of weather changes. Rain as close as the day before picking will provide fat berries with a pale flavor; a sunny afternoon, sweetness and intense flavor. The best, most consistently sweet berries rest under the leaves where the sunlight dapples. There they get an even share of sun, rain, wind, shade, and protection. It is also helpful to know that a raspberry cane likes to be picked. Raspberries have the ability to multiply like bees in a hive: The more you take away, the faster and fuller the berries seem to grow.

Before long, I knew what to expect from each shape of berry in the row. There were those that reminded me of the uniform berries we buy in plastic boxes, perfect in shape but bland; small soft buttons that were sweet; and large mutant raspberries with a rich winy taste (they rotted the soonest). The best were the squat berries with supple, overgrown cells. They had a velvety fuzz all over their swollen cells that collapsed on your tongue.

With June's maturation came the glint of depression that followed. I almost didn't want the cherries to redden. I liked their waxy, firm exteriors. I felt overwhelmed by the burgeoning growth around me, as if life were passing too quickly—even if it was just the life of a pea plant. I wondered if Monsieur Milbert felt the same this time of year, or if he was just too busy to worry about it. He kept at his pace, like the tortoise who won the race. (And I was definitely the hare. One day I was fixated on raspberries, the next I ran around trying to take mental notes on all the growth in the garden, the next I was lost in jelly making . . . .) He did, however, develop new patterns, spending the early-morning hours watering and the late morning sowing, ensuring future growth. He planted the seeds from the gourd, the squashes, and the zucchini. They made quick progress. The garden had a pulse. Fruits, vegetables, and herbs simply moved forward.

So did the weeds. For every inch of growth the vegetables were making that June, I think the weeds advanced two. They ravaged the garden like a wildfire. Monsieur Milbert would pass over clumps of them unfazed, then he would clean them out in spurts to feed to his rabbits. He razed their stalks, making "good" and "bad" piles for them, just as he did with the pea plants, cutting them just at the root, dropping the last peas (the first planting) into a bucket and bundling up the shoots and greens for his rabbits.

One afternoon, while we were bending over the peas to survey the damage done by the mice, he grabbed a weed and yanked it from the ground angrily. "What's wrong?" I asked.

"You see this?" he growled, pinching a tiny pink flower from the weed. "It can kill the rabbits. It's deadly. I can't even grow safe weeds in this garden." He continued, getting more cross: *"Les mauvaises herbes prennent tous!! Ah, c'est une saloperle! Oui."* The weeds are taking over!! Ah, it's a filthy mess! Yes. Well, his weeds may not be safe for his rabbits, but they are pretty. I grew to like the weeds and all their chaos.

Late June yielded a crowded, cluttered mess of beauty. It was very Milbertesque, although I'm not sure he knew it. Perhaps the garden didn't seem very French in appearance, but it was. Beneath the clutter was a decided order and arrangement to all the rows, trees, and shrubs that spattered across Monsieur Milbert's canvas. Sorrel, parsley, and spinach formed definitive sections in the large beds; the currant bushes alternated colors along a path; the peach trees slouched lightly, shading the sage in the corner and protecting the young cabbages from the unforgiving summer sun.

I looked around the garden and saw, at various stages of growth, nearly all the foods that would feed us through the year. The activity in the garden was staggered harmoniously. While harvesting proceeded at a brisk tempo, some plants were just germinating, others dying. Frail leeks and carrot greens dotted several rows. The pears were still tight knots on their branches, mere children compared to the asparagus which were up to my shoulders, looking like needleless pine trees on their way to seed.

Some herbs, like sage, produced flowers, which Monsieur Milbert ignored. He refused to trim off the flower heads, which any gardening book will tell you to do. This had clearly caused a rift between gardening and cooking bands at the château. But he could care less that trimming back the herbs would save their flavor. The flowers added color and beauty to his world, so he left them.

June is a golden month for the gooseberries and currants. The currants first sprinted to full size before they rounded that final corner and turned red, white, and deep purple. The gooseberries took a different route: They grew in color from the very beginning, ballooning and softening with age. The raspberries, cherries, and strawberries also ripened in force.

The fruits didn't begin to stockpile until the end of the month. By then it was clear that summer, with all of its voluptuousness, had overtaken us. Although the mornings were still crisp, the freshness and innocence of spring was gone. June and all its fervent life had filled the sparse garden little by little. . . .

• • •

Fried Zucchini Flowers Stuffed with Goat's Milk Cheese, Tarragon, and Parsley

There are two types of gardeners: those who grow too much zucchini year after year and those who do not. Hasn't everyone, at one point or another, been harassed by a zucchini grower trying to pawn off his surplus? Doubtless, he gives you the biggest, fattest, most tasteless ones, and sheer guilt causes you to salvage them by baking countless loaves of zucchini bread, which you proceed to push on visitors and neighbors . . . and so begins the cycle.

Fortunately, Monsieur Milbert is not one of the pushers. He is a hoarder. And if I didn't nag him so often for more zucchini, he would let a few go to seed to guarantee supply for next year. I try to request zucchini frequently so he is forced to give me small young zucchini. When he resists I sometimes even lie and tell him *les patrons* (my bosses) made a special request. This is a cheap but necessary tactic. And I almost had to resort to it for the zucchini flowers.

This was the first year Monsieur Milbert ever parted with his zucchini flowers. The first few days I put *fleurs de courge* (zucchini flowers) on my list, he conveniently ignored the request altogether. Determined as I was to get them before they wilted, I confronted him. He paused and then slowly knit his right brow, causing me much internal pain and angst. Then he headed toward the garden.

I don't think he ever understood why I wanted to eat the shriveled orange flowers hanging over the beefy zucchini, but he showed me how to pick the flowers anyway. We squatted together over the broad plant while Monsieur Milbert taught me the birds and bees of zucchini mating, pointing first to a female flower that had a short bulb backing its flower, then to the male flowers, which do not grow zucchini but merely bloom forth from a thin, prickly lime-colored stem. These, he explained, were the ones that should be cut. *"Les femelles—Jamais!!"* (The females—Never!!)

The males grow on the end of a long stem and are best if cut off close to the ground so the life remaining in the stem will help them make it back to the kitchen for cooking. After working with these for awhile, always fresh from a garden, I have no idea how grocers are able to keep them alive for so long in stores. I find they tighten up, die, and dry almost instantly.

I later learned that, in contrast to Monsieur Milbert's opinion, harvesting some of the female flowers is actually a good idea if you wish to curtail an overload of zucchini. Alternate harvesting zucchini and female flowers, and the zucchini will mature at a pace you can deal with.

This recipe has been influenced by many cultures. It was taught to me by Hiro, a Japanese chef with whom I cooked in Maleo, Italy. He combined the cooking of his homeland with French training and Italian flair to make these neatly stuffed and fried, fresh-tasting zucchini flowers: a sort of tempura meets *la campagna* tempered with chèvre. Serve alone as an appetizer, or on top of greens dressed with good olive oil and seasoned with coarse salt.

Serves 4

12 zucchini flowers
4 ounces goat's milk cheese (needs to be fresh, tangy, and slightly cakey in consistency)
1 tablespoon chopped tarragon leaves (about 2 branches)
1 tablespoon chopped flat-leaf parsley leaves (3 sprigs)
1 clove garlic, crushed and chopped
4–5 tablespoons all-purpose flour
Coarse or kosher salt
Freshly ground black pepper
Vegetable oil
1 slice bread (optional, if you do not have a candy thermometer)

1. If the zucchini flowers have stems, trim them to 1 inch.

2. In a small bowl use a fork to mix the cheese, tarragon, parsley, and garlic. Use your hands to shape the mixture into tight balls the size of marbles (about 1 teaspoon each). Carefully open the flower petals and push a ball of cheese firmly into the base of each flower cavity. This helps them stay together during cooking.

3. Sift the flour in small additions over ½ cup of water in a small bowl, whisking after each addition, until the batter resembles thick cream. You do not want it to be too thick or it will mask the bright colors of the flower petals when they are fried. Season the batter well with salt and pepper.

4. Fill a medium heavy-based sauté pan, large enough to fit half the stuffed flowers, to a depth of ¾ inch with vegetable oil and heat slowly. To test the oil for readiness, add a small bread cube to the hot oil. It should brown in 30 seconds. Or, use a candy thermometer. The oil is ready when the temperature registers 350°F. Adjust the heat accordingly to maintain this temperature, and test after each batch of zucchini flowers is fried so the temperature and cooking times are consistent.

5. Put several layers of paper towels on a plate and have it ready by the stove. Then, holding the flower stems, dip the flowers into the batter, holding them up to drain for 2 to 3 seconds before adding them to the hot oil. Fry for 3 to 5 minutes, until browned on both sides, using a slotted spoon to remove them to the paper towels. Fry them in two batches. Serve hot.

6. If you are serving them on salad or with some other accompaniment, it should be ready before you begin frying the zucchini flowers. They do not hold well once cooked. . . .

Tomato Jelly

Several times during the summer I had to contend with an avalanche of fruits or vegetables. One time, late in August, it was tomatoes. And Madame Maria, the housekeeper, came to the rescue by teaching me this recipe.

It was a Monday morning, and Maria was in one of her naughty moods, poking fun at my screwy hair and tired eyes while I got coffee. To change the subject, I asked her about her tomato dessert, one of the many legends I had caught wind of. She was always coming into the kitchen when I was cooking to brag about her own cooking, implying that mine and any French cooking was, of course, inferior. (If it were anyone else, I might have put up a fight, but Maria seemed to hassle the people she liked. I took her behavior as a compliment.)

Her eyes got squinty and glassy, creased by her smile. *"Oui! C'est une confiture!"*, she barked at me with her hard Portuguese-accented syllables. I did manage to get out a "Can you explain to me?" She replied, *"Oui, c'est simple. . ."* and off she went. If only I had a franc for every time she said this before teaching me something—how to peel beans, clean a floor, live life. But she wasn't being her normal sly self. She was about to share a recipe she had made countless times for her children to spread with butter on their morning baguettes.

And so we began, she giving me a few instructions, then running off to scrub some bathrooms or change the laundry and then sneaking back to be sure I was peeling the tomatoes correctly or stirring with enough vigor. The jelly turned out beautifully, a rich red, bright and racy like the colors of her floral housedresses.

Makes 4 ½ pints

Special Equipment: Food processor

Proportions:
1 quart tomato juice (about 6 ½ pounds of tomatoes should yield 1 quart of juice—do not use canned)
3 cups sugar
1 cup water

1. Purée the tomatoes in a food processor, in batches if necessary. Pass the pulp through a sieve, pressing with the rounded side of a ladle or a wooden spoon to extract as much juice as possible. Measure out 1 quart of the juice.

2. Using the above proportions, figure out how much sugar and water you need and combine them (not with the tomato juice) in a pot twice the volume. Heat the pot, dissolving the sugar to make a syrup, and bring the syrup to a boil. Boil to string stage (240°F on a jelly thermometer). You can test this by using a spoon to drop a little syrup in ice water. Dip your fingers in the ice water and take a small bit of syrup off the spoon. Quickly press it between your index finger and thumb, then pull them apart. If a thread of sugar, or *ficelle*, as Maria calls it, forms, the sugar is ready. Maria simply licked her thick fingers, stuck them in the hot sugar, tested for the *ficelles*, and then smacked her fingers against her thigh—to kill the pain, I suppose. I wouldn't recommend this method.

3. When the sugar reaches 240°F, take the pot off the heat, pour in the tomato juice, and stir quickly to dissolve the sugar lumps that form. Return the pot to the stove and keep stirring with the pot over high heat, until it reaches jell stage (220°F), 20 to 25 minutes. Do pay careful attention because this jelly will rise up in the pot and will need constant knocking down by stirring with a wooden spoon.

4. As it cooks, the syrup progresses from a pale peachy color to a russet red. As time passes the color darkens more rapidly, turning this russet red just at jell point. Nearing this crucial point, you will also begin to hear the snap and crackle of air bubbles breaking at the surface and popping against the thick syrup. This means you're almost there. If you wish to test the jell point, pull the pot off the heat. Spoon a little jelly onto a plate to see if it sets up in a minute or two.

5. When ready, pour into sterilized jars. The jelly, curiously, does not set up clear like other jellies but is a solid red that is dotted

with a fine-grained texture. As a result, pouring it into jars rather than ladling does not change its finished appearance.
6. Process the jars in a boiling-water bath for 10 minutes.

Serving suggestion: In a restaurant I once ate tomato jelly spread on peppered flatbread with a baked goat-cheese *crottin*. It was a surprisingly good combination—sweet, tart, peppery, and yeasty.

The Smoky Trail to a Great Bacon

by R. W. Apple Jr.
from *The New York Times*

In 1999, Pulitzer Prize–winning *New York Times* journalist R. W. Apple Jr. acquired a new beat— the food scene—which he took to with gusto. Apple's lively, wide- ranging articles on food sources around the world prove that a talented writer can write superbly about anything he loves.

S in is in, gastronomically speaking. Which is why I found myself pulling up to Nueske's Hillcrest Farm, about 65 miles west of Green Bay, Wisconsin, at midmorning one crystalline day in January, with the car's digital thermometer stuck at 5 implacable degrees below zero.

I was there in pursuit of postgraduate studies in bacon.

Chefs everywhere are reaching for real bacon, with its deep, smoky flavor, to jump-start their oyster stews and their terrines, their collard greens and their roasted birds. The bacon cheese-burger has turned into a fast-food icon (Burger King alone buys more than five billion pounds of bacon a year), and the high-protein, sugar-busting diet faddists positively applaud bacon binges. Fatty, allegedly artery-clogging bacon, which a few years ago stood at the head of the diet cops' hate list, is suddenly back in fashion.

I love bacon. Sizzle! Pop! My mother used to insist on Rath's, which was packed, as I recall, in Waterloo, Iowa, but Rath's is no more. What most supermarkets sell these days is more liquid than solid, a consequence of injecting curing agents into the meat with needles to speed the process.

It shrivels pitifully in the skillet and tastes mostly of chemicals. It doesn't even have the alluring aromas of the bacon of my childhood.

When Nueske's bacon started showing up in a few stores in Washington, where I live, I was startled. We found it first at the Safeway on Wisconsin Avenue (known to Beltway types as the Social Safeway) and then, to our astonishment, at the little Korean-owned market on our street corner in Georgetown. The sweet, thick slices held their shape as they crackled on the stove. They tasted pure, porky and intensely smoky, in the Midwestern style. Best of all, they didn't pucker your mouth with saltiness.

I don't want to go whole hog here, but Nueske's struck me as the beluga of bacon, the Rolls-Royce of rashers. It makes a memorable B.L.T., one of the supreme inventions of American shortorder cookery, and its crunchiness provides an ideal counterpoint to the richness of calf's liver or shad roe. It was invented, or might have been, for breakfast—bacon and eggs, which my wife, Betsey, allows me (and herself) a morning or two a month. It is one of those food products, I have discovered, that is known to and cherished by chefs across the country, if not to most home cooks—a product of a fine rural smokehouse, a modern place using old-fashioned methods that turns out bacon worth throwing caution to the winds for, at least once in a while.

This is bacon that cries out, now that I think of it, for a revival of those half-forgotten comfort foods of the 1950's like cheese dreams (open-faced grilled cheese sandwiches with slices of tomato and crisscrossed bacon slices on top) and traditional English savories like angels on horseback (oysters wrapped in strips of bacon, skewered with toothpicks and then broiled) or devils on horseback (in which the oysters are supplanted by pitted prunes).

There are other high-quality American bacons on the market, smoked with hickory or corncobs, flavored with red pepper or molasses or even cinnamon. Some are sweeter, some saltier. They come from the Ozarks, from New England and from the upper South—mainly Kentucky, North Carolina, Tennessee and Virginia. An enterprising California mail-order operative named Dan Philips has started a Bacon of the Month Club: a pound or so of a different bacon each month for $140 a year (through the Grateful Palate, 888/472-5283, or on the Web at www.gratefulpalate.com). None of them, rest assured, bear any resemblance to the wan, watery product that dominates the supermarket shelves.

When I bring home the bacon these days, it's usually Nueske's, so I thought I'd better try to find out why it tastes the way it does.

Two Nueske brothers, Robert D., 52, and James A., 50, run the place. Their great-grandparents, Jim told me, came to Wisconsin from Prussia in 1882, settling near Wittenberg, a village named for the city in Germany where Martin Luther nailed his 95 Theses to the door of the castle church, touching off the Reformation. Like all the other immigrants hereabouts, they brought spicing and curing formulas with them, and quickly built a smokehouse.

But it was not until the Depression that R. C. Nueske, the brothers' father, started marketing bacon, sausages, hams and smoked turkeys, peddling them from a panel truck at the little resorts across northern Wisconsin. And it was not until the present generation—and Jim Nueske's devilishly effective country-boy salesmanship—that the Nueske brand (pronounced NOO-ski) spread across the nation.

Hillcrest Farm raises no pigs of its own. This is dairy country. Instead, it buys pork bellies, the fatty flaps that lie across the pig's ribs, from hogs raised to its specifications in Iowa, North Dakota, South Dakota and Canada. But not in Wisconsin.

"Here in Wisconsin," said Jim Nueske, who was dressed in a baseball cap and a work shirt emblazoned with Green Bay Packers logos, "we're meatheads among cheeseheads."

The hogs whose bellies are bound for Nueske are fed a larger-than-normal percentage of barley, along with corn, and are slaughtered at certain weights, Mr. Nueske explained, to minimize fattiness without destroying the taste. The brine in which the bellies are soaked is simple—sugar, as little salt as possible and several sodium compounds, among them sodium nitrite, which are included as preservatives and flavorings. Sodium nitrite content is regulated by the Agriculture Department, and Nueske bacon contains only 4 percent of the permitted maximum. It could be eliminated altogether, which might be marginally healthier, but nitrites provide some of the characteristic bacon flavor, and the only nitrite-free bacon I have sampled tasted more like roast pork.

The slabs of bacon spend about 24 hours in the brine, as much as 1,800 pounds to each yellow plastic vat. But the key to the flavor and consistency of Nueske bacon, unlike some country bacons, which are cured with dry rubs, lies in the smokehouse and not in the curing tanks.

Most bacon is smoked in stainless-steel machines, fired with sawdust, that do the job in four to six hours; Nueske uses 16 steel-lined concrete-block smokehouses, heated by open fires of applewood logs, and keeps the meat over the coals 20 to 24 hours. The bacon goes in on special racks fitted with wheels, 80 sides at a time, about 16,000 pounds a day. It emerges lean and cordovan-colored, ready to be hand-trimmed and then machine-sliced, roughly 18 one-eighth inch slices to a pound.

"The point is to render most of the fat here and not in the frying pan," Mr. Nueske said as he led me on a tour of the plant. "For that, and for maximum flavor, you have to finish at very high temperatures."

A pound of most run-of-the-mill raw bacon produces as little as a quarter to a third of a pound of cooked bacon; Nueske shoots for about three-quarters of a pound, he said.

While bacon consumption in restaurants is rising, consumption in American homes is still dropping. Harry Balzer of the NPD Group, a market research firm near Chicago, said 47 percent of all Americans cooked bacon at home in 1984, but only 34 percent did so in 1999. Households that use it treat it as restaurants do, more as a taste-enhancing ingredient than as an everyday breakfast meat.

Jim Nueske is no exception.

"I think mostly Kellogg's in the morning," he said. "Bacon and eggs we save mostly for the weekends."

The boom in bacon sales has come from its use in sandwiches, salads, soup, pasta dishes and the like, which put a premium, of course, on flavor. That has opened a lot of doors for Mr. Nueske, starting with grocers and restaurateurs in Milwaukee and Minneapolis in the late 1970's.

"I'm selling a flavoring, not bacon as such," he told me. "That's my sales technique. I drop a pound of bacon off, ask the guy to try it. I don't mention price—half the time I don't know the current price—and tell them I'll be back to check with them in a week. Then I have them."

Almost from the start, he hooked enough customers that 20 years ago the Nueske brothers and their families mortgaged their houses, their cars and their weekend cottages to build a big new smoking plant. "I'm going to give you an opportunity to fail," their cheerful banker told them.

Now, from this little town of 1,140 people, Nueske bacon is shipped to restaurants like the Mansion on Turtle Creek in Dallas, Balthazar and An American Place in New York, Commander's

Palace in New Orleans, Clio and Olives in Boston, and Pinot in Los Angeles. It goes into everything from quiche Lorraine to wine-based sauces for eggs and poultry.

Availability through retail channels is spotty, and in the New York area, so far nonexistent. But direct-mail shipments, based until three years ago in a garage, have taken off, and Nueske is now sending out a million catalogs four times a year. Available either in standard slices, 18 to a pound, or thin-sliced, 24 to a pound, bacon costs $19.95 for two pounds, or $20.95 coated with cracked pepper. (Orders can be placed by calling a 24-hour number, 800/392-2266, or at www.nueske.com)

It's a far cry from the old days.

"There's this woman who's worked for us for years," Mr. Nueske said over a lunchtime B.L.T. at Al & Mary's cafe at Wittenberg's main (and only) crossroads. "She's 85 now, still going strong. Anyway, 25 years ago, she and I were the shipping department. I wrapped and she labeled. Our main retail outlet was this place. They'd let us put some bacon in their soft-drinks cooler, and when people ordered a B.L.T. or a bacon cheeseburger and asked where they could get that bacon, why, they'd just point across the room.

"Now, people order the stuff from Japan and Russia and we have 120 people working for us. Who would have thought bacon could do that?"

Corn in
the USA

by Warren Schultz
from *Saveur*

An old adage urges writers to write about what they know best. We all know about food, of course, and most of us have special memories of that quintessentially American food, sweet corn on the cob. But Warren Schultz *really* knows corn, and his recollections of summers in a cornfield richly bring the season home.

W hen my brothers and I were kids on the family farm in Colonie, near Albany in upstate New York, we used to spend most of our summer days picking corn under the hot sun—feeling our sweat sting the hundreds of scratches that the sharp leaves left on our arms. We grew about a dozen varieties of old-fashioned sweet corn, the type whose sugars start diminishing as soon as the ear is picked, and it was our job to harvest several times a day so that the ears we sold would be as fresh and sweet as possible. The three of us would fill dozens of big burlap bags and baskets, load them on the tractor, and haul them to the farm stand. I'd jump at the chance to drive, to roar down the road astride that International Harvester, bringing in the corn—shirttails flapping in the wind, hair slicked back with sweat.

Around five o'clock in the afternoon, regular customers would start lining up at the stand. They knew we came in with the last picking then—the only one of the day's deliveries that had a scheduled time. This not only was convenient for folks on their way home from work, but also helped them estimate how many minutes of the corn's sweetness they had left before they'd be able to get their teeth into an ear or two. Sometimes they'd hear us driving down the road, and we'd see them craning their necks, pointing, nudging each other. Sometimes—I swear—they'd even cheer as we turned, gravel flying, into the parking lot (a little faster than necessary, I admit). The customers would crowd around the tractor, grabbing the corn as we unloaded the harvest, pulling back the husks to inspect the ears. It was easy to see how the venerable heirloom corn "Howling Mob" got its name.

When corn season started, in mid- to late July, we were always just as excited about it as the customers were. It was what we had been waiting for since the first seed was dropped into the spring soil months earlier. It was what all that painstaking feeding, weeding, and watering had been for. (If you think watering is a pleasant pastime, try hauling 30-foot-long metal pipes into a cornfield in 90-degree heat, hooking them up to sprinklers, and then moving them every few hours to reach a different part of the field.)

No matter how much we sweated over the harvest, though, we never resented the corn. Other crops were different. When tomatoes flooded the market in late summer and prices got too low for us to bother picking them, we'd breathe a sigh of relief; you had to stoop to gather tomatoes, and there were always so damn many of them. When frost shriveled the melons on the vine, we'd rejoice; they were heavy to lug, especially by the bushelful. But we always tried to coax one more day out of corn season. It was easy picking and pleased the customers like no other crop we sold—and we never, ever grew tired of the way it tasted.

For about two months we'd pick every day, all day, rain or shine, and when we brought in the last load of the day, we'd take a turn behind the corn counter to fill in for Mom. She'd gather up a dozen ears, maybe two, and start husking them for dinner. More often than not, she'd also husk an ear for our farm cat, the corn-loving Montana, who spent most afternoons dozing on the counter. Montana would eagerly gnaw the kernels off an entire ear of corn right where she sat. This display was always a crowd pleaser and a great testimonial for our corn—so creamy even cats loved it!

Corn clarified our lives in those days. It was the hub around which we revolved. We'd begin picking early in the morning, while the stalks were still wet with dew. That would be the first of six or eight or ten trips to the fields. When we weren't picking corn, we were thinking or talking about it. Would the next planting ripen on time? Which field needed watering next? Why was it that the "Sweet Sue" or "NK-199" was so much better this year than last? Then, at the end of the day, we'd eat fresh sweet corn, steaming on a platter at the center of the table; after all that work, those ears seemed like a reward. And then, without fail, someone would razz Dad for eating corn the "wrong" way—he liked to chew around the ear instead of across it. It's no wonder that when I closed my eyes at night, I would see ears of corn floating in front of my face.

Corn defined our farm. It separated us from those tailgate vegetable stands that cropped up in midsummer, offering zucchini and tomatoes but no corn—because their proprietors didn't have the land. Corn needs space. It needs sprawling fields and open skies full of sunshine. That's what we tasted in each kernel—the product of vast green fields capturing and working the sun's energy, converting the sunshine into sugar. Eating corn was the closest we could ever come to tasting the flavor of strong summer sunlight. Somehow that flavor seemed connected to corn's ephemeral nature—to the fact that the second those ears were ripped from the stalk, their sugar started to disappear. Would our craving for corn on the cob have been as fervent if the ears had held their sweetness, in the stolid, reliable way carrots do? I don't think so.

Now, of course, the nature of sweet corn has radically changed. More than forty years ago, corn breeders began tinkering with the plant's genetic mechanisms to prolong the sweet moment, and in the early 1960s announced the arrival of supersweet varieties that would retain their sucrose for days, even a week, in the refrigerator. There was only one problem: These varieties had a saccharin-like sweetness that didn't really taste like corn. Yes, they stayed sweet in storage, but in the same way that Diet Coke stays sweet in the can. The corn lost something when it gained its sweet staying power. It lost its depth of flavor, its essential corn-ness. We never grew supersweet corn on our farm. Today, though, farmers grow it and ship it to supermarkets by the ton—where it winds up on counters beside hard, cardboard-tasting tomatoes, another diminished vegetable.

These days, I stay away from supersweets, but I do buy corn. Our family farm is gone—my mother sold it 15 years ago, after my dad died—and though I grow tomatoes, eggplant, peppers, and melons in my little backyard garden, I don't have the heart to plant corn—or the room. I have only a tiny patch of land, which would yield but a few fresh ears and would feel like a futile attempt to recapture those corn summers. Instead, I seek out the best local grower.

Naturally, I'm pretty particular. In fact, I'm probably the kind of customer I would have found annoying when I was on the other side of the counter. For instance, I have a list of conditions that must be met before I will shell out my cash. I want a place where nobody minds if I peel back the tip of an ear or two to make sure the kernels are young and tender and the corn is worm-free. I'm also searching for rich green husks, a sign of freshness. I won't buy prehusked corn because husking removes the long stem end—the place where the corn was ripped from the stalk, and the best clue to freshness: Its tip turns brown and dry at roughly the same speed that the sugars in the kernels turn starchy. A truly fresh stem-end, promising truly sweet corn, should be pearly white and beaded with moisture.

What else? I prefer buying from a farmer who knows my name and what kinds of corn I like—someone who's eager to talk about corn varieties and weather conditions. I shop for corn around five in the afternoon—and when I walk up to a stand, I find myself listening for the sound of a tractor roaring in from the fields with a load of corn on its back. I like it when I see someone behind the counter husking a dozen or two for their own dinner. And I always look for a cat on the counter, though I haven't found one yet.

Pasta Meets the Tomato

by Lynne Rossetto Kasper

from *The Italian Country Table*

As a cookbook writer and host of the radio program "The Splendid Table," Lynne Rossetto Kasper knows whereof she speaks when it comes to the food of her ancestral homeland, Italy. Perhaps nothing seems more basic, and more Italian, than pasta in red sauce—but Kasper reawakens our appreciation of this fundamental dish.

I must begin with a confession: There is nothing, absolutely nothing that pleasures me more than a bowl of pasta and tomato sauce. When I want to reach out with all my love to my husband, a dish of pasta and tomatoes is almost always in my hands. When I am worn out and the world isn't such a nice place to be in, I make tomato sauce and pasta. When time is short but dear friends must be fed with joy and not pressure, I make pasta with tomato sauce. Never are any two of these pastas alike, because for me, this is the food of instinct. I cook listening to something beyond a recipe—the tomatoes always seem to tell me what kind of sauce they want to be this time. Pasta and tomatoes restores me. I believe every tomato sauce tastes like a new experience. And I believe the tomato and tomato sauces with pasta have never been given their due.

In the years of exploring Italy's countryside, I cannot think of a farmhouse or country home I have visited where I did not see tomatoes preserved in some way or another. I remember September in my Tuscan cousin Edda's kitchen, and a year's worth of bright scarlet tomato sauce cooling in canning jars on the old marble counter. In Umbria, I watched from afar as a woman simmered her garden's tomatoes in a huge battered pot set on a brazier outdoors, under a tree. Next to her on a table, bottles and jars were lined up waiting for the tomato puree. Elizabetta Del Monaco, a farmwoman who, with her brother, runs one of Puglia's oldest pottery businesses, hangs branches of whole small tomatoes in the cool grotto that is also their workshop. The tomatoes will winter there, shriveling slightly, their flavors intensifying with each passing week. Nine hundred miles to the north, farmwomen in Romagna twist small tomatoes from their stems, thread them on strings and hang them like garlands across the mantles of their homes.

Everyone I met reminisced about putting up tomatoes—drying them or boiling them, making paste or hanging the whole fruit on its branches in cool pantries. No other single food has become so much a part of Italy's country cooking. The tomato grows everywhere, from the Alps of the Alto Adige at Austria's border to Sicily in the middle of the Mediterranean Sea.

Tomatoes flavor countless foods—pizza, polenta, rice, beans, meats, seafood and all kinds of vegetables. But at every table, in every home, no matter what else I was offered, eventually a bowl of pasta with some kind of tomato sauce was set down before me. Even in places like Lombardy's high mountain valleys near the Swiss border, where the tomato was a latecomer and pasta was not part of the local tradition, the two were served.

Pasta twirls on the fork, wonderfully messy, chewy, wheaten, lively. Add tomato—bursting with taste, juicy, tart, sweet, meaty—and the whole becomes greater than its parts. Far more than just good eating, the coupling of pasta and tomatoes is enormously satisfying. Scientifically, the carbohydrates in wheat and tomatoes stimulate the production of serotonin—our body's "feel-good" chemical. But I believe, beyond science in a realm of the subconscious, we respond to the genius of perfect simplicity in two foods meant for each other but kept apart until relatively recently by an accident of botany. Wheat of the Mediterranean and tomatoes from the Americas belie the idea of what grows together goes together. These two ancient foods came together from two ancient worlds separated by an ocean. In their joining, identified a nation. To the world in this century, a plate of pasta with a tomato sauce is Italy.

Since the ancient Carthaginians first sold wheat to the Romans, it has been Italy's most valuable grain both in the marketplace and in the kitchen. Yet in over three thousand years, no single food had brought to pasta and bread what the tomato did. Although tomatoes arrived in Italy in the 1500s from the Americas via Spain, their pairing with pasta did not become popular for three centuries. Instead, tomatoes immediately stirred controversy. Vivid, exotic and new, they were grist for debate among botanists over how edible, nourishing or deadly they might be. They remained a curiosity of the wealthy, eventually eaten stuffed, sautéed, stewed or as salad. Early tomato sauces were for meat. The first written recipe of tomato sauce for pasta did not appear until 1839, published by Ippolito Cavalcanti, the Duke of Buonvicino, in his cookbook, *Cucina Teòrico-Pratica (Cooking Theory and Practice)*.

Tomatoes gradually moved from the tables of the wealthy to the gardens of middle and lower classes. Many other foods had traveled this path, yet nothing took over kitchens like the tomato in nineteenth-century Italy. Why? After two centuries of cultivation, tomatoes had probably come to taste better, and they've always been easy to grow. A year's worth grew in the garden patch a landowner usually allotted to his sharecroppers to feed their families. Except for what they raised on this piece of ground, everything else they harvested had to be shared with the landowner. Farmwomen discovered how delicious tomatoes are on their own and also learned they stretched a little meat into good-tasting, plentiful sauces. Tomatoes brought unique sumptuousness to minestrone, bean or bread dishes, almost anything made with polenta and stews of fish or meat. No other single, easily had ingredient—except salt—married flavors as the tomato did.

By the mid-1800s, the fragrance of cooking tomatoes meant summer in the countryside. In farmyards and back gardens, cauldrons of tomatoes simmered over outdoor fires as families put up bushels and bushels for winter. Although few country people probably thought of vitamins back then, they knew tomatoes made them feel good and made their food taste better.

Countless tomato sauces for pasta evolved in a matter of decades, not centuries. Nearly every savory food successfully joined tomatoes in the sauce pot. Tomatoes and pasta had their detractors, who called them commonplace, the result of tasteless cooking and overindulgence. Few Italians paid much attention.

Pasta traveled north and west into Europe long before the tomato's acceptance, yet not until tomato sauces joined pasta in foreign parts did its popularity climb. Pasta and tomatoes were the siren's song, drawing foreigners into Italian restaurants. Once there, they learned to love other things Italian. Interestingly, initially most of them had tomato too—pizza, Chicken Cacciatora, Steak Pizzaiola and the Parmigiano family of eggplant, veal and poultry. Today, no city in Europe—and in much of the world beyond—is without an eating place serving spaghetti with some kind of tomato sauce. This pair is the foreigner's talisman of Italy. And for most Italians, pasta with tomato is the talisman of family and home. . . .

It Takes a Village to Kill a Pig

by Jeffrey Steingarten
from *Vogue*

A man of prodigious appetite and strong enthusiasms, food critic Jeffrey Steingarten spices the pages of American *Vogue* with monthly dispatches from the world of serious eating. Depicting himself (in the title of a previous collection of his essays) as *The Man Who Ate Everything*, Steingarten here tracks down a delicacy that is not for the faint of palate.

I went down to Chinatown looking for blood. They say you can buy anything or anyone in Gotham City if you're willing to pay the price, but not this time, not when you're looking for fresh pig's blood and getting desperate. I had shot the morning on the telephone. One of the two French butchers in Manhattan had vanished, and the other pretended not to understand. Ditto the old Italian pork stores on Ninth Avenue, on Bleecker Street, on Arthur Avenue in the Bronx. "Forget about it," one Italian butcher advised. "Pig's blood is against the law. In Jersey, they make blood sausages with beef blood.

If anybody says otherwise, either they got it illegally or they're lying."

And so it was down to Chinatown, where they live by other rules—south on Mulberry, left on Bayard, north on Mott, right on Canal, south on Elizabeth, and right on Bayard. I could have gone directly to Bayard, but I was sure that USDA commandos were following me. At last I darted into Bayard Meats, and there it was, way in the back, frozen and maroon in quart-size plastic tubs. The label said PIG'S BLOOD in ballpoint pen. How could I tell for sure it wasn't beef or sheep blood? Is frozen blood as nice as fresh? And now I would have to search for les poumons, le coeur, le rate, and les joues of some pig. I needed a French-Chinese dictionary, and fast. I was feeling overwhelmed. I reeled out onto Bayard Street and disappeared into the teeming crowd. Once again I was faceless in Gotham, and I sighed with relief. I felt like the Icarus of gastronomy. A guy should never hunger for what he cannot have.

It had all started so innocently, as these things often do, with a simple appetite, a modest craving. It was three years ago, and I was at a dinner party just outside Paris. Before we sat down to eat, we drank wine and nibbled on rich charcuterie from Béarn, in southwest France, served with slices of warm, wheaty bread. There were rillettes of goose, a pork pâté, and boudin noir, blood sausage. All three were memorable, but the boudin noir was the finest I had ever tasted. It was so phenomenally good that I quickly added it to my list of the hundred greatest foods of the world, tearfully removing the Frozen Milky Way Bar from my pantheon.

Upon subjecting the remaining scraps of boudin to minute inspection, I guessed that it was composed of long-cooked onions, tiny cubes of white pig's fat and skin, and ground pork—all held together by pig's blood, which, when poached, solidifies into a kind of custard. It was wonderfully spiced with cinnamon, nutmeg, clove, and black pepper (a quartet the French call quatre-épices) and, as I later learned, with the hot red Espelette pepper for which the Basque country is famous. Our boudin noir had come in an unlabeled gold-tone metal can the size of a medium can of tuna. Its texture was loose, unlike that of most boudins, which are densely packed into casings. In southwest France, boudin noir has long been preserved in jars and, in this century, metal cans.

Our hosts were Frédérick Grasser Hermé and her husband, Pierre. Frédérick is a wonderful cook and food writer who has worked from time to time with Superchef Alain Ducasse, to whom she addressed her most recent cookbook, *La Cuisinière du Cuisinier*. Pierre is the greatest pastry chef in France, with shops in Tokyo, clients in New York, and an award-winning book in English (written with Dorie Greenspan) called *Desserts*. We three have organized little food adventures all around Europe and in New York City. Fred, as I have come to call her, and Pierre always bring their own salt to dinner—the white fleur de sel from Guérande or the pink stuff from the Île de Ré—even to the fanciest restaurants. Pierre also brings his own knife. Yet neither of them is in any way pretentious.

After dinner, in the guise of using the men's room, I rifled through their pantry and discovered that they still had a good supply of metal cans filled with blood sausage, which I stopped just short of sharing. A few ounces of this inconceivable sausage meat had aroused in me an irrepressible craving, an appetite that could not long be denied. Frédérick and Pierre agreed. "Il est top," they said, using the French slang popular then. But they were unusually guarded about the source of their boudin. They did reveal that it could not be bought in any shop and that the recipe was a complete and total secret. I taught myself to be content with the shards and crumbs of boudin to which I was treated at their dinners, and lay in wait.

A year later, Fred and Pierre made an astounding announcement. Their boudin is the famous boudin of Christian Parra, proprietor of the Michelin two-star restaurant Auberge de la Galupe, in the microscopic village of Urt, near the city of Bayonne, in the southwest corner of France. Out of love for Frédérick and Pierre, Christian and his older foster brother, Joseph Bordus (the guardian of the secret family recipe), had decided to pass on their great and incomparable boudin noir. So when we were ready Christian would arrange the ancient ceremony known as la tue-cochon, "the killing of the pig."

Pork is the most popular meat in France. Grimod de la Reynière, the very first restaurant critic, wrote in the early 1800s, "The pig is an encyclopedic animal. It is a veritable meal on hooves. One throws away nothing." Half the French say, "Dans le cochon, tout est bon": "Every part of the pig is good to eat." The other half say, "Tout est bon dans le cochon." By law, most French pigs are now killed in government-inspected slaughterhouses. But in rural France, traditional pig slaughters are still permitted on farms, where they have apparently changed very little for the last 2,000 years. (After the Romans conquered Gaul, in 51 A.D., they so admired the Gallic way with pigs that they brought home both the famous hams of Bayonne and the methods for curing them. These are said to have been the inspiration for Italian prosciutto.)

When a farmer's pig is ready for slaughter, always in the cold months between fall and spring and only when the moon is waning, he confers with his neighbors, and a day is chosen. That morning, the men take care of bleeding, killing, cleaning, eviscerating, and dismembering the animal. Then there is a cassecroûte, a snack in mid-morning. In this part of France it was traditionally the pig's liver, sliced and grilled. Meanwhile, the womenfolk make the charcuterie (chair means "meat" and cuit means "cooked")—sufficient sausages, salamis, pâtés, bacon, white and black boudins, salt pork, and hams to last the winter. If the village is small, a professional charcutier from a neighboring town may come to help. Everybody's reward comes that evening at la fête du cochon, "the feast of the pig."

In March 1998, Frédérick, Pierre, and I flew from Paris to

Biarritz, rented a car, and checked into an exceedingly grand seaside hotel offering low winter rates. With us was Patrice Hardy, a chef who had worked for Pierre, and Patrice's wife. We drove in the gathering darkness to Auberge de la Galupe to meet Christian and his wife, Anne-Marie, and share a pre-slaughter supper of ham from Spain (an hour's drive away), puff-pastry treats flavored with cracklings, rillettes of duck and of goose, small potatoes with black truffles, bluefin-tuna belly cooked with hot green peppers, a salad dressed up with little pieces of foie gras, and more black truffles, ravioli filled with deeply flavored braised duck, a tender shank of veal, and thin slices of crumbly sheep cheese from the nearby Pyrenees. Christian's cooking is much lighter than it sounds, and everything was extremely fine.

But where was the boudin noir? I saw it on Christian's menu but nowhere on our dinner table. I had expected it with each succeeding course. Even after dessert, I kept the hope alive that someone would soon carry in a huge platter weighed down with all the blood sausage you could ever eat. Only when we had driven halfway back to our hotel did I give up the ghost. I need not have worried. The following day, after la tue-cochon, the treasure was to be ours forever.

In France boudin noir, while the cheapest of all sausages, can become almost an object of veneration and worship. I have an entire little book called *Le Boudin, Récits et recettes de la cuisine du sang*— "narratives and recipes of the cuisine of blood." The author compares boudin eaters to Masai warriors, to Aztec noblemen drinking the blood of human sacrifices. The essential formula for blood sausage is equal proportions of onions, pork fat, and pork blood, plus flavorings, and often cream. Every region of France has its own version—*Larousse Gastronomique* lists sixteen, and my collection of French pig books gives recipes for others. In southwest France and in the Parra family, boudin is made from the pig's entire head, neck, and organs, and it contains as much meat as any other ingredient. Unlike some boudins in this region, the meat is not stretched with cream or bread (or, as in English black pudding, with rice and oatmeal). I have read that blood pudding was invented by Aphtonite, a cook of ancient Greece.

Christian is a large, jolly-looking man with a well-trimmed salt-and-pepper beard. He received his first Michelin star in 1989. When the great chef Michel Guérard tasted the Parra family boudin noir, he insisted that Christian add it to the menu. Christian agreed, and it was probably no coincidence that shortly thereafter La Galupe was promoted to two stars. His is the only recipe for boudin noir included in the latest *Larousse Gastronomique*. And in Christian's own volume, *Mon Cochon*, published last year, it is the very first recipe. The problem is, they are wildly different. And Christian made us promise not to publish a recipe that gives precise quantities.

The next morning we rose at dawn and drove back to Urt. Three extremely large rubicund farmers, in their late 40s, I guessed, wearing berets and rubber boots and rubber trousers or aprons, were standing in a courtyard between some farm buildings, and together we waited for the pig and watched our breaths in the bright, cold air. In one corner a large copper cauldron had been set on a portable gas burner and filled with water that had nearly reached the boil. In the center was a rectangular, flat-bottomed, galvanized zinc trough, which would serve as a pig-size bathtub for cleaning the animal. Inverted, as it was now, it would be a platform on which to kill and bleed it. Soon Christian, his sous chef, and Joseph showed up. Someday I may possibly understand why everything involving farms or farmers must begin in the unpleasant hours just after dawn, though I have my doubts.

I had heard that the killing and bleeding of a pig is pretty rough stuff, and I wondered whether I could take it. I have long felt, at least in theory, that carefree meat eaters like me need to face the reality of slaughter. We shouldn't think of meat as something that originates in shrink-wrapped packages at the supermarket and imagine that we can escape the karma of killing by paying someone else to do it. The more we understand where meat and fish come from, the less we will eat in a casual, mindless way and the less we will waste. Am I wrong?

At last a large truck rolled into the driveway, back end first. The doors were opened, and a wooden ramp was pulled down into the courtyard. Now the three farmers dragged the pig off the truck against strong resistance. It seemed to know that it was about to die. Maybe it had heard the adage of animal husbandry Christian taught me: When a pig cannot get any fatter, it is necessary to kill it. Put another way, a farmer cannot afford to feed a pig that has stopped growing.

Our pig was over five feet long and weighed 400 pounds, a male castrated at the age of one month or so. He had been trucked that morning from the Pyrenees. Free-range Pyrenees pigs fattened on corn and barley are especially prized for the making of the finest dry-cured hams and other charcuterie. Our pig's skin was off-white with an uneven growth of dirty bristles, and his eyes were tiny. His ugliness made it easier not to sympathize with him.

The three farmers had tied ropes around the pig's ankles, and with the help of an iron grappling hook were able to pull him across the courtyard to the inverted zinc trough, and, by tying his feet together, to haul all 400 pounds of him onto the platform, lying on his side. Then the largest of the farmers pulled back the pig's head with his iron hook, baring its neck from chest to chin. Joseph had brought a broad, deep sauté pan to collect the blood. For the moment, our pig had stopped struggling.

The farmer tugging on the hook held a knife in his right hand. He plunged it in, just above the pig's chest, and drew it up, toward the head. Immediately the blood began to flow, and Joseph caught most of it in his pan. With one hand he continuously stirred the blood so that it would not coagulate in the cold air. Later he would pour it into a bright-blue plastic pail, mix in some salt, and put it in the refrigerator.

The pig began struggling again, and I became nauseated and dizzy. I had not bargained for his grunts and his hoarse cries. The sounds came close to unhinging me. Pierre and Fred were not doing much better. Bleeding the pig took at least 20 minutes, and then he was dead. His tongue poked out of the side of his mouth, just as in a cartoon.

At first I felt a deep sadness and a sense of shame. But doesn't a pig, a chicken, or a lobster die every day of the week for my dinner? Is there a difference between the deaths I witness and those I don't? It is true that commercially slaughtered pigs are stunned before they are bled. The USDA considers this a humane method of slaughter, required of everyone except kosher and halal butchers, who will have nothing at all to do with pigs. But is this more humane or a matter of convenience? I recently spoke to a friend who years ago nearly bled to death. Her pain had lessened as consciousness drained out of her. With each minute, she became less aware that she was watching her own death.

Cleaning the pig was an elaborate affair. First he was rolled onto a wooden frame with a sort of stretcher on it. Then the platform was inverted, and six people grappled with the stretcher to roll the pig into what had now become a trough again. Half the boiling water in the copper cauldron was poured over the pig as the farmers scraped his skin to remove the bristles. To speed the process, the pig was dusted with a powdered pine resin, a precursor to turpentine. Then the rest of the boiling water was poured over him, and the scraping resumed, followed by a singeing with a blowtorch for those problem areas, and then another bath.

The outcome was amazing. What had started as a filthy beast deserving of demolition had become . . . a gigantic baby! Its skin was creamy white and spotless, every square inch perfectly smooth and supple, wrinkled at the joints and neck, and absolutely clean. If he only could have looked this way in life! Only now would the farmers dare to disembowel him.

They rolled the pig onto his back, made one incision from the belly downward, and another up to the chest. First they carefully removed the intestines. If they had broken, the waste inside could have contaminated everything else. The breastbone was sawed through and the major organs removed—the lungs, heart, thymus, spleen, and liver. All these but the liver would become part of our boudin noir. Then the pig's head, throat and the flaps on both sides of the chest incision were severed, and the pig was opened wide, almost flat. His legs were tied to the four corners of the wooden rack. All three farmers were needed to bring the rack and its pig upright; then the largest farmer held the rack against his own back, walked it to a barn ten feet away, and rested it against the wall. They covered the pig with a blue-and-white Basque cloth, hosed down the courtyard, and disappeared briefly to remove their blood-spotted boots and rubber trousers and aprons.

Meanwhile, a table was brought out and set with three places for the farmers' casse-croûte. Soon they were feasting on a giant cépes omelet that Christian had prepared—it must have taken a dozen eggs—plus two crisp baguettes and two bottles of red wine. For the rest of us there was nothing. I had not eaten for twelve hours, and my hunger was becoming bothersome, I question a value system that rewards physical labor with cépes omelets while guiltlessly starving those whose vital work consists of taking notes and contemplating the meaning of blood sausage.

Now the pig was lowered and untied and dismembered into the primal cuts of pork, the shoulder, ribs, loin, filet mignon, belly, legs, shanks, and so forth. In the old days, the filet was given to the village doctor or priest, but today it was destined for our lunch. Joseph immediately salted the hind legs. In eighteen months, they will have become two Bayonne hams of the highest quality. The farmers disappeared again, this time to shower and change into jackets, slacks, and ties.

Work on the boudin had begun in the kitchen two hours earlier. The goula—the neck or throat—of another pig had been chopped and sautéed in a very large pan for a half hour, until all the fat had rendered out. Great quantities of chopped onion were mixed into the fat and slowly cooked for an hour or so, sending out irresistible aromas. More than a pound of chopped garlic was added, plus thyme and parsley near the end of the cooking.

As soon as the pig's head was severed, Joseph went to work on it, partially splitting it with a hatchet, removing the tongue and the brain, and cutting off the ears. The copper cauldron had been refilled with 30 or so quarts of water, along with several onions stuck with cloves and five long, dried, red Espelette peppers, and brought to a boil. Joseph gently released the head into the boiling water, then the lungs, heart, goula, spleen, thymus, tongue, and ears. The brain and liver would be saved for other uses. On top of everything went four thick bundles of beautiful leeks from Joseph's garden, trimmed and tied with string.

After an hour, the leeks were done; Joseph squeezed the excess water out of them and, in the kitchen, fed them through a large electric meat grinder under which the pan holding the onions, garlic, and rendered fat had been put. After an hour and a half, the ears, tongue, and assorted organs were removed; the ears were skinned and the cartilage discarded; the tongue was skinned and the skin discarded; the organs were chopped into large pieces and their largest arteries and nerves removed; then everything was fed through the meat grinder and into the pan. After two hours, the goula and meat from the chest were done and soon afterward, the head. Joseph tested them by seeing how hard he had to press before his finger could pass through the meat.

Standing at his table in the courtyard, he first removed the skin from the head, goula, and chest flaps. The skin was lined with a quarter-inch layer of fat, in some places more, and Joseph carefully cut the skin and its fat into hundreds of cubes about ⅜ inch on each side, and he slid them directly into the pan under the meat grinder so that they would remain whole in the boudin.

Finally, he cut off every scrap of meat and fat remaining on the pig's jaw and skull; the most substantial pieces were les joues, the jowls or cheeks. "Les yeux?" I asked Joseph—what about the eyes? He looked at me as though I were a barbarian.

We were nearly done. We all crowded into the kitchen as Joseph removed the bright-blue pail of blood from the refrigerator. The pan, now full of everything good, had been pulled out from under the meat grinder. Joseph poured in the blood, mixing it in with his hand, a process that must have taken at least five minutes and left him bloody up to the elbow. Now it was time to season the mixture Joseph added salt, black pepper, quartre-épices and ground Espelette peppers, measuring with his eyes, and mixed them in thoroughly. For the first time all morning, Fortune smiled. To test the seasoning, Joseph needed to fry up a handful or two of the boudin mixture—eating raw pork and fresh blood is not considered safe. At long last, I had a taste of the epiphanic boudin noir. Then Fortune smiled again when Joseph added a little more of something and cooked another test batch. The boudin was spicier than I had remembered it. Everybody agreed that it would mellow after it was canned.

Now, at two in the afternoon, we returned to La Galupe for lunch, our fête du cochon, with the three farmers and several friends. Drinking lots of good local red wine, we ate two pâtés Joseph had made from the family's recipes, a plate of Bayonne ham, wild freshwater shrimp from the Guadalquivir River delta in southern Spain, and then the boudin noir—a dark-red disk about three inches in diameter and ¾ inch high, sautéed crisp on top and bottom, and served with very fine, rich mashed potatoes and an apple compote, the traditional accompaniments, and a grilled pig's rib. The main course was the pig's filet mignon, sliced, sautéed, and served with a vinegar sauce and diced potatoes, crisply browned with garlic and parsley. We finished off with sheep cheese, two desserts, and a glass or two of Armagnac.

All I wanted to do was stagger into a soft bed and lose consciousness for a day or two. But fickle Fortune had temporarily stopped smiling. The boudin noir over which we had slaved since dawn had to be immediately preserved. Joseph had cleaned several lengths of the pig's intestines, stuffed them with boudin, attached them to willow branches, and poached them in the strongly flavored broth from the copper cauldron. But most of the boudin remained. We drove to Maison Montauzer in the nearby town of Guiche, a small factory for the making of traditional, unadulterated charcuterie and prizewinning Bayonne hams. It was M. Montauzer who had arranged for the delivery of our pig that morning.

Christian and Joseph rarely use live pigs when they make boudin noir; they buy only the parts they need from M. Montauzer—the head, throat, blood, and organs, the cheapest parts that might otherwise go to waste. On the second floor of Maison Montauzer was a small mechanical canning line. The entire crew from the restaurant had come with us, and Joseph supervised as they spooned the boudin noir into 166 shallow metal cans. The cans were then placed on a short moving belt that passed slowly through the sealing machine. Later, M. Montauzer's son would put them into a hot-water bath, maintained at the boiling point, for two hours. This would finish cooking the boudin, sterilize it, and solidify the blood.

On our last evening, Frédérick, Pierre, and I said goodbye to Christian and Anne-Marie, who gave us each twelve cans of the Parra family's peerless boudin noir. As to whether they also arranged for us to feast on the forbidden ortolan or the prohibited bécasse, or both, crisply roasted, I have no comment.

Miserly though I was with my cans of boudin when I returned to New York City, it was inevitable that before long they would vanish, which is why I had embarked on my pursuit of fresh, clean, local pig's blood. I now realize that I had become unnecessarily discouraged by the man at the Italian pork store and by my nightmare in Chinatown. Last week I telephoned the USDA in Washington, spoke with Robert Post, director of the labeling and additive policy division, and learned that pig's blood is totally legal! The frozen blood at Bayard Meats was probably genuine after all.

I exchanged frequent e-mail with Frédérick and Pierre, who were suffering the same withdrawal pains as I. There was only one solution: I would fly to Paris, we would buy all the supplies we needed, and we would make boudin noir in Pierre and Fred's backyard. Besides the dizzying prospect of getting my hands on 80 cans of boudin, this was also the only way to test whether we had learned well the ancient lessons of Urt.

Making the arrangements fell to Frédérick, and even after it became clear that she had bitten off more than any one human could chew, her mood remained cheerful at least half the time. She had to rent and transport a portable gas burner, a huge cauldron, 160 empty metal cans, an industrial-strength meat grinder fitted with screen number ten (just like Joseph's), and a hand-operated machine for sealing the cans. She had to find all the pig parts we needed and make sure they came from a 400-pound pig. She had to shop for leeks, onions, garlic, spices, and herbs. And she had to find seven quarts of clean, fresh pig's blood. It was our good fortune that the local butcher is quite distinguished—he supplies several cuts of meat to Alain Ducasse. Under Frédérick's constant vigilance, he was able to find all the animal matter we needed.

Three of us had taken detailed notes in Urt—me, Frédérick, and Patrice Hardy. Now each of us composed a complete recipe and faxed it to the others. Miraculously, our recipes were extremely close, with five or six disagreements. The event was set for June 18, 1999, at nine o'clock in the morning. None of us had any idea how to operate a canning machine.

We were five men and one to three women, depending on their whim, and yet it took us twice as long as Joseph to make the boudin mixture, six hours in all. This cannot be explained entirely by the fact that all the men had brought their cellular phones—it was Friday, after all, a working day. Whenever there was an incoming call, all five of us would lunge for our phones.

Frédérick had been in touch with Christian all week. He seemed less than happy about aiding us, probably because he was having second thoughts about letting go of his family's priceless boudin noir. After both Fred and I again pledged that we would not publish a recipe giving exact quantities, he relented, remaining slippery on only one or two matters.

Mixing in the blood required more effort than any of us were prepared for, but otherwise it went without a hitch. At last came the spicing. Those of us who had polished off many cans of Christian's boudin noir were able to get the balance of salt, pepper, quatre-épices, and hot pepper just right—though we felt that Christian had not sent us the real Espelette pepper, as he had promised, and though we had to fry up many succulent handfuls of boudin before we succeeded, remembering that the spices would soften after we had canned and cooked the boudin, but that the salt would not.

The canning machine was a vibrant French blue, and with the aid of a completely confusing French diagram, I finally figured it out—just in the nick of time because the others had already filled 126 of the cans with all of our boudin mixture. Christian and Joseph had produced 166 cans. We were 40 short. Forty times, say, seven ounces per can meant that we had omitted 17.5 pounds of something. Had Christian and Joseph added 17.5 pounds of fat or meat to the cauldron or the meat grinder while our backs were turned? Had our Parisian butcher used a 300-pound pig?

In case you're new to these things, let me tell you that operating a manual canning machine takes much more strength and energy than you can possibly imagine. At 7:00 p.m., 126 cans later, all five men were totally depleted, staring listlessly into space. Frédérick bustled about, collecting the sealed cans and dropping them into fresh, boiling water in the cauldron, where they would remain for three hours of cooking and sterilization. We held our breaths. We had no reason to believe that the cans were really, truly sealed. At any minute they could burst open and spill their treasure into the water, or water could seep in and ruin everything. But they held. And one by one, the slightly concave lids became slightly convex as the air and blood inside expanded. Then we all left and went back to the center of Paris. Frédérick stayed up until midnight, taking care of everything.

Before I left Paris with my sanguinary hoard, Fred, Pierre, and I opened a can of our boudin noir, sautéed it until it was crusty, and tasted it. We were in heaven, at least at first. Our more mature judgment was that the taste and texture were nearly perfect, but that there was a bit too much blood in proportion to meat. The extra blood had pooled here and there like a crimson custard. Adding 17.5 pounds of something else would surely have done the trick. We were certain we could make an absolutely perfect boudin noir in the style of Urt if we tried again, but we were overcome with narcolepsy at the very thought. Perhaps we'll change our tune when we have gone through 60 cans apiece, but for now, the expense and effort seem too awful to contemplate. You might say that it takes a village to kill a pig.

The Flavor of Autumn

by Lori Zimring De Mori

from *Saveur*

Fennel may still be a bit exotic in the United States, but in Tuscany—American-born cookbook writer Lori Zimring De Mori's adopted homeland—it's one of those ingredients that define a season.

A small box on the bookshelf in my parents' room holds, among other cherished memorabilia, a stack of crumbling, yellowed aerograms sent from Italy 20 summers ago. At the time, I was one of a dozen UCLA undergraduates spending eight weeks in Florence. My letters home—written in bold, girlish script, the *i*'s dotted with circles or hearts, exclamation marks everywhere—concentrated on three recurrent themes: Lori's Ongoing Struggle with the Italian Language, the learning of which was the stated purpose of the trip; Lori's Italian Boyfriend, Jean-Louis, whom I met at his family's café in Florence (where he worked the cash register during tourist season); and finally, Lori's Gastronomic Adventures, ranging from updates on my daily gelato intake to glowing accounts of the meals at Pensione Alessandra, our little group's temporary home in Florence.

This small hotel occupied the top two floors of a timeworn palazzo just steps from the Ponte Vecchio, the famed jewelry-shop-and-tourist-covered old bridge across the Arno River in the Centro Historico, Florence's historical district. Although the building was about as shabby as shabby comes, it felt authentic to us. Our rooms were light and airy, and we thought the food spectacular. Never in our short lives had we eaten so well, so regularly—from the steaming pitchers of caffellatte that began each day, to the supper of Tuscan bread soup, ravioli with butter and sage, and other local delectables that we were offered each night.

It was at the Pensione Alessandra that we were introduced to the art of the leisurely Italian meal; and it was there, in the brightly lit, tile-floored dining room late one August, that I began my love affair with that most Florentine of vegetables: fennel. It was brought to the table one evening as a not altogether appetizing-looking side dish—unidentifiable, even to the most sophisticated of our group. It appeared to be some sort of cooked, celery-like substance, a pale creamy yellow in color.

That this mysterious fare was sprinkled with parmigiano was a good sign; that it smelled faintly of licorice (*anise* was not yet part of our vocabulary), which I detested, was not. "Finocchio," the proprietor replied in answer to our blank stares. Hmmm. More blank stares. I took my first bite cautiously—and discovered that finocchio was like nothing I had ever eaten. Its flavor was subtle yet rich and warm, and its juices were infused with butter, cheese, and a hint of black pepper. It tasted like licorice about as much as a ripe red cherry fresh from the tree tastes like a cherry gumdrop.

Although it was new to our young palates, fennel, which is native to the Mediterranean, is actually one of the world's oldest known edible plants. Common fennel, *Foeniculum vulgare,* was eaten over a thousand years ago by the Romans, who prized it for its medicinal qualities as well as for its unique flavor. Roman women used fennel as a diuretic; their warrior men dined frequently on the herb to guard against poor health. The Roman gastronome Apicius favored fennel as well, and he often used the seeds in his seasoning mixtures and added the stems to various stews and pickles. In fact, so many and great were fennel's virtues in ancient times that it was popularly known to the Romans as erba bona, the "good herb."

Unlike the fennel we know in America, common fennel, which grows wild, does not produce a bulb. The plant looks much like a taller, sturdier version of dill (in fact, their seeds will cross pollinate if the plants are grown close together), with bright green, feathery leaves and clusters of yellow flowers that bloom in the spring. Its ribbed, aromatic seeds—among the four "hot" seeds (along with anise, caraway, and coriander) considered by the Romans to have digestive properties—are not gathered until the end of the summer. These seeds are still used throughout Italy today, sprinkled in the cooking water with simmering chestnuts, and in the salty brine in which green olives are cured. They also impart their subtle aniselike flavor to breads, biscotti, and liqueurs. Finocchiona, a soft salami flavored with fennel seeds, is standard in any Tuscan affettato misto, the ubiquitous assortment of cured meats that begins many informal meals. Nursing mothers have found their own use for the seeds: They steep them in boiling water and sip on the fennel tisane, which, passed through the mother's milk, helps to alleviate the pain of colic.

The fennel that brought us such gustatory delight so many years ago, however, was actually wild fennel's diminutive sibling, *Foeniculum vulgare dulce*—also known as Florence or bulb fennel. It is cultivated more for its pale, bulbous stem base—

which is eaten as a vegetable—than for its leaves or seeds. In late August, just as summer's vegetables are petering out, this fennel makes its first appearance in markets all over Italy. It is enormously popular there, and for good reason: No other vegetable is so equally delicious raw or cooked. Raw, it is crisp, assertively aromatic; its springlike freshness belies winter's impending arrival. A salad pairing sliced fennel bulbs with wild chicory, black olives, and sanguinelli, the crimson fleshed Sicilian blood oranges, is popular in southern Italy, and in some parts of Tuscany, people still follow the old custom of eating raw fennel at the end of a meal to refresh the palate. When cooked, fennel's taste and texture are transformed into something altogether different. The crunch mellows to a tender, melt-in-your-mouth softness, and the bold flavor becomes more delicate and restrained. Fennel will go happily almost anywhere you put it: in soups; dipped in batter or bread crumbs and fried; braised in butter, milk, or olive oil; baked in a rich gratin with besciamella (béchamel sauce) and parmigian-oreggiano. (The traditional Sicilian fennel-and-sardine-sauced pasta con le sarde, on the other hand, is made only with the wild variety—as are most Italian pasta sauces that call for fennel.)

Back in Los Angeles after my eight weeks in Italy, I thought constantly about Florence (and about Jean-Louis, who was coming to spend a year with me on my home turf)—but I can't honestly say that fennel crossed my mind until many years later. Those were the dark ages for Italian cooking in America—arugula and radicchio had yet to make an appearance—and fennel simply wasn't available.

Today, however, nearly two decades later, fennel can be found in almost any grocery store in America—and I have since returned to Italy. Jean-Louis and I are at home now in Tuscany, just south of Florence, near a tiny town called Mercatale, living in a small farmhouse we rescued from ruin and brought back to life. As we sit in the crisp fall sunshine watching our children,

Julien, 10, and Michela, 7, traipse off to the garden, I am reminded of that dinner at Pensione Alessandra so long ago. Silvano, our gardener, has been here since dawn, raking leaves, pulling up the spent remains of summer's squash vines and tomato plants, working with the good humor and dogged determination needed to care for the nearly four acres of fertile soil. As he works, the bambinos head to the brightest spot in the garden—a mass of green, lacy leaves wedged in between the broccoli, the kale, and the tilled earth where our summer vegetables grew only a few weeks ago. The harvesting is easy: They simply close their fists around the waist-high stems and pull, releasing the pale white bulbs from the soil. Julien and Michela have a plan for their bounty: finocchio in pinzimonio, which they will make by cutting the fennel bulbs into thick, crunchy wedges and dipping them into little ramekins of olive oil sprinkled with salt. It is not just any oil, but a clear glass bottle of jewel-green olio nuovo, just pressed—thick and cloudy, with a bite that catches in the back of the throat as it goes down—given to us by our neighbor Bea from the olive groves at her family's vineyard.

Fifty steps from our garden, the cut grass yields to a few acres of uncultivated farmland—a tangle of yellow broom, thorny blackberry vines, wildflowers, even patches of wild fennel, which thrive there all summer long. Against this Tuscan landscape, I see Julien and Michela walking towards the house, their faces hidden behind the brilliant green stalks of garden fennel that fill their arms. I am reminded that for everything there is a season—and I am grateful that for this season there is fennel.

Getting Sauced

by Michael Hood
from *Seattle Weekly*

Hot sauce aficionados make up one of those specialty markets that is a highly partisan food world unto itself. Intrepid *Seattle Weekly* contributor Michael Hood wades into the fray, rating the field of bottled sauces with a finely honed sense of the absurd.

In the white, middle-class, *Reader's Digest* world in which I was raised, the joke was: "They've been married so long, they're on their second bottle of Tabasco." In those days, the stuff lingered in cupboards until it oxidized pond-water brown, which further lowered the possibility that someone might actually consume it. Later, consumption of hot sauces became a guy thing—a measure of masculinity—weightier in some circles than quiche rejection or penile heft. Real men drank sauces right out of the bottle and put Mexi-Pep in their beer.

But times, they are a-changin'. The new *machisma* is not

only giving women solid biceps and male stress disorders; it seems they're going at hot sauces as hard as they are at their sparring partners. Women account for 25 to 35 percent of sales at **The Firehouse** (219 Broadway, Alley Building, 568-0144), a Capitol Hill emporium crammed with over 900 hot sauces and a bevy of marinades, pepper rubs, powdered blends, and custom gift packs.

Though tiny, The Firehouse is sort of a community center. It's fun to stand around and listen as the junkies wander in and the talk gets hot. People swap recipes, swig from sauce bottles, and tell war stories. Adam Karlin, a partner in the venture, says, "We have the brutally hot, but these days it's all about flavor."

Hotness comes from a substance called capsaicin, which collects in the veins of peppers. Like heroin, tolerance is gained by using. In other words, the more you eat, the hotter you can stand or crave. Crackheads and fire-eaters live by this concept.

The heat of peppers is measured in multiples of 100 "Scoville units." The little thermometers on some salsa bottles are roughly based on the Scoville scale. Although there's some pretense of science to this measurement, it's a subjective rating based on the consensus of panels of three people who rate pepper power. The wimpiest peppers, like paprika or cherry peppers, measure around 100; jalapeños, serranos, and chili oils come in at 10,000, Tabasco and cayenne at 12,000, while Texas Fireballs and Bahama Mamas go way up to 20,000.

Ten years ago, however, Americans were exposed to another pepper that measures in megatonnage. It's known variously as Señor Bombasta, the Caribbean Sweat Curse, La Contusion, or the Scotch Bonnet. It's the baddest pepper of them all—the Jamaican red *savina habanero,* which pushes the mercury up to 300,000 units. It's considered inedible by some meek horticulturists, but you can find it in produce departments of many local supermarkets these days. It's two inches in diameter and looks deceptively innocent, like a little Chinese lantern in yellow, green, or red. It smiles dishonestly as it marks you for the kill. As word of the habanero and its machismatic possibilities spread, a new industry sprang up to meet the needs of the new fire-eaters. Hundreds of sauces with elaborate labels (and brewed in unlikely places like New Jersey) have created a bottled renaissance of styles, flavors, and firepower.

Here are a few, starting with the hottest.

Dave's Insanity Sauce ($5.99): This stuff separates the peppergrrls from the boys. Dave, who customarily wears a straitjacket, made national headlines a few years ago when he and his Insanity Sauce were kicked out of Albuquerque's prestigious National Fiery Foods Show. Officials said Dave's sauce was dangerous to public health. Then there's the guy who put it on his terrarium to keep his parrot from bothering his turtle. After pecking the sauce, the bird reportedly jumped back in its cage and yelled, "Asshole!" Even CBS' Bryant Gumbel, breaking his vow of blandness, once said, "Boy, this stuff is hot."

On the shelves in time for Christmas, **Dave's Ultimate Insanity** ($9.99) is reputedly three times hotter than the original. These extreme sauces don't depend on habaneros for power; nowadays, they're kicked with pure capsaicin.

(NOTE: There's a delicate matter I'd be remiss not to mention here. These very hot sauces truly are gifts that keep on giving, if you get my drift. If you don't, it probably more than suffices to say that, like the match that burns twice, or the dog whose bark echoes in your next life, the egress can be as attention-getting as the ingest. You have been warned.)

If you're not trying to prove anything—you just want heat and flavor, or a gift for a friendship that needs heating up—here are some other suggestions.

Pepper Girl Brand Big Top Fantasy ($5.99): A unique habanero sauce with finely minced cucumbers, basil, garlic, and red onion, it's great in potato or pasta salad, and a natural for sandwiches. Somehow the subtle flavor of the cucumbers and basil comes through the fire. Pepper Girls Brand is an innovative company that favors flavor over heat. Try their "Bad Girls in Heat," a papaya-pumpkin habanero sauce, or "Fifi's Nasty Little Secret," with pineapples and jalapeños. These are the only sauces I know of that claim to be aphrodisiacal, hence their motto: "Our sauces arouse more than taste buds."

Craig's Chipotle Sauce ($4.99): "New Jersey's finest," and a first place winner at the 1997 Fiery Foods Show. It's a rich, ruddy red sauce made from smokey chipotle peppers and tangy with peaches and brown sugar. Chipotles (pronounced chip-OAT-lees) are smoked Sonorran jalepeños with moderate heat and lots of extra flavor. They've become popular in recent years and are found crushed in a great variety of forms besides sauces—powders, salsas, and seasoning blends.

Amazon Hot 'n' Sweet Mango Sauce ($4.99): Another deadly substance from Colombia—but this one's legal. This sauce is one of a genre of translucent, fruit-based Caribbean sauces made with mangoes, passion fruit, and habaneros. A sweet sauce, it's good with cured meats like sausages or ham, or on almost any fish, and it comes in varying temperatures. This can be a gateway drug—start your jones by beginning mild and working your way up the Scoville.

Scorned Woman ($4.99): I know, "hell hath no fury," but you have nothing to fear with this well-crafted sauce from Atlanta's Oak Hill Farms. In a perfect world, it would replace Tabasco as the everyday table sauce in the breakfast places, barbecue joints, and motherly cupboards of America. It's hotter than Tabasco, but without the rough vinegary twang that turns off lots of pepper-sauce fans. Try it as a condiment for omelets or tacos, or as a way to vitalize a listless salsa. You can cook with it as well; use it in stir-frys, chili, soups, stews, or extreme desserts.

Alligator Bayou Louisiana Barbecue Sauce ($5.99): There are lots of sauces for grilling meats and fish. Alligator Bayou is a certified Cajun sauce and, with typical Cajun understatement, claims to be "pretty hot." It's actually only jalapeño hot, but also spicy with Cajun seasonings and reduced nice and thick, sweet but tangy. It's made of ketchup, like so many other good things in life that come from Louisiana. This is a good starter sauce for intermediate pepper bellies—a healthy step up from the old Kraft Hickory Smoke.

Nothing Is Better than Butter

by Al Martinez

from *Bon Appetit*

Los Angeles Times columnist Al Martinez is not afraid of letting his readers know where he stands, and in his frequent writings on food, he lets his personal tastes hang out. Here he staunchly argues the case for a much-maligned foodstuff.

My attitude toward butter is essentially this: Anything good enough for Cleopatra to bathe in is good enough for me. The idea that history's most enduring beauty moistened her skin with the silkiest of food substances sends the kind of chill through me that only a Chardonnay-butter sauce can usually generate.

Even if this tidbit about Cleopatra isn't true, we know that butter, in one form or another, did exist during her time. Scholars have traced it to 3,500 years before the Christian era.

And, like the Queen of the Nile, it has always been versatile and tantalizing.

Without butter, fine cooking would disappear from the face of the earth. Butter is the ultimate flavor, the "mouth feel" that silkens and mellows and glazes. Butter is to food what love is to romance. Without it, there is only lard and emptiness. "I wouldn't want to live in a world without butter," says Julia Child. Me neither.

And don't talk to me about margarine. Health experts, who once celebrated that pallid butter substitute, are discovering that the taste-deficient, oil-based chemical creation may not be so healthful after all. Recent medical reports find that margarine contains compounds that increase harmful blood cholesterol levels. So, to the endless butter versus oleo debate add this lofty observation from the American Butter Institute's John Whetten: "I'd rather trust a cow than a chemist."

But it hasn't always been cows, John. In the beginning, even before Cleopatra was beguiling Mark Antony with her buttery complexion, butter came from camels. In Tibet, it's still made from yak's milk. In Egypt, it comes from the milk of sheep and goats. In India, a form of liquid butter called ghee starts with the water buffalo. In other parts of the world, butter is made from the milk of horses and donkeys, but, like Scotch, the taste for it must be acquired.

America favors the cow. Butter emerges from the animal not in sticks or tubs or pats, of course, and certainly not garlicked or herbed or otherwise flavored. Butter is made from the cream of the milk that cows produce. The cream is pasteurized, chilled, churned and drained, and what emerges is—voilà!—God's butter, the gold standard of taste.

Throughout our history, butter has achieved mythic status. East Indians of the pre-Christian Vedic era invoked it as a deity. "Tongue of the gods," they chanted, "navel of the Immortal. Let us praise the name of butter. . . ." Tibetans simmered their dead priests in boiling butter before embalming them. In medieval France, people feared that butter made one vulnerable to leprosy But—the French being French—they ate it anyhow.

Tested by time, butter has emerged without peer. Since 1991, consumption in the United States has risen from an annual 3.7 pounds to 4.2 pounds per person. In France, where everything but the wine contains butter, the intake is three times that. "Today," says Suzanne Goin, co-owner and chef of Lucques restaurant in Los Angeles, "even the skinny people of L.A. like butter." Goin says she uses butter in 80 percent of her creations. "Life," she sighs, "would be so lonely without butter."

Butter. The word slides off the tongue. Eat butter salted or unsalted, whipped or unwhipped. Use it in soup or sandwich. Fry eggs in it. Bake cakes or baste chicken with it. Cook fish in it. Sauté steaks or drench vegetables in it. "There is no substitute for butter," says Julia Child. "The sweetness, the creaminess . . . the mouth feel comes from nothing else," says Goin. "It's even in the Bible," says Whetten, reverentially quoting a line from Judges: "She brought forth butter in a lordly dish."

Finally I turned to my own wonderful cook, the lady in my kitchen, the love of my life. "Nothing," she says, her eyes glowing, "is better than butter. Except, of course, you, dear."

Ah, butter. Oh, butter.

Smell the Coffee

by Dara Moskowitz
from *City Pages*

Reviewing restaurants in the Twin Cities for the weekly magazine *City Pages*, Dara Moskowitz addresses her readers with a lively, slangy, anecdotal style, like a trusted friend giving you the gossipy scoop on where she ate last night.

Everybody makes such a big stinking deal about curare. Oooh, it's such a deadly poisonous root, but people in South America figured out that they could eat it if they boiled it, pounded it, buried it, and then boiled it some more. Wow, that's so *crazy*—I mean, who were the recipe testers on the first versions? (Haw-haw.)

But get this: There's another tropical plant, an evergreen that grows high up in the mountains of Africa, and this evergreen makes a little berry that takes *seven* months to ripen, and there's barely any berry to it at all, it's mostly just two seeds that fit together into a ball, and around that there's a parchment membrane and some sticky pulp and then a tough outer skin. It's not an attractive fruit—as twigs are to zucchini, so are these meager nubs to peaches, passion fruit, papayas.

Still, people figured out that if they collected enough of these things and let them dry in the sun, and then worked them over with rocks and pulled the double-thick skins off, and finally collected about fifty of those seeds, and roasted them till they spilled smoke all over the place, and then they took the charred things, ground them up into a fine powder, and boiled that powder with water, it would yield a non-nutritive beverage, and everyone would want it. Go figure.

Now, somehow, I've managed to go to a bunch of coffee tastings, or "cuppings," as they're known in the trade, but I never managed to absorb what an amazing discovery coffee really is. For one thing, that tortuous route from wild thing to food makes you realize how much of our diet began as a quixotic experiment—I mean, I can't think of the last time I looked at something and said, "You know, I'm going to take that little tiny thing there and dry it, and really break my back trying to husk it, and then roast it, and then grind it up, boil it, and see if it's any good then." (For all I know, this would make the cassette tapes and paperbacks that line my shelves delicious.)

For another, remember the environmentalist refrain that we can't afford to destroy the rain forest because we don't know what treasures lurk within it: Thinking about coffee's origins, the only response can be: Jumping jahoozefats, yes! Get in there and taste it all! And finally, examining the twisty tale of coffee has an unnerving way of knitting together all of human history, from prehistoric nibbling in the mountains of Ethiopia to the double latte spilled on your mouse pad.

Ethiopian coffee is particularly close to those prehistoric origins: It grows on the same line of trees, in the same soil and much the same climate as it did tens of thousands of years ago. Most important, it is also processed the same way—the ripe fruit picked by hand, dried in the sun, and then painstakingly stripped down to the bean. In contrast, most South American coffees are processed by soaking the ripe fruits in water, which allows the outer layers to ferment off. This is a big deal in coffee circles, with some arguing that "wet processing" removes subtle flavor while others maintain that a dry process can allow the fruit to overripen and the beans to sour.

Nessim Bohbot, president of Alakef Coffee, a local roaster, says it's not simply a matter of which method is better or whether Ethiopian coffee is really superior to any other: "It is true that most of the time Ethiopian coffee has a very rich body," he explains. "But coffee is like wine—you like one for one reason, another for another reason. People like Ethiopian coffee for its profile and complexity, but even people who love a certain Costa Rican coffee might like an Ethiopian sometimes for a change."

That change is easy to come by: A quick run around Loring Park recently scared up three varieties of Ethiopian coffee. Dunn Bros. was selling a batch of big, whole, beautiful, and freshly roasted beans imported from the highlands near the Ethiopian city of Sidamo, for $9.15 a pound. Across the park, Starbucks offered another, darker-roasted Sidamo at $9.95 a pound. They also had a water-processed Lekempti, which despite the steep $13.65-a-pound price tag looked dismayingly bashed up and broken.

Back home I cupped all three coffees—a goofy process whereby you douse fresh-ground beans with boiling water, let them cool for a minute or two, break the crust of grounds that forms on top with a spoon, and slurp up the liquid making a lot of noise and endeavoring to spray the coffee over all the regions of your mouth at once. My first discovery was that all my finds made beautiful brews. The Dunn Bros. Sidamo was one of the fullest coffees I've ever had, the grassy, herbal top notes and bright acidity rounding out essential, strong bass notes. The Lekempti from Starbucks was a delicate, beautiful thing smelling faintly of lavender and finishing with a chocolatey fullness. The Starbucks Sidamo basically didn't stand up to the other two, though it might have done fine had I tested it against less noble beans.

Having sealed my flavor adventures, the next thing I discovered was that I remain a lousy cupper: You're supposed to swish and spit, not swallow the coffee grounds and all, but, of course, I did, so I had to spend the rest of the night running circles round the chandelier and gibbering to the tune of "Tie a Yellow Ribbon."

Later in the week, mostly recovered, I made a pilgrimage to Addis Ababa, the bright little storefront of an Ethiopian restaurant situated across from Fairview-Riverside Hospital. This little place, which dishes up fresh, lively versions of Ethiopian stews for around $7 a meal, also serves an Ethiopian coffee that is truly a revelation. (The menu says the coffee service is only done weekdays, but the staff assures me it can be had anytime; one $5.95 order is enough for one or two people.)

The adventure begins with your server roasting a handful of beans in a small pot with a long handle and a screen bottom; at one point the server brings them to your table, shaking the pot so the beans make a skittering noise like maracas and gray smoke spills out like a waterfall. The server then disappears into the kitchen, giving you time to contemplate that people around the world prepared coffee in a similar contraption until the early twentieth century: If Wild Bill Hickok or Charles Dickens drank coffee, it was roasted like this.

The coffee eventually returns to your table on a tray that holds two small espresso-sized cups, a pitcher of sugar, a beautiful, black, round-bottomed earthenware pot resting in a straw base, and, most dramatic, an hourglass-shaped stand of glowing incense. It's a terribly impressive display: In the billowing cloud of smoke, coffee seems magical the way it must have been back when the first cups were brewed and people dreamed up the story of the dancing goats. (Legend has it that the effect of caffeine was discovered when a goatherd found his charges hippity-hopping around a particular tree. He figured out they had munched the berries, soon he did the same, and a few millennia later there I was, circling the chandelier.)

The Addis Ababa coffee tastes mainly big and smoky, and a few herbal notes may or may not be detectable—it's hard to taste anything when your nose is full of incense. I tried filling my cup up with sugar, and the doubly potent brew made me feel awfully exotic, even more so since *Xena, Warrior Princess* was playing on the TV in the corner. After a lot of sipping and sniffing, I emerged back on the streets quick-hearted and bright-eyed, a little goat-like, and maybe a little less attractive to bugs.

See, it turns out that one of science's best guesses as to the role of caffeine is that it's nature's own Deep Woods Off!, keeping insects from devouring the otherwise tasty beans. But nature's best-laid plans went awry: What bugs found distasteful commuters found highly desirable, and the rest is history.

Food Court

by Nancy Harmon Jenkins

from *Food & Wine*

As the world grows smaller and markets more global, local producers wage a heated political battle to protect their turf. Seasoned food journalist Nancy Harmon Jenkins has an admirable grasp of the big picture and deftly reminds us why it matters.

I was in Naples, Italy, last November, eating my favorite Neapolitan food (pizza—did you really have to ask?), when I heard startling news: if the mayor of this delightfully anarchic town has his way, tens of thousands of pizzerias all over Europe might be changing their menus, if not their very names. Mayor Antonio Bassolino, it seems, has petitioned the Italian government, and thereby the European Union, for controlled-name status for Neapolitan pizza.

Now, I need no convincing that the best pizza in the whole wide world comes from Naples, but much as I love it, I can happily make do with Neapolitan pizza from New Haven, Chicago, even Naples, Maine. But if Bassolino is successful, the only pizzas that can legally be called *pizza napoletana* will be those from Naples, Italy—made with Neapolitan flour, Neapolitan yeast and Neapolitan water and baked in a Neapolitan wood-fired oven. For the rest of the world, "flat bread in the Neapolitan style" may become the accepted name. Somehow, it doesn't have the same ring to it.

While it seems silly to legislate the definition of *pizza*, what's happening in Naples is a very small part of an important European movement to protect traditional foods from the galloping globalism that threatens the entire world of food and wine. And for that reason alone, I'm all for it, even though the movement sometimes comes off as ridiculous.

The issue at hand is the coveted Protected Designation of Origin (PDO), as the European Union clumsily refers to it. Currently the European Union recognizes more than 500 foods and beverages as worthy of this rare status and more are added constantly. What all these products have in common is the official recognition that something about them is inherently special and inimitable and that attempts to duplicate them elsewhere or to change the way they're produced should be prevented by law.

Exactly what makes a food deserving of protected status was spelled out for me by Denis Richard, export director of Société Roquefort, when I stopped for lunch in the cheese-obsessed village of Roquefort in France last September: *terroir, matière première, savoir-faire* and *tradition*. The first two requisites are easy to control—*terroir,* the region where the product is made and the soil in which it grows, and *matière première,* the raw materials from which it's created, whether milk, meat, sweet chile peppers, olives, honey or fragrant lavender. But savoir-faire—knowing how to do something, to translate the term literally—and *tradition,* the knowledge and sensibility built up over generations, these are much more difficult to define.

In other words, you can't make just any old cheese and call it

Roquefort. You can't even make a sheep's milk cheese, inject it with *Penicillium roqueforti* mold and call it Roquefort. Only a cheese made from the milk of the Lacaune sheep native to the Massif Central in France, injected with blue penicillin cultured from moldy rye bread in the village of Roquefort and then aged a specified number of weeks in the Cambalou Caves that honeycomb the region, only that cheese may be designated Roquefort. And the controlled-name status has the force of law around the world.

This concept has been familiar to wine lovers for most of the 20th century, since a movement to control France's fine-wine production began by strictly classifying wines and awarding *appellations d'origine contrôlée* according to vineyard location, grape varieties used, yield, vinification methods, aging time and other variables. The translation of such rules from wine to food isn't hard to understand. In 1926, Roquefort's *appellation d'origine contrôlée* was confirmed, the first French law establishing a controlled name for a cheese.

Other countries were slower to recognize the importance of protecting traditional foods and wines. Italy, for instance, didn't safeguard wines with *denominazione di origine controllata*, its version of this protected status, until 1966, and Spain was slower still to set up its *denominación de origen*. But as revered traditions are increasingly threatened, more and more producers are taking steps to procure this kind of security. In the new Europe, it has become the task of the European Union's complex bureaucracy, headquartered in Brussels, to regulate and protect controlled names, along with every other aspect of food and wine production.

The story of *culatello di Zibello,* Italy's Po Valley ham, is a good example of how a controlled name rescued a national food treasure from what seemed almost certain extinction. A boneless wedge from the upper haunch of the pig, *culatello* is rubbed with salt, pepper and sometimes garlic and white wine and is tied in a tight net of twine that, as the ham loses moisture and decreases in size, loosens and drapes like a thick, graceful spiderweb on the outside of the meat. The ham is traditionally cured in dank stone basements in the Bassa Parmense, the right bank of the Po between Parma and Piacenza, a region where cotton-thick winter fogs and hot summer humidity add a special sweetness to the meat, according to Massimo Spigaroli, chef, *culatello*-maker and president of the *culatello di Zibello* consortium. This natural environment, Spigaroli explained to me over a plate of exquisitely curled slices of culatello, simply cannot be copied outside the region, though attempts have been made.

Early in this decade, the disapproving gaze of sanitary inspectors fell on the dark, damp, mold-crusted curing cellars, and for a while it looked as though *culatello* would become but a memory. That was before Spigaroli and his fellow *culatello*-makers organized to defend their beloved ham. Now, with its *denominazione di origine protetta, culatello di Zibello* is safeguarded—which does not, of course, mean that it is produced in an unsanitary manner, but rather that unreasonable sanitary regulations that would have entirely changed its nature cannot be foisted on this gastronomic prize of ancient origin. (Because of U.S. Department of Agriculture regulations, American importers are not able to bring *culatello* into this country; all the more reason to make a trip to the Bassa Parmense, perhaps to Al Cavallino Bianco, the restaurant in Polesine Parmense where Spigaroli serves his own satiny *culatello* from a menu of regional specialties.)

Pimentón de La Vera, paprika from Spain's western region of Extremadura, wasn't exactly facing extinction, but it did receive a new lease on life with the acquisition of a *denominación de origen.* The first aromatic seasoning to acquire the coveted status, the production of *pimentón de La Vera* has almost tripled in the past five years. That says a lot for the kind of market guarantee that a controlled name can offer. The paprika is produced from mature red peppers, which are dried and smoked over oak fires, then stone ground to a uniquely smooth, almost talclike texture. Even the spicy-hot version has a warm, rounded flavor, one that lacks the fierce heat of Mexican chiles. Traditionally used to season sausages and other cured meats, smoky brick-red *pimentón* also gives a characteristic meatlike fragrance to vegetarian and seafood dishes. Chefs in the United States are beginning to understand this quality now that sweet, bittersweet and spicy-hot *picante* versions of the paprika are all available here.

As the list of name-controlled products grows, consumers may be apt to think of this protection as a guarantee of high quality. This isn't necessarily so. As any wine lover knows, even though all Champagne is made according to norms established by the *appellation d'origine contrôlée* for Champagne, not all Champagne is great Champagne; just so, the quality of Roquefort, *culatello*, *pimentón* and other traditional foods varies from one producer to another. In the end, as with any food, it's individual taste that counts. But it's comforting to know that many of Europe's best-loved and highly prestigious culinary traditions are being given the added protection of a fierce watchdog in Brussels.

The Primal Feast

by Susan Allport
from *The Primal Feast*

Borrowing from neurobiology, cultural anthropology, and behavioral psychology, Susan Allport has written a fascinating study of how we humans have evolved from our hunter-gatherer roots. Are the impulses to forage, hoard, and gorge hard-wired in our brains?

T hese thoughts about food and the quest for food began one night a few years ago, over a wine-dark lamb stew and a question posed by my husband. We were having friends to dinner, and at some point during the evening, he asked us all what role we would have played in a much simpler, subsistence society. In truth, no one in such a society would have had the option of spending their days in any other way than in the near-constant quest for food. But my husband got across the idea that what he wanted from us was what we thought our deepest talents were, what we could contribute in a subsistence society and be happy in the doing.

My husband was sure how he would have been occupied ten or twenty thousand years ago. He would have been a toolmaker and a tinkerer. He would have been busy inventing new ways to build shelters, haul water, pick berries, and scrape the meat off carcasses. There were no declared hunters in our group that night; our friends saw themselves as storytellers, shamans, or medicine men. But I immediately knew that I would have been a forager—a gatherer of wild foods.

I answered "scavenger" at dinner, but I didn't mean scavenger in the sense of one that feeds on dead animals. Rather, to scavenge or search for usable goods—in this case, food—at no cost. That's how I spent my summers when I was much younger and working at odd, poorly paid jobs on Cape Cod. During a bottle-washing stint at the Marine Biological Laboratories in Woods Hole, I lived in a tent and ate the giant clams called quahogs that a friend and I used to dive for, then stuff with various store-bought and wild ingredients. My favorite at the time was quahogs with black beans and wild onions, though I now suspect it was something that only a forager could love. Other summers, with Euell Gibbon's *Stalking the Wild Asparagus* as my guide, I fed my friends and myself on chowders and stews made from mussels and oysters I had collected and on pies filled with hand-picked huckleberries. By then I might have been a better cook (or at least I knew to add lots of butter and cream to my concoctions), and one of those summer chowders is still remembered longingly by a certain Epicurean in my family.

Still, I had never thought of myself as either a scavenger or a forager before that night. I was a writer, a wife, and a mother, and foraging was just something I do every now and then to put food—food that is a little different, a little more interesting—on the table. So I was surprised at how quickly the answer to my husband's question popped into my mind—and how sure I was that it was right. It made so much sense that I suddenly found myself counting the ways in which I knew it was true.

I know that I am a forager because I can't start work in the morning until I have settled the question of what I'll be cooking for dinner.

I know that I am a forager because although I can't remember where I parked my car in a parking lot, I can always remember the exact spot where I found a stand of ostrich fern, a patch of lemony curly dock.

I know that I am a forager because, during the summer while other people are off playing golf or tennis, I spend my time searching for mushrooms. There are others like me, I also know, because I've spotted them in the woods with their baskets and pails. I've read their articles on morelists and fine foraging in magazines. I've even seen a cartoon about them in *The New Yorker*. In it, three people are outside on a porch with rain pouring down around them. A man and a woman sit despondently with golf club and tennis racket in hand, as a very cheerful woman stands in the doorway. "Well, it has been a great summer for chanterelles," she says.

I know that I am a forager because the books I like tend to be about food and the effect that food can have on a person's destiny. I'm thinking, of course, of *Growth of the Soil, The Good Earth,* and the chapter in *Far From the Madding Crowd* in which Gabriel Oak's sheepdog eats a dead lamb and then uses his new-found vigor and energy to drive all of Oak's sheep over the cliff. Some of my favorite movies also have to do with food: *Eat, Drink, Man, Woman, La Grande Bouffe, Big Night,* and *Babette's Feast,* in which Babette, a French chef and refugee, teaches the people of a small village in Denmark that food is more than just nourishment. It is pleasure, forgiveness, gratitude, and love. And I can't forget *Ermo,* a film out of Communist China, in which a woman who makes twisted noodles winds up selling her body, blood, and soul in order to buy her son a television set. One of my favorite pieces of sculpture, carved out of quartz by an Inuit artist, is also about food. It is called *Four Hungry Bears Dreaming of a Whale,* and I saw it on Baffin Island when I was on my way to an island in Hudson Bay to observe a colony of thick-billed murres. Four white bears are walking upright and in a straight line. A white whale seems to float above their heads.

I know that I am a forager because one of my favorite things about my house—a house with many charms—is that it has a small spring in the woods that is carpeted with fresh peppery watercress in the spring and the fall.

I know that I am a forager because my favorite color is green.

I know that I am a forager because of the profession I've chosen. For how better to describe science writing than foraging for discoveries in different fields, scavenging for the ideas and research of others?

Most of all, however, I know that I'm a forager because of a very peculiar mental tug or nag that food exerts on my brain.

Let me try to explain. Let's say that I am snacking on a piece of toast or a cracker with cheese, but then I get sidetracked by something—a telephone call perhaps, or a request from one of my daughters to help her find her book or her socks. I put the half-eaten morsel down on the table or a windowsill and seemingly forget about it. But sometime later, something inside my head won't let me rest until I've gone and retrieved that bit of food. I don't need to try to remember where I put it down. I usually walk straight to the spot, guided by this peculiar sensation of unfinished ingestive business.

I can't be the only one to experience this near-magnetic attraction toward half-eaten food. Everyone, I think, must be built this way. But none of the people to whom I tried describing this phenomenon seemed to recognize it. That is, until I spoke with Lewis Barker, a professor of psychology and neuroscience at Baylor University in Texas. I called Barker especially to ask him about this because I knew from his writings that he was interested in both food and memory and had, at one time, thought a

lot about something he called the "Mom's apple pie is best" phenomenon. How, he wondered, had the taste, look, and texture of
his mother's apple pie gotten into his memory in the first place,
and how had it managed to persist there for decades? Barker, I
know, would have had a great deal to talk about with Marcel
Proust. And with Lin Yutang, the Chinese writer who said that
patriotism is the memory of foods eaten in childhood.

"Sure, I've experienced that," Barker said during a telephone
conversation in which I described my mental tug to him. Then
we discussed how losing food could provoke this tug, but not
losing our glasses or our keys. Those we had to find by a much
more conscious reenactment of our movements—or if that failed,
a thorough search of the house. What did Barker think was the
reason for that tug, that mental honing in on lost food? He had
always attributed it, he told me, to the fact that he was a tidy
person and liked to finish what he started. But he also thought
it might have to do with the fact that his parents grew up in the
Depression and that when he was growing up, he was made to
finish everything on his plate.

"But I'm a fairly messy person," I told him, "and I grew up
with an indulgent mother."

He was quiet for a moment, and then he began to slowly muse.
"Okay," he began again. "So there could be an entirely different
slant to this. Like other animals, we humans have evolved in
order to solve survival problems, and the most important of
these problems is finding enough food to eat. Our brains have
evolved to help us in this search. They are wired to sense food
and to remember where to find food. And even though we've
spent the last one thousand or five thousand years in a city, our
brains haven't changed at all. They are still wired in the same
way. We are still foraging animals."

You can really see this in children, Barker went on to say,
because of their increased nutritional and calorie needs. From
the time his children were very little, they had always known
everything there was to know about the food in the kitchen and

where it was stashed: the chocolates on the top shelf, the cookies in the cupboard. "A teenager doesn't know where the dishwasher is, but she knows exactly what's in the refrigerator," Barker observed. "She may not know where to find an auto parts store, but she knows every place to eat in town."

That night at dinner, I repeated parts of the conversation I had had with Barker, and though my own daughter resented the comment about the auto repair store, she agreed to a very informal test of the idea that children have an increased consciousness about food. I asked both her and my husband to write down on a piece of paper the foods that were in our refrigerator. Not the foods that were usually in our refrigerator, but the foods that they knew to be in there that very night. I thought my husband would have a fighting chance in this little test since he had put the groceries away just the day before. But still, he listed only items that were routinely in the refrigerator—cheese, fruit, milk. My daughter listed the foods that were actually there—Brie cheese, blueberries, two percent milk, raspberry and cherry yogurt, packaged and bottled yeast, et cetera, et cetera.

The next time I talked to my older daughter, a teenager with a remarkable memory for the events of her early childhood, I also asked her what she remembered about the kitchen and its contents. She was puzzled because very little came to mind. Then, a day or two later, she called me from school with a rush of food memories. But they were outside memories, foraging memories, memories of her and her sister collecting honeysuckle and clover blossoms, acorns, and hickory nuts and stashing them in their treehouse or in empty flowerpots. I could remember those stashes too, remembered cleaning out those pots in order to fill them in the summer and stopping to wonder at the strange assemblages inside. My daughter had also asked her friends at school about their early memories regarding food. "That's the game that we all played," she told me, "finding food."

It is more than a game for children in other parts of the world. Among the Alor of Indonesia, children are not given any food between their morning and evening meals, and they soon learn to forage for themselves by scraping food from cooking pots, raiding the fields for vegetables, and collecting insects that would be spurned by adults. Young Tallensi children in Ghana satisfy their hungry stomachs by eating toads and snakes, animals that are disgusting to older children and adults and that they too will spurn in time. Young Hadza in Tanzania, hunters and gatherers who live the way all humans lived before the advent of agriculture, are active foragers, collecting berries, the fruit of the baobab tree, and digging for tubers. These children make significant contributions to their families' resources.

It used to be thought that children only foraged for themselves in agricultural societies and that, in societies in which people lived by hunting and gathering wild resources, children relied on their parents for food until they were adolescents. But this was a mistaken view that arose among anthropologists when too much emphasis was placed on the studies of just one group of contemporary hunter-gatherers, the !Kung San of Africa's Kalahari Desert. Among the !Kung, children do not forage because of the nature of the !Kung resources and the long distances that !Kung women must travel to collect food. It is more efficient for them to stay in camp after they are weaned and crack mongondo nuts, the staple food of the Kung. Studies of other hunter-gatherers, though, including the Hadza, have found that even very young children are active foragers. My daughters would have been happy growing up with the Hadza, though they might have objected to the fact that only boys are allowed to hunt with bows and arrows. . . .

. . . During wars, famines, or any time of shortage, people turn—return—to foraging to fill their bellies. Many countries in Africa still have what they call their "hunger season," a time of year when inhabitants run short of the foods that they have grown and stored and must find wild things to put in the pot. At the end of the American Civil War, Southerners were helped in their search for food by Frederick Aldolphus Porcher's *Resources of the Southern Fields and Forests,* a book written expressly and hurriedly for that purpose. During the Irish potato famine, country people survived on "hedge nutrition," a knowledge of what leaves and berries could be combed from hedges and other wild places.

Some Irish families are ashamed of what they had to do during the famine to keep hunger at bay, and Marie Smyth, an Irish professor born in the early 1950s in the north of Ireland, observes that "to this day, in parts of rural Ireland, a 'respectable' family would prefer pie made with apples that were bought in a shop. A 'respectable' family would not wish to acknowledge that they too knew about foraging in the hedges and ditches for wild foods to eat." But others think it important to pass on those tricks of survival. Of her own family, Smyth remembers, "As a child walking in the Irish countryside, my mother taught me that hawthorn berries and leaves are edible, but rowan is not. Blackberries, fitches (vetch), dandelion are also edible; soup made from nettles is full of iron, the fruit of the black thorn—the sloe—is edible but slow to ripen and bitter before it is ripe."

Like Marie Smyth's family and foragers around the world, I too prefer to keep my food-finding equipment in good operating condition. And I also enjoy being reminded, by that insistent little tug, that I am a forager in my heart and in my genes; that we all were foragers, hunters and gatherers, until a change in the human way of life allowed many of us to put foraging behind us, leaving food production to others while we moved on into new and different realms of thought and activity. But there's another reason why we shouldn't be too quick to leave our foraging pasts behind. For if human nature was forged during our existence as hunters and gatherers, as we know it must have been, then understanding how humans and other animals forage for food may better our understanding of human nature and of the way that humans, men and women, interact with each other and the rest of the world. Understanding that "finding food" has shaped our human selves and turned us into the people who we are today may help us to unravel some of the many mysteries surrounding food and the consumption of food.

Home
Cooking

Recipes from My Mother

by Sallie Tisdale

from *The Best Thing I Ever Tasted*

Cultural journalist Sallie Tisdale ranges over many topics in her absorbing book, always coming back to the question of how we feel about the food we eat. It's an insightful work of social history, especially when flavored with Tisdale's own memories of the food she grew up with.

S ince my mother's death several years ago, I've gathered a pile of hundreds of recipes from the derangement of papers every death leaves behind. I added a few hundred more when my grandmother—her mother-in-law—died a few years ago. This last cache of papers surprised me; I don't remember my grandmother ever cooking a meal for anyone. She lived next door to my mother and father for the last twenty years of her life, a perpetual guest in my mother's living room, subsisting mainly on cigarettes and beer and the hot dishes cooked by other women and brought to her like peace offerings.

Still, here they are: recipes, hundreds of recipes, cut out of newspapers and magazines, from the bottom of advertisements and off can labels and on index cards and notepaper. Some are in my grandmother's crabbed, backward writing, but most are in my mother's meticulous schoolteacher's penmanship. A few are in mysterious hands, gifts from long-gone friends and neighbors scribbled on the backs of envelopes, bits of stationery, handed on, copied again and again.

These aren't last classics or great secrets. Most of them share a single quality—speed. Here is Vegetable A La Supreme, requiring cream of mushroom soup, frozen broccoli, Minute rice, and an entire bottle of Cheez Whiz. Here is Tomato Soup Salad, with canned soup, Knox gelatin, cottage cheese, mayonnaise, and stuffed olives. Here is Easy Deviled Ham 'n' Cheesewich, Saccharin Pickles, Chicken Spaghetti. There are a great many recipes using zucchini: zucchini with tomato juice, with fried onion rings, with cream cheese, with whipped cream, with cream of mushroom soup, with nuts and crushed pineapple. These dishes are based in convenience, the ingenuity of making do with a few odd cans and boxes, combining anything and everything you can put your hands on so as to avoid yet another trip to the store. Here are the endless reinventions of fusion cuisine, the creativity of limited ethnic poverty, the surprise of nouvelle, the patent simplicity of country people, all wrapped into a Jet Age suburban gift box. Weird and wonderful, this criminal's urge to avoid work, this wily feminine conspiracy of 3 x 5 cards. My mother worked a lot. At the end of the day what my mother wanted wasn't food but *time*—time out of her labor, time to goof off in her armchair reading romances and drinking coffee, smoking while she watched Mike Douglas watch someone else cook something.

In this whole pile are only a few familiar items, like Porcupine Meatballs—hamburger and rice rolled into balls and baked in a sauce of canned tomato soup—and Pigs in Blankets. I don't know if I loved the name, evocative of luxury and comfort, or the doughy combination of Vienna sausages and Bisquick, but they were one of my favorite treats, rarely had. The fact is that she cooked the same few things over and over. After a few swings at Porcupine Meatballs or Scalloped-Potatoes-and-Spam you don't need a recipe. You don't even need a shopping list, and so you don't need to plan too much or think too far ahead. She kept a pantry stocked well enough for cataclysmic natural disasters, but the hundreds of boxes and cans were simply variations on a few basic things. (You can make Porcupine Meatballs with tomato soup, with mushroom soup, with cheese soup, and call it something different every time.)

So why did she keep a recipe for eggplant stuffed with lunch meat, something our entire family (and perhaps the whole human race) would have loathed? Why did she save how-to plans for time-consuming, multilayer tortes when she never baked? Why menus for party foods and coffee klatches written in the careful hand of a woman who rarely went to parties and never entertained? I wonder if my mother indulged in what Rosalind Coward, decades later, coined "food pornography." "All the women I have talked to about food have confessed to enjoying it," wrote Coward. "Few activities it seems rival relaxing in bed with a good recipe book. Some indulged in full colour pictures of gleaming bodies of Cold Mackerel Basquaise lying invitingly on a bed of peppers, or perfectly formed chocolate mousse topped with mounds of cream. The intellectuals expressed a preference for erotica, Elizabeth David's historical and literary titillation. All of us used the recipe books as aids to oral gratification, stimulants to imagine new combinations of food, ideas for producing a lovely meal."

I keep a thick folder of untried recipes, too, torn from the newspaper and various magazines, handed to me by friends or scribbled from conversations. There are elaborate desserts meant to be served on linen tablecloths by candlelight, and hearty family suppers for a family I no longer have to feed. I'm still caught, like her, between what I've imagined and what I've known, what's been given and what I've been able to take. I rarely use any of them. Like impulsively chosen lovers, a lot of recipes look less appetizing in the cold light of day.

One of my mother's old recipes is on a bit of stationery from a hotel in Reno. I don't remember her going to Reno, and when I found it, I was suddenly, unreasonably glad that she went there, I could see her, laughing, drinking a martini, playing slot machines, staying up late with other secretly dissident women, smoking cigarettes, and not missing their husbands. But I was struck as well by a sudden small grief that she spent even one minute there in Reno copying down a recipe. When I think of her, I never see her in the kitchen. I see her loafing around the living room with a cup of coffee, putting off supper for a few minutes more, I see her rising heavily, dutifully, to begin.

I asked my sister, Susan, what she remembered of the suppers of our childhood. She was quiet for a long moment and then said, in a very small voice, "What I remember is that she wasn't a very good cook." Susan said this as though she were speaking betrayal, and I know how she felt. Our mother was easily hurt, and she knew she wasn't a good cook, which to her somehow meant she wasn't entirely a good woman.

She did her needlework in the weary evening hours while my father slept stretched out loosely across the couch. Women's work is all details, a lot of small stitches put into life one at a time. Needles keep the hands busy while the heart stirs in its difficult sleep; they weave a hypnotic and deliberate calm. Women have always done these things, made scarves, gloves, headdresses, quivers, swaddling boards, vestments, moccasins, veils, christening gowns, beaded necklaces to rattle in the dance— inner turmoil brought to ground and herded into pattern. Women rein in their sorrows, their loneliness and denial, and make it into beautiful things bursting with erotic, joyful color, beautiful things not called art because they are useful. My weary, educated mother not only collected useless recipes but she bought craft kits and sequins and felt and fabric paint and Rit dye. She took up embroidery in middle age. I was disap-

pointed in her when she did, of course. I was too restless for needles, too mad about the world. I wanted her to complain—not
cook and clean, not sew.

I was a fool.

I believe now that my mother's life was one of wrenchingly
difficult choices. Only the fearful need courage, and only the
lazy need discipline. Her courage was to go on, day by day, in
spite of hungers buried deep. The needlework she tried (and
failed) to master may have been a last-ditch attempt to be what
she was not, what she could not be but spent her whole life trying to become.

After dinner she cleared the table, put away food, washed the
pots and pans, wiped the counter, and then closed the kitchen
door against the sloshing roar of the dishwasher.

Such discipline—day in and day out, for many long years.

One Knife, One Pot

by John Thorne
from *Gourmet*

Simple Cooking is John Thorne's thing. That's the name of his newsletter and his web site; that's the kind of down-to-earth food he celebrates. His straightforward, personal writing is a refreshing change from fussy gourmandizing; he holds fast to kitchen basics and reminds us to do the same.

Cooks, at least serious cooks, can be divided roughly into two groups: pot cooks and knife cooks. Of course, each sort uses both implements; it is a matter of which serves as the lodestone of their kitchen, the piece of cookware that, in case of a fire, they would rescue first. There is no doubt that I would save my knives. Not only am I a knife cook, but it wasn't until I found the right knife that I became any sort of cook at all.

I fell into cooking as many do: by necessity. I was nineteen, a college dropout, living alone in a dirt-cheap fifth-floor walk-up on New York's Lower East Side. I had no experience, no kitchen equipment, no money, but none of that mattered, because I had no palate then, either. Everything I made tasted good to me because everything I made was an adventure. At that time, frozen corn and frozen peas were five boxes to the dollar; a pound of hamburger was even less. So, until I discovered rice, a weekday meal was simply a box of the one cooked with a fifth of a pound of the other, and I ate it feeling amazed at what a clever fellow I was.

But even if I didn't know what to think about what I ate, I had definite opinions about the kitchen equipment I cooked it with. Most of my tiny collection had been bought at a store on East Fourteenth Street. It was different from other junk stores only in that everything it sold was brand-new—instant junk. My single kitchen knife was far from sharp, but, even worse, it *felt* dull, as if it had been made to look like a knife rather than to be one. It was little better than a toy—and so were the cheap pans that warped at once if put empty on the flame and scorched any-thing, even soup, if you weren't careful.

This upset me. I had an adolescent's volatile sensitivity to anything that threatened my *amour-propre*. Aspiring to become a novelist, I knew I needed a decent, solid typewriter, and I had sacrificed everything to get one. Then, when it was stolen from my apartment a week later, I found a way to buy another, and discovered that sacrifice could pull even more out of me than I knew I had to give. Now I yearned almost as much for two things more: one good knife and one good pot.

This was in the early 1960s, and at that time there was a cook's store on the Avenue of the Americas near Twenty-first Street called Bazar Français. I had come across it on one of my rambles, and I could tell it was the right sort of place as soon as I walked in the door. The store itself was austere and slightly scary; the customers and the equipment they were examining looked seri-ous and professional.

I began to browse, with trepidation. The smallest copper pot cost more than I earned in a week, working as I did then in the mail room of a steamship line. The kitchen utensils—the spatulas, ladles, skimmers—were made for pots and pans whose dimensions seemed larger than life. I couldn't have put one in any pot or pan I owned without causing it to tumble off the stove.

Then I came to the knives. Of course, there were many of these that were also beyond the timid reach of my wallet. But this didn't matter. Almost at once I saw a knife that I both desired intensely and could easily afford. Although there was no mark on it that said so, the store claimed it was made in France. If it was, it was certainly not at the top of the manufacturer's line. No knife could have been more utilitarian: It had a blade and a handle, and that was all. I don't remember exactly what it cost, but I know that the price was less than ten dollars.

This knife, three decades later, sits beside me on the desk as I write. It is made of carbon steel, with a full tang—the metal extending the entire length of the knife, with the two halves of the wooden handle clamped to it with brass rivets. Not in shape, size, or hauteur would it ever be confused with a chef's knife: It makes no statement whatsoever about the taste or expertise of the person who uses it. It is simply a tool, and all it says is "I cut."

That, it proved, was enough. The synonyms for *cut* in my thesaurus smack, almost all, of the rough and violent—"gash," "pierce," "slash," "cleave," "sever," "rip," "lacerate"—but with this knife the experience became eerily sensuous. The blade slid through a piece of meat almost as if it were cutting butter, and the slithery ease of it had a giddy edginess: One slip, and it would as easily slide into me. No matter how many times you've done it before, picking up a razor-sharp knife puts the nerves on alert, and practice teaches you to feel rather than cut your way around gristle and bone.

In other words, that knife brought the act of cooking to life. I don't doubt that a skilled cook can prepare good meals with the crummiest of kitchenware, because I have done this myself. But after the challenge has been met, there is no real pleasure in doing so. Cheap stuff is never neutral; it constantly drags at your self-respect by demeaning the job at hand. Only if you start a life of cooking knowing that dead weight can you truly appreciate the feeling of release, even joy, when you finally lay hands on your first good knife, your first good pot.

Eventually, I retired that first knife. The same metal that could be honed sharp enough to shave with also stained the moment it touched a tomato, rusted if not dried immediately, and gave any onion it sliced the faint taste of metal. When knives made of a new high-carbon stainless steel appeared on the market, with blades that could be kept sharp by regular honing and that were far less vulnerable to everyday use, I searched one out and put the older knife away. However, while I may have been done with it, it was hardly done with me. That first good knife had become a partner as much as a possession. With it close by, I knew I could make myself at home in any kitchen. Were it to disappear, I would feel like a stranger on my own.

The road to my first good pot turned out to be a much longer one. To begin with, pots are far more complicated than knives. Even when they are tucked away in a cupboard, their presence looms in the kitchen the way a knife's never does. A pot is the kitchen itself made small. After all, it is inside the pot that the actual cooking takes place.

Consequently, it is the pot—really, the set of pots—that is the kitchen's pride. The more self-aware the cook, the more those pots take center stage, not hidden in kitchen cabinets but hung proudly from open racks—sturdy, gleaming, clean. And, let's admit it, expensive. Acquired as wedding presents, they are often less participants in the cook's first fumbling efforts than silent, slightly intimidating witnesses. Spouses are easy to please; the cook's real task is to live up to a set of All-Clad or Calphalon.

As a teenager, one of my household chores had been to wash the dinner dishes, a task that always culminated in the ritual cleaning of the pans. My mother's pride and joy was a set of stainless-steel, copper-bottomed cookware, and there was no escaping the kitchen until these pots sparkled . . . a process that began with steel wool, went on to copper polish, and ended with the nervous rush to get each one dry and put away before its bottom was stained with a single water spot.

I wanted no such bullying presence in my free-and-easy bachelor's kitchen. In fact, the first pan I acquired, a small cast-iron frying pan, was in appearance and temperament the very antithesis of "house-proud." It entered my apartment greasy inside and rust-stained without, looking as surly as a junkyard dog. I cleaned it up a bit and taught it how to do a few basic tricks—the skillet equivalents of "sit" and "beg"—and tried to give it as few chances to bite me as I could.

Still, we got along all right. I found that I felt at ease with the lesser breeds of cookware: other, larger, equally grumpy cast-iron skillets, a cheap aluminum pasta pot, an unmatching assortment of saucepans made of thin steel and coated with cream-colored or blue-speckled enamel.

The truth is, I had a lot of growing up to do before I understood what good pots are all about. Knives are easy to understand. They are about cutting the Gordian knot. They offer immediate gratification, the opportunity to make decisions first and live with the consequences later. The sharper the knife, the quicker that choice is made. Pots, on the other hand, are about patience, about resolving things through mediation, taking the time to get something just right. The better a pot, the less it can be hurried.

I might never have learned this had I not, in my forties, finally gotten married. At this point in our lives, the problem was not one of quickly acquiring a *batterie de cuisine* but one of merging two very different ones. Since my wife, Matt, owned pots and pans of a much higher quality than my own, I was quite content to get rid of almost all of mine. In return, I was introduced to what would become, for me, *the* pot: a solid, stainless-steel, four-quart Italian-made saucepan with a thick aluminum plate welded to its base.

As with the knife, it was love at first sight, perhaps because the pot's serious cookware look was tempered by a pair of jug ears—two oversize steel handles—that gave it a gawky sweetness. More than that, though, its particular proportions drew me to it. I just loved to feed that pot. Our ideal cooking vessel must surely be shaped in some mysterious way to fit our appetite, and this one was a perfect measure to mine.

Like the knife, it asserted a simple, unintimidating confidence that somehow was transferred to me. By tolerating my capricious kitchen ways—refusing, say, to let a risotto scorch merely because my attention had lapsed at a crucial moment or to boil a cut of beef into shoe leather because I had forgotten to check how the temperature was holding—it got me to tolerate them more myself and, thus, to stop letting them get in my way.

It was also a delight to use. The heavy bottom not only made hot spots a thing of the past, it absorbed and then radiated heat in a way that made tasks like searing meat or browning onions seem rewarding rather than tedious, especially since the results were so compellingly delicious. Matt and I suddenly found ourselves eating chowder or cioppino, some curry or another, butterbean soup, or hoppin' John almost every night—dishes that seemed conceived for no other purpose than for me to take the pot through its paces. And so it was that this knife cook finally found his pot and discovered that, with it, his kitchen was complete.

Bottom-Drawer Blues

by Kim Severson

from *The San Francisco Chronicle*

If John Thorne needs only one knife and one pot, then what's all that clutter in our kitchen drawers? In the hands of an energetic food reporter like the *San Francisco Chronicle*'s Kim Severson, it's a question that reveals a lot about how Americans cook.

Cookware guru Chuck Williams held up a slim, three-pronged kitchen gadget and sighed. He was certain the French tool, designed to make it easier to peel a hot, boiled potato, would be a hit at his Williams-Sonoma stores.

Instead, it bombed.

"I don't understand it," he said, a wistful look crossing his 84-year-old eyes. "Maybe it's because we don't eat as many boiled potatoes as the Europeans do."

Or maybe it's because peeling the darn thing with a knife is easier.

So it goes in the mercurial world of kitchen gadgets. More often than not, tools that offer a clever solution to a vexing kitchen problem are used once or twice and then relegated to the place all bad kitchen gadgets go to die—the bottom drawer.

Don't look so smug. You know you have one. Likely, it's filled with olive grabbers, cherry pitters, butter curlers and bundt pans.

The bottom drawer has a corollary—the bottom shelf. That's reserved for kitchen appliances that once held the promise of certain culinary glory, only to be shoved in the pantry after a few uses. The items are often so heavy and bulky, their sheer weight keeps them from being pulled out for use. Count among the candidates food processors, electric juicers, yogurt makers and electric pasta machines.

Although we ought to know better, cooks just can't stop buying gadgets, ever hopeful that the olive will be easier to pit, the cheese easier to grate. Last year, according to the National Housewares Manufacturers Association, Americans spent almost $15.75 billion on kitchen cookware—including pots and pans and basic tools like spatulas—but also including more esoteric items. And the trend shows no sign of slowing.

So what makes a gadget go bad? Why does an item that seems so promising in the store end up in the bottom drawer? After interviewing dozens of cooks and sellers of kitchen tools, some broad—albeit completely unscientific—theories emerged:

It's simply easier to do the task by hand.

Williams' boiled potato holder falls into this category. So do egg separators. Remember when tasting spoons were popular? They had a hollowed handle so soup or sauce could cool as it flowed from the bowl down the handle to your lips. Somehow, just using a regular spoon seems a lot easier.

Stephanie Connelly, an avid San Francisco home cook, offers a perfect example. "The one gadget that I bought that I tried to use to no avail was a shrimp deveiner—a little plastic thing with a metal prong that you are supposed to scrape along the bottom of the shrimp to remove the vein. The thing was more trouble than it was worth. Just stick with your fingers; they work better."

Food fashion changes.

Still have your larding needles? How about that terra cotta garlic roaster or your sea salt grinder? Food trends change as fast as fashion trends, and the bottom drawer is a mini-museum of the way we once cooked.

Williams doesn't sell many of those two-piece wire baskets used make deep-fried shredded potato nests anymore. Nor does he sell a lot of escargot equipment or vertical chicken roasters. He does sell truckloads of oil misters, a gadget that reflects today's lighter cooking style.

But like bell-bottoms, keep a gadget in the drawer long enough and it might come back in fashion. Just look at the crepe pan and the fondue pot.

It's easier to buy the food than to make it.

Many a cook has discovered this truth after buying a pasta maker, bread machine, beef jerky maker or counter-top potato chip fryer.

Allex Gruman, a division merchandising director for Macy's, puts pizza stones in this category. "Pizza stones were big when thin-crust Italian pizza became fashionable five or six years ago. But people realized it was a pain to roll out the crust and it never tasted like the pizzas from the wood ovens anyway."

But that wasn't the worst entry in this category, he says. "The total ultimate dog was the seltzer maker. I'll never forget it. It was 1989. We found out nobody wants to make seltzer water at home."

You rarely or never make the food for which the tool is designed.

Holiday-specific cooking gadgets comprise much of this category. Just shuffle through a drawer full of Pilgrim-shaped cookie cutters, heart-shaped gelatin molds and cast-iron rosette irons. Alongside, you'll find zucchini ballers, soft-boiled egg cups, turkey roasting accessories and donut making equipment.

Maybe it's time you admit you're never going to curl butter. **Cleaning the tool is too much work.**

Although some people swear by them, garlic presses might be the poster children for this problem. Spend time with a tooth-pick trying to get garlic bits out of the holes and you'll be back to using a knife in no time.

Home cook Jon Dickson of Oakland offers the combination pasta and sausage maker as an example of a kitchen tool that got consigned to the bottom shelf not only because cleanup was a hassle, but because making the food wasn't worth the trouble.

"I bought it, used it twice for pasta and once to make sausages. It took more time to use than if I'd made pasta and sausages by hand," he says. "And the clean-up . . . let's not even go there."

You can't resist the pitch.

It slices, it dices—and it usually doesn't work. This is the uni-verse of gadget sellers like Ron Popeil, and where bottom drawer items are likely to be born.

Whether as complex as a half-hour infomercial or as simple as a well-written packaging claim, the pitch on some kitchen items can be too strong to resist. Of course you want a simple way to get garlic odors off your fingers. But is a piece of polished stain-less steel really the answer?

Instant frothers, little glass disks that keep pots from boiling over, in-the-shell egg scramblers, devices to make hard-boiled eggs square, counter-top hamburger grills and knives that can cut a soft-drink can then slice a tomato—they all sound so promising, so necessary. And how about those machines that cut segments of citrus with the turn of a handle or slice onions into perfect blossoms, just like you see in restaurants. Brilliant—until you find out that they don't work, they're too much has-sle or you never really liked those deep-fried onions anyway.

Clearly, weak moments fill bottom drawers. But good tools are as essential to cooking as fresh ingredients. So how can a smart cook balance the temptation to buy time-saving gadgets against the need to have the right tools?

Easy. Be a smart shopper and go for solid kitchenware that will endure.

"The basic tools are what you'll always use," Williams says. "Good knives, slicers and vegetable peelers, a zester, a whisk."

Of course, that doesn't mean his stores will never stock candidates for the bottom drawer. Among the kitchen items stacked in his office for consideration recently was a wide-bladed knife designed specifically to cut and serve cottage cheese.

Williams admitted it was a rather esoteric item. But then he got a twinkle in his eye. "Well," he said, "you can get a lot of cottage cheese up with it."

Herbs at the Kitchen Door

by Jerry Traunfeld

from *The Herbfarm Cookbook*

Outside of Seattle, the Herbfarm Restaurant astounds its guests with a flavorful, highly-wrought cuisine inspired by the extensive surrounding herb gardens. The presiding genius, Jerry Traunfeld, conveys his fervor for fresh herbs in this remarkably readable cookbook.

Whether you have a few pots of herbs on a tiny balcony or an elaborate *potager* (kitchen garden), growing and cooking with fresh herbs brings incomparable vibrancy to the food you make. Herbs are easy to grow—they're undemanding and practically take care of themselves. If you love to cook and have any sort of sunny outdoor space—balcony, deck, yard or acreage—there is no reason not to plant at least a few. When newly cut, herbs have vividly fresh flavors, full of both strength and subtlety and noticeably more intense than the fresh herbs in supermarkets. And then there's the satisfaction of knowing you raised that herb yourself.

From a gardener's perspective, herbs are worth growing just for the simple delights of what they are. They are beautiful plants: from sprawling gnarled thyme, to anise hyssop crowned with furry royal purple spikes, to towering angelica with strapping leaves and great umbels of chartreuse seeds. Both ornamental and useful, they're at home in the flower border, vegetable garden, and window box. And just as a perfumed rose has ten times the charm of a scentless blossom, herbs captivate because they add fragrance to the garden. Lemon verbena permeates the air with piercing lemon scent each time you brush by it. The silvered deep green needles of a rosemary shrub send out a clean and bracing piney fragrance that you can smell from yards away. Lavender charms not just with graceful flower spikes but also with its sweet, alluring perfume. Herbs are the great seducers of the garden.

From a cook's perspective, the herb garden is a source of endless culinary inspiration. When you rub and sniff your way down the paths, the fragrances whet your appetite and you soon have the itch to cook. Run your hand over the lush variegated mounds of lemon thyme edging a path, and the provocative scent they release might have you thinking of a marinade for fresh tuna. Pinch off a bit of the lacy yellow fennel blossom, chew it for a moment, and it will suggest just the right touch of anise flavor for sprinkling over broiled shrimp or a grilled peach. Rub the fuzzy rose-geranium leaf, and you'll remember last summer's crisp raspberry tart scented with its floral leaves.

The ultimate pleasure of having your own herb garden is its proximity to your kitchen. You have the luxury of being able to run out to pick herbs as the inspiration comes to you, If you need a few sprigs of thyme for the stock, a shower of basil for your pasta, or a tablespoon of rosemary for the foccacia, it's right outside the door. And when you shop for recipe ingredients, you won't have to search all over town for the tablespoon of fresh oregano that's called for and end up paying a fortune for a bunch of tired sprigs.

The flavor in a freshly picked herb comes from the concentration of essential oils. Some of the oils are contained in the leaf itself, but much of them are held in little sacs (glands) on the surfaces of the leaves and stems. These oils are volatile, meaning they evaporate into the air. As soon as you pick herbs, their fragrant oils begin to dissipate, so the longer they sit after being harvested, the weaker their flavor. This is the reason the taste of dried herbs only vaguely resembles that of fresh. Some herbs are more vulnerable to losing essential oils than others. Lemon thyme, tarragon, and lemon verbena will be noticeably less intense after a couple of days, while in rosemary, sage, and thyme the difference will be subtle. Fresh herbs in the supermarket are often more than a week old when you buy them.

And then, even if the herbs in your market are harvested daily, many kinds will be nearly impossible to find unless you grow them yourself. Most of the time, you can find fresh rosemary, sage, basil, and thyme, but chervil, lovage, rose geranium, lemon verbena, fresh lavender, and fresh bay leaves rarely make it to markets—there's simply not enough public demand.

As a bonus, when you grow your own herbs, you will discover they offer more than just their leaves. Sage bursts into bloom each spring with delicious-tasting, vivid purple blossoms that are superb sprinkled on pasta or over a salad. Fennel produces copious amounts of potent aniselike seeds at summer's end that add fabulous flavor to seafood and vegetable dishes, and their bamboolike stalks make an aromatic bed on which to cook a whole fish. Basil withers away in October, but you can gather and dry its sturdy stems and use them as fuel in a stovetop smoker. . . .

• • •

Choosing An Herb

The first house I grew up in had herb wallpaper in the kitchen. Bold fifties-style graphics spelled out the names of all the herbs that could be found in the kitchen cupboard, and below each name were listed the foods that the herb could be used in— marjoram for omelets, pot roast, and peas; sage for stuffing, meat loaf, and gravies; and tarragon for chicken fricassee, mushroom soup, and chowder. Quaintly retro, yes, but it was a very handy reference. After all, the question I'm most often asked is, "How do you know which herb to use in what dish?"

As in all pursuits, it's best to start with the classics. Take a look at familiar combinations of herbs and foods in cuisines worldwide. Tomatoes and basil from Italy, salmon and dill from Scandinavia, chicken and tarragon from France, lamb and mint from Great Britain, epazote and beans from Mexico, and cilantro and chiles from many parts of Asia are a few of these classic pairings. Each of these unions has become an integral part of their particular cuisine because the flavors make sense with each other and the two together transcend the individual elements. They are yours to borrow and integrate into your own cooking.

The key to successfully pairing herbs with other ingredients is to match and balance robust and delicate flavors. Unless the herbs are the focus of the dish, such as pasta with pesto sauce or a parsley salad, the flavor of the herbs should complement the other flavors in the recipe, not overpower them or disappear. The mild fresh flavor of poached halibut fillet will be smothered by a handful of rosemary, while a shower of tender chervil will exalt it. On the other hand, the gentle flavor of the chervil will be lost in a boldly flavored braise of lamb shanks, but rosemary will contribute a harmonious astringency and spice. Once you develop a sensitivity to how the intensities of flavor interact in a dish, it will be hard to make a mistake. . . .

• • •

Chopped, Torn, Snipped, or Puréed

It's midsummer, the herb garden is in full force, and you're inspired to make fettuccine sauced only with herbs and extra-virgin olive oil. Ask five cooks to make this dish, and you will end up with five very different results because of the way each cook treats the herbs. They can be pounded to a fine paste with the oil, minced to a powdery sprinkle, given a few coarse chops, cut into shreds with scissors, torn into ragged pieces, or tossed in whole. Each of these treatments will affect the flavor and character of the final dish.

As a first criterion for whether to chop, tear, or purée consider the style of the dish. A rustic, robust dish, like a garlicky bread soup, calls for generous handfuls of coarsely chopped herbs, while a more refined dish, let's say a seafood mousseline, would be better with a restrained and finely minced sprinkle. And just as a dish has a personality, so does the cook. Some are bold and impulsive, while others are painstaking and measured. It's these differences in approach that make cooking a form of self-expression.

The way an herb flavors a dish subtly changes with the way it's cut. The finer an herb is chopped the more surface area is exposed, the faster its essential oils blend into the food, and the faster they will dissipate as the dish cooks. This means you get a strong and more immediate stroke of flavor but less impact in a long-cooked dish. A fine chop integrates the herbs with other ingredients, both visually and texturally, while a coarse chop makes the herbs more prominent, lends more flavor contrast, and allows the herbs to hold up better in the cooking process.

Let's say you choose oregano, parsley, chives, and sage for your fettuccine. At one extreme, you could make a pesto sauce and purée the herbs with the oil in a food processor. The individual herb flavors will all meld, but they will lose their distinction and will be perceived on the tongue as very strong tasting. The fine purée will accentuate the bitter resinous flavors of the sage, the heat of the oregano, and the acrid onion flavor of the chives.

Once it's tossed with the pasta, the flavor will be powerful, sharp, and without nuance. (This combination of herbs is not suited for this treatment, but less aggressive herbs will work superbly, particularly the classic—fresh basil.)

At the other end of the spectrum, you could remove the leaves from their stems, give them a very coarse chop, and then toss them with the fettuccine as is. In this dish the leaves of the herbs will look attractive and will slowly release their flavor into the oil, but the large pieces will distract from the texture of the delicate fresh noodles, stick in your teeth, and be overly strong and unpleasant when chewed.

Clearly the dish will be most appealing with an approach somewhere in between. My own tendency would be to give the herbs a coarse chop. The more I cook with fresh herbs, the more I like to allow their individual shapes and personalities to make a statement in the dish. Coarse pieces of nearly raw sage, however, would be strong tasting and rough textured, so I would lightly toast that particular herb in the olive oil over low heat, then toss it with the carefully cooked pasta and the freshly and casually chopped oregano, parsley, and chives.

When you are chopping fresh herbs and are wondering when to stop, remember this: Coarsely chopped, the herbs will be visually exciting and their individual flavors will come forth distinctly and individually, but they will blend with other flavors more slowly and might distract from a smooth-textured dish. Finely chopped, the herbs will blend in quickly to achieve an integrated taste and unobtrusive texture, but they will lose some of their fresh appeal and identity.

Chopping Fresh Herbs The essential tool for chopping fresh herbs is a sharp chef's knife. If your knife is dull, you'll end up smashing and bruising the leaves instead of cutting them cleanly. They oxidize quickly, which means they discolor and the flavor will not be as clear. Take a few sprigs of lemon thyme and pound half of them with a mallet or the back of a knife to bruise the leaves. After ten minutes compare the scents. You'll notice the unbruised sprigs smell clean and bright, while the smashed sprigs have a muddier grassy scent.

Be sure your knife is free of a concave bow, which is caused by a poor sharpening job. Choose a large cutting board, either wood or plastic, so you don't need to worry about the herbs falling off the edge, and make sure the board is not warped. If there is not perfect contact between the knife and the board, some leaves will be scored rather than cut all the way through. If the cutting board slides on the counter, lay a damp cloth underneath to anchor it. Grasp the knife firmly with one hand, choking up and gripping the lower blade with your thumb and the top of your index finger for extra control, and place the extended fingers of your other hand over the front end of the blade to act as a pivot. Use the knife in a rocking motion, traveling with the blade to and fro. Don't be afraid to use a good amount of pressure and determination. The herbs will naturally spread out across the cutting board. Every once in a while, after a dozen chops or so, stop and use the side of the knife to scrape the material back into a pile.

Some cooks prefer to use a mezzaluna, or half-moon chopper, to chop herbs. This tool is specifically designed for chopping with its curved blade and vertical handles at either end. You hold both handles and rock the blade back and forth over the herbs. They work beautifully if they are sharp, but most aren't. It's very difficult to keep a good edge on these knives because you can't use a sharpening steel on the rounded blade. Once the blade is dull, you have the same problems of bruising instead of slicing that you have with a dull chef's knife, but if you're good with a sharpening stone or diligent about taking it to a skilled knife sharpener, a mezzaluna is a worthwhile tool.

Yes, you can use a food processor to chop fresh herbs, but it will never do as good a job as you can with a knife and board.

You have little control over how fine the herbs are chopped, the pieces of leaf will end up in very uneven sizes, and they will often be smashed and halfway to pesto instead of cleanly cut. Unless you're chopping a huge quantity of herbs, mini processors are the preferred choice. The key is to keep a sharp blade. It's best to buy a second blade and reserve it exclusively for chopping herbs.

The type of cut that delivers large-leafed herbs, like basil, sorrel, or mint, into very thin strips is called chiffonade, and it's a good way to treat the herbs if you want an elegant cut where the leaf is still prominent, such as in salads, stirred into a light soup or sauce, or to sprinkle over a dish as a finishing touch. Remove the leaves from the stems and stack four to six leaves in a pile. Fold the pile in half, or if the leaves are large, roll them tightly in a bundle. Using a very sharp, thin-bladed knife, slice the leaves as thin as possible. If the leaves have thick center veins, as sorrel often does, cut them out with the tip of a paring knife before you stack them. You can also cut the leaves into thicker strips, about one-quarter inch wide, as I often do with sage before I toast it in butter or olive oil, or with basil for a tomato sauce.

If your knife skills are not yet at an accomplished level, use a pair of sharp scissors to cut strips from the leaves. Scissors are also handy for snipping chives—just hold a bunch that's about half an inch thick in your hand and cut them to whatever length you like.

To treat soft-leafed herbs in a very casual way, you can simply tear the leaves into large pieces. This works particularly well with basil, whose tender leaves are similar to lettuce and easily discolor, but you can treat other large-leafed herbs, like sorrel, perilla, dill, fennel, or mint, this way. It's perhaps the most satisfying way of handling a fresh herb; you just gently rip away—right into the dish if you like—and enjoy the fragrance.

Always chop, cut, snip, or tear your herbs just before using them. All those newly cut surfaces exposed to the air are likely to brown and the flavor will begin to dissipate, especially with herbs like lemon thyme, tarragon, and marjoram. If you end up chopping more than you can use, refrigerate the leftovers in a small cup tightly covered with plastic wrap and use them within a day. Or keep a jar of olive oil in the refrigerator and every time you have leftover robustly flavored herbs, like rosemary, thyme, sage, savory or oregano, add them to the jar. You'll soon have a flavorful oil that's especially good for grilling.

Eggs

by Madhur Jaffrey

from Madhur Jaffrey's World Vegetarian Cookbook

Actress and cookbook writer Madhur Jaffrey moves beyond the Indian cooking that first won her culinary fame in a comprehensive volume packed with smart vegetarian recipes from around the globe. Her direct, enthusiastic, down-to-earth manner makes this the sort of book one uses over and over, with the stained pages and scribbled notes in the margin signifying a real cook's book.

When looking for a quick, easy meal, how many of us turn without thought to eggs: an omelet, perhaps with herbs, served with a salad, or a pair of eggs, scrambled quickly and served on toast.

I have always found great satisfaction in a single boiled egg, done just to my taste with the white set but the yolk still flowing thick and molten. I serve myself in an old egg cup, slicing off the top of the egg and sprinkling some salt and pepper over the opening. I wait, each time with equal excitement, for my first mouthful, which must include a bit of the white, a bit of the yolk, and a touch of the salt and pepper; a bite of toast has to follow. My mother always kept a special salt on the table that included some ground and roasted cumin seeds. This went well with most things but on eggs, it was heaven. I do the same. You will always find my mother's salt mixture on my table, especially at breakfast.

While I have always been partial to boiled or scrambled eggs, my father was strictly a fried egg man, and he ate them strangely. He would work all around the egg yolks, eating first one white, then the second. When only the yolks were left, glistening yellow orbs dotted with my mother's salt, he would ease his fork under one, pick it up whole, and deposit it in his mouth. He chewed slowly and long.

The fork would go next to the second yolk, which would also be picked up whole, shaking like Jell-O, and it too would disappear. My five brothers and sisters and I were mesmerized. More chewing would follow, with the veins near my father's temples throbbing all the time. My father loved his fried eggs. He ate them in total silence. If you asked him a question before he started on his eggs, he would answer only when he had finished. If he himself were in midstory at the start, we would all have to wait until he had finished his egg ritual to hear its conclusion.

Eggs may be quick and easy to cook, but they require care and timing.

For poached, boiled, and fried eggs, use the freshest eggs you can find or the top-grade ones. They fill their shells if they are boiled and so have a perfect "egg" shape with no depression at the top. Because the white and yolks are well bound together at this stage, they hold their shapes when broken into a pan for frying and poaching. However, all upsides have a downside and very fresh hard-boiled eggs are sometimes hard to peel, as the shell can stick to the whites.

Eggs may be poached and covered with all manner of sauces or served over cooked vegetables, or they may be poached in the sauce itself as is common in Irani villages. They may be scrambled with a variety of spicy seasonings (coconut, chiles, ginger, mustard seeds) as is common in India or with cooked vegetables such as cauliflower, asparagus, and the best of wild mushrooms.

In many parts of the world they are made into pancakes or cakelike pies. Known variously as *kookoo* (Iran), *tortilla* (Spain), *torta, tortina,* and *frittata* (Italy), and *eggah* (Middle East), these pies sometimes have a little flour in them and sometimes not. They may be flavored with herbs, or with tomatoes, zucchini, mushrooms, potatoes, asparagus, or even sliced and fried artichoke hearts. In India, they are frequently flavored with fresh coconut and fresh curry leaves.

Because their own flavor is mild, the fat used in the preparation of eggs makes a great difference. Tuscan fried eggs cooked in generous amounts of excellent virgin olive oil (sometimes with a clove of garlic slipped into the oil) have one flavor whereas a French-style omelet cooked in butter has another. French toast in America is all buttery, cinnamony, and sweet whereas the French toast of Bengal with its strong taste of onion, green chiles, and mustard oil is a world apart. The Far East, where eggs are sometimes seasoned with drops of oriental sesame oil, soy sauce, and even scallions, offers yet another group of flavorings.

What you serve with eggs also affects their final taste. In the Mediterranean, eggs are generally eaten with crusty bread: The last mouthful is invariably part egg and part olive oil, cleaned off the plate with a bit of bread. Middle Eastern egg pies are often served with yogurt and naanlike flatbreads. In India, hard-boiled eggs are thrown into curry sauces and served with rice, while scrambled eggs may be served with a range of flatbreads. In Japan, eggs (poached or made into omelets) are often placed decorously over a bowl of rice or noodles to make meals-in-a-bowl. There is always a little lubrication for the rice in the form of a sweet-salty sauce or a stock. In Indonesia, Thailand, and even Korea, flat omelets are cut into fine strips and used to both garnish and flavor all manner of foods from soups to fried rice. The eggs leave just a hint of taste and texture, while adding immensely to the nutritional value.

For reasons of safety, buy eggs from a reliable source and keep them refrigerated until you are ready to use them. Leaving eggs decorative in a bowl in the kitchen, in loving memory of lives in old farmhouses, is no longer a sound idea.

SOFT- AND HARD-BOILED EGGS
Use only fresh, top-grade eggs for boiling.

Soft-boiled eggs: Fill a pan with enough water to cover all the eggs you wish to cook. Bring to a boil, then turn the heat down to low so that there are just a few gentle bubbles rising to the surface. Now lower as many eggs as you wish to boil, one at a time, into the water with the help of a spoon. Set your timer for 4 minutes if you want the whites soft and semiclear, 5 to 5 ½ minutes if you want the whites almost but not quite set, and 6 minutes if you want the whites fully set. (I like the 5 ½-minute egg.) The yolks get consistently thicker with each passing minute but they remain runny even at 6 minutes. Remove the eggs with a spoon and serve immediately, either in egg cups or remove the eggs from their shells and serve them in a cup. These eggs are generally eaten with just salt and pepper though some people, like my husband, throw in a pat of butter as well. In Eastern Asia, soft-boiled eggs are served in a cup mixed with a few drops of soy sauce and oriental sesame oil. At my home in India, we served them with a cumin-flavored salt mixture. . . .

• • •

An Indian Salt Mixture
Here is a very pleasing salt mixture to have on the table.

> 1 teaspoon whole cumin seeds
> 1 teaspoon whole coriander seeds
> 1 teaspoon whole black peppercorns
> 1 tablespoon kosher salt

Put the cumin, coriander, and peppercorns in a small cast-iron frying pan over medium-high heat. Stir and roast for 2 to 3 minutes, or until the cumin seeds turn a shade darker. Turn off the heat and cool off. Grind the seeds finely in a clean coffee grinder or spice grinder. Add the salt and mix. Store in a tightly lidded jar.
Makes about 2 tablespoons. . . .

Hard-boiled (hard-cooked) eggs: These eggs have firm, opaque whites and firm yolks that set into balls. To make them, fill a pan with enough water to cover all the eggs you wish to cook. Bring to a boil. Turn the heat down to low so that there are just a few gentle bubbles rising to the surface. Now lower as many eggs as you wish to boil, one at a time, into the water with the help of a spoon. Set your timer for 12 minutes. Once the eggs are done, remove them immediately with a spoon and run them very briefly under cold water if you wish to eat them hot or you may run them under cold water long enough to cool them off thoroughly if you wish to eat them cold. They may now be cracked and peeled or left in their shells and refrigerated if you wish to take them on a picnic.

Hard-boiled eggs may be put into curry sauces; they may be deviled, their yolks creamed with mustard and then mounded back into the halved whites; they may be fried in a Southeast Asian style and put into fragrant chile sauces; or the shells may be cracked and eggs cooked in tea or soy sauce in a Chinese manner that leaves the whites quite marbled. . . .

POACHED EGGS

I hate to say this, but fussy French culinary technique has made home cooks wary of poaching eggs. I love poached eggs and I do not care to have them served to me in neat oval shapes. In fact, the oval shape seems unnatural and unnecessary. I certainly do not like the taste of vinegar in the poaching water, a commonly suggested trick for coagulating the whites.

So how do I poach my eggs? This is a method I learned some decades ago in Japan. My eggs turn out looking like fried eggs, only instead of oil, I use water.

I use a nonstick frying pan, preferably with a lid. It is important that the pan be of a size that just accommodates the number of eggs being cooked with ease; it should not be too large or too small. For a single egg, you need a 5-inch frying pan. For 4 eggs, a 9-inch pan is best, although one that is a bit larger or smaller would also work.

Ideally, poached eggs should be served as soon as they are made. However, if you wish to hold them for a while, place them side by side on a lightly greased plate, which may be covered with an upturned plate and even refrigerated. When ready to eat, slip the eggs back into a frying pan filled with hot but not boiling water, keeping them in a single layer. As soon as they are warmed through, they may be removed with a slotted spoon and served.

Poached eggs may be served over all manner of cooked vegetables such as artichoke hearts, spinach, asparagus, and even lightly grilled tomato slices.

Put ¾ inch of water in a 9-inch nonstick frying pan and bring it to a low simmer. Break 4 eggs into the water in such a way that they sit side by side. Let the water simmer very gently until the egg whites are almost set. Now turn the heat off and cover very loosely. Allow the eggs to set to the consistency you like. Separate the eggs, lift them out of the water with a slotted spatula, and serve on toast or over vegetables as desired. . . .

FRIED EGGS

Our cooks in India always fried our eggs over high heat in lots of oil so that the edges of the whites turned crisp and brown. I never developed a taste for these eggs, but my children succumbed on their very first visit when they were tiny mites. (Perhaps it was India that they really succumbed to!) Even today when my children, now with children of their own, come to visit, I have to cook their fried eggs karara, or "crisp."

Fried eggs taste best with toast, though I have seen them fried in green olive oil in Italy and then eaten with crusty bread. They may be accompanied, if you like, with grilled tomato halves and sautéed mushrooms.

Western Fried Eggs

Here is a recipe for the more common fried eggs. The secret to their success is in keeping the heat low and basting the eggs with the hot fat. The frying pan you choose should just about hold the eggs with ease, being neither too big nor too small. For 2 eggs, a 7-inch pan is perfect. The eggs should be fresh and of top quality.

    1 tablespoon olive or canola oil
    2 eggs

Put the oil in a medium, nonstick frying pan and set it over medium-low heat. When hot, break the eggs into it, side by side.

Let the bottoms set. Now baste the top of the eggs with the hot oil, tilting the pan to get at the oil, if needed, until the whites set completely. You could also partially cover the pan for a brief period, especially if you want to set or partially set the yolks. Lift the eggs out with a slotted spatula and serve immediately. (If you wish to turn the eggs over, slide the spatula carefully under them and turn them over. Cook for 20 seconds, then turn them over again and serve.)

Serves 1 to 2. . .

SCRAMBLED EGGS AND OMELETS

Scrambled eggs mean different things to different peoples. In China, eggs are lightly cooked in a wok with scallions, Chinese chives, or tomatoes and then seasoned with salt or a few drops of soy sauce and sesame oil. They are generally eaten with rice. In North India, the eggs may be cooked with anything from tomatoes and onions to mushrooms and cauliflower but they are nearly always cooked until they are fairly firm so they can be easily eaten with flatbreads. They tend to be very spicy (and so good!). In the West, eggs are often scrambled with the addition of just a little cream, milk, or water. They are very lightly cooked and remain creamy. Indeed, the cooking is often stopped with the addition of a little cold butter. Scrambled eggs are best made in a nonstick frying pan.

French Omelet
Omelette

The traditional French omelet is a work of art, a light, puffy cocoon-shaped creation, just about firm on the outside but vulnerably soft and creamy inside, born in a very brief burst of activity over fairly high heat. This is the omelet many of us aspire to but make with varying degrees of success.

When I first started teaching cooking, I began with Indian food—naturally. This is what I really knew best or, I should say, better than most people around me. I was teaching in James Beard's house, with him not only watching over me in an avuncular manner, but as he grew old and infirm, sending down for a taste of everything I was preparing on the ground floor of his four-storied brownstone home. At first he kept up with his own classes at least a few times a year but later he would ask me to teach the actual class while he sat in a high director's chair, watching and giving advice.

The first class he asked me to teach was Sauces, Crepes, Soufflés, and Omelets—all very French, of course. It was not that I hadn't cooked these things at home many times. But teach them? Not one to say no, I agreed and then rushed home in an absolute panic and fell on my already well-worn copy of *Mastering the Art of French Cooking* by Julia Child et al.

I made hollandaises again and again, crepes by the dozen were swirled into pans (the wrist, the wrist), soufflés were rising (and falling), and omelets were dissected for proper creaminess within. I realized then that tossing omelets into the air and catching them again was an iffy matter for me. I needed to keep matters in hand with forks and spatulas.

Over the years, I have developed my own approach to the cooking of an omelet based on what I know I can do with ease. All egg cooking requires timing and practice, and omelets are no different. But first we need to relax. This is my simplified way of going about it.

For a 2-egg omelet, I use a nonstick pan that is about 6 inches at the bottom and 8 inches at the top. It is best to use a wooden fork so it does not scratch the pan as well as a wooden or plastic spatula. The omelet cooks in less than a minute, so read the recipe thoroughly before you begin.

French omelets are traditionally cooked in butter. You may certainly do so. I use olive oil.

2 eggs
Freshly ground black pepper
generous pinch of salt
2 teaspoons olive oil

Beat the eggs until the whites and yolks are well blended. Add the salt and pepper to taste and mix well.

Put the oil in a nonstick omelet pan and set over medium-high heat. As soon as the oil is hot, pour in the beaten eggs. Allow them to set at the bottom for just a few seconds, then scramble the eggs lightly with the back of your fork, allowing them to stay spread out at the bottom of the pan.

Holding the handle of the pan, tilt it very slightly away from you and begin to jerk the omelet toward you. The omelet will begin to fold up on itself but stay at the far end of the pan. Keep doing this until a cocoon has formed at the far end. If you cannot manage this, use your spatula, and while the top of the omelet is still quite wet, fold it in thirds and then quickly turn it over. Roll the omelet onto a warm plate and serve immediately.

Makes 1

One Bite Won't Kill You

by Ann Hodgman

from *One Bite Won't Kill You*

Cooking for children is an art in and of itself, as any mother knows. Food writer Ann Hodgman throws a lifeline to exasperated parents of picky eaters in her snarkily funny, but dead-on-target, cookbook.

I had a very healthy breakfast this morning," said my son, John, recently. "Lemonade and Nutter Butters." From which it will be seen that I was still sleeping while John broke his fast. Unfortunately, I'm always sleeping while my children stock up on the nutrition they need for the busy day ahead. My husband wakes up with them on school mornings; on weekends, they forage for themselves on yew berries and pine sap from the yard. Or Nutter Butters, as the case may be. Breakfast just isn't that big a deal in our house. Naturally this makes me feel guilty and ashamed, though not as guilty as another mother I know should feel: her son, at a friend's house for the night, ate Lucky Charms *with Pepsi on them* for breakfast.

Still, breakfast isn't really a problem meal—at least as far as getting kids to eat it. When I was a horrible, eating-disordered teen, my breakfast was a cup of water that I drank with a spoon. But my mother left me alone, thank God. You may have a struggle on your hands if you insist on serving eggs to your children (or to me), especially soft-boiled ones. And working in enough milk might cause a little trouble. But most breakfast foods are easy to like. Cereal, toast, pancakes, muffins, bacon, sausage— what's the problem?

Speaking of bacon: my friends Andy and Barbara were once eating breakfast with their son, Will, when he was about two and a half. Scrambled eggs and bacon were on the menu. After he had cleaned his plate, Will asked for some more eggs, and Barbara obliged. "No," said Will. "I want more of *those* eggs"—he pointed at the bacon. "That's bacon," said Andy. Will said firmly, "Daddy, *we need more bacon.*"

Anyway, I doubt you need much breakfast advice from me, even if I were qualified to give it. Keep the meal simple during the week. Train your children to get as much of their breakfast ready for themselves as possible—and certainly to pour their own cereal and toast and butter their own bagels. Remember that if they want to eat foods that aren't traditionally "breakfasty," that's fine. Is there any reason that leftover lasagna, one of my favorite breakfasts, is unsuitable? Don't make a big deal about table manners this early in the morning; it's important not to start the day fighting. Dreamily reading the back of the cereal box with their elbows on the table is as much as most children can manage. Remember, they don't have the benefits of caffeine to get them going. "Why can't humans hibernate?" growled a six-year-old I know one morning when his father was trying to drag him out of bed.

And for the times when you actually want to cook a nice breakfast, here are a few recipes that are worth the effort.

Amish Friendship Bread

This recipe, from my friend Lisa Lasagna in Victoria, B.C., is one of those pass-it-along affairs. You give some of the batter to friends so they can start their own friendship bread, which they pass on to friends, and soon everyone in the world is Amish. As the batter bubbles, rises, bakes, gets eaten, and gets turned into more batter that goes into more bags, so do the friendships. The bread itself is more like a loaf cake than bread—you can serve it for dessert if you want.

I'm not sure I want someone handing me a bag of batter without warning. It would be like one of those health-class assignments where you have to take care of a pretend baby for a few weeks. Or like a living chain letter—one I'd feel even guiltier about breaking than I do regular chain letters (which I always break and always have, so don't anyone ever send me one). But the bread is good for breakfast, dessert, or snacks, and it's *way* fun to make from scratch. And, as Lisa says, you've got to love a recipe whose main direction is "Mush the bag." There was never a better cooking instruction for children.

"When gas builds up in the bag, let it out" is a good one, too.

I'm assuming you're starting this recipe from the beginning. In other words, no one has given you any batter—which means you have to make your own sourdough starter before you do aaaaaaanything else. The Internet has hundreds of versions of Amish Starter, including several recipes you have to pay for. Huh! Really *friendly*. Some of the versions take 17 to 22 days because you rely entirely on the batter's fermenting by itself; some take only 10, because you cheat and use a little yeast at the beginning. Guess which version I picked?

Day 1: In a nonmetallic bowl, mix together 1 cup flour, ½ cup sugar, and 1 envelope (2 ½ teaspoons) active dry yeast. Stir in 1 cup lukewarm water. Blend the ingredients well. Pour/scrape the batter into a 1-gallon zipper-lock bag, which you should then put into another bag, because if the first bag broke, you'd go insane. Put the double bag into a bowl, for the same reason, and let it sit, sealed, for 24 hours. It will begin to fizz and bubble and look ugly. Don't worry.

(Never use a metal bowl or spoon for mixing the batter. Never refrigerate the batter.)

Day 2: Mush the bag. Let out any gas that's built up.

Day 3: Mush the bag. Let out the gas.

Day 4: Mush the bag. Let out the gas.

Day 5: Mush the bag. Let out the gas.

Day 6: Heads up! Add 1 cup *each* flour, sugar, and milk to the bag. Mush the bag.

Day 7: Mush the bag. Let out the gas.

Day 8: Mush the bag. Let out the gas.

Day 9: Mush the bag. Let out the gas.

Day 10: Pour the batter into a large nonmetallic bowl and add 1 cup *each*—yes—flour, sugar, and milk. Mix well. Pour 1 cup of the batter into each of four 1-gallon zipper-lock bags. (Don't cheat and use a lesser plastic bag, the kind you use a twist-tie on.) One's for you; the others are for three friends, or enemies, *along with a set of instructions.* Write the date on each bag. This is important, because *the date for your friends is the new Day 1.*

Now preheat the oven to 325 degrees. Lavishly grease two 9-x-5-inch loaf pans or one large Bundt pan. Coat the inside of the pan(s) with 3 tablespoons sugar mixed with 1 teaspoon cinnamon. (It won't all stick. Save the remainder for the top.)

To your 1 cup of batter, in a large bowl, add:

> 2 cups flour, sifted with:
> 2 teaspoons cinnamon
> 1 ½ teaspoons baking powder
> ½ teaspoon baking soda
> ½ teaspoon salt
> 1 cup sugar
> 1 3-to-4-ounce box instant vanilla pudding
> 3 large eggs
> 1 cup vegetable oil
> ½ cup milk
> 1 teaspoon vanilla

Beat well. Stir in:
> 1 cup chocolate chips, raisins, or chopped nuts.

Scrape the batter into the prepared pan(s) and sprinkle the top with the remaining cinnamon sugar.

Bake for 1 hour; or, if you use the Bundt pan, about 1 ¼ hours. In either case, a toothpick inserted into the middle of the bread should come out clean.

Let the bread stand for 20 to 30 minutes before you take it out of the pan(s) and cool it on a rack. It would be a shame if it broke in half at this point.

Makes 2 loaves or 1 Bundt pan.

Vegetarian Turkey

by Fran Gage
from *Bread and Chocolate*

Longtime proprietor of San Francisco's acclaimed Pâtisserie Française bakery, Fran Gage surveys the highly-evolved Bay Area food scene in a sharp and spirited collection of essays. In this one, she and her husband rise to the challenge of vegetarian offspring arriving for a big holiday meal with some fresh thinking.

Thanksgiving dinner is always at our house. We have cooked turkeys every way possible—in an O'Keefe and Merritt oven, starting breast side down, basting frequently; in our commercial convection oven, which produced the crispiest skin; in a Weber barbecue; in *nouvelle cuisine* fashion, cutting up the bird, roasting the breast meat, and eating that as one course while the legs continued to cook; after a twenty-four-hour brine treatment; and in our outdoor adobe oven at our country house. Friends bring other components of the meal, but Sidney and I are always in charge of the bird.

Usually ten to fifteen people sit down at the table. During the years when the children were young, it was a boisterous affair, parents cutting up food and mediating disagreements, and usually at least one parent missing, soothing a fretful infant. As the children grew, it was the adults who talked and laughed the loudest, fueled by special bottles of wine that everyone brought from their cellars. During their high school years, the kids ate politely, and then escaped as soon as possible, to congregate in Casey and Claire's rooms, playing guitars, listening to music, or watching television.

Then last year, Sidney and I faced a special Thanksgiving dilemma—all the teenagers had become vegetarians. Turkey was out. Tofu was in. The change was predictable with Claire, our animal-loving daughter. First she stopped eating red meat. But chickens were still acceptable; she would still carve the ones we frequently roasted for dinner, vying with her brother for the "oysters," the sweet morsels on either side of the backbone. "It's because they're so stupid," she explained. "Cows are smart?" I asked myself. But over time chickens were excluded too. Claire would still eat cheese, eggs, and selected vegetables, and she had never liked fish of any kind.

Casey's conversion took a different course. It was a radical, blink-of-the-eye change. Before he left for college, he was a junk food maven, although he also appreciated well-prepared food, especially large steaks. Then he moved to Santa Cruz, one of the last bastions of hippiedom in the state, to attend the university there. In a flash, he was buying bagfuls of vegetables and shopping at the organic farmers' market. All meat was out. He actually cooked and ate tofu. I love vegetables and probably eat more than the rest of my family combined, but I draw the line at tofu.

Our friends' daughters were on the same food trajectory. And to bolster the vegetarian ranks, Casey had invited a friend from school for dinner. For me, the meal had to be as special as it had always been; relegating them to eating side dishes of vegetables wouldn't be a Thanksgiving dinner. We had to come up with something spectacular that would please everyone. The thinking process began. We had a month.

I leafed through the vegetable sections of cookbooks without inspiration. The vegetarians couldn't help. When asked for ideas, they were mute. "Just cook a bunch of vegetables, Mom," was their answer. A bunch of vegetables for Thanksgiving dinner? We could do better—but what?

Two weeks went by. We were at a standstill. Various vegetable casseroles and exotic lasagnes didn't seem right. Then one evening, Sidney, returning from a business trip, burst into the house. "I have it, I have it!" he yelled as he ran up the stairs. "What are you talking about?" I asked. "Thanksgiving dinner. Let's make a *timpano!* Remember the timpano that Primo made in the movie *Big Night?* It came to me on the plane, sandwiched in the middle seat between two large people. It would be perfect." I thought about the film and recalled the triumphant moment when the *timpano* was brought to the table, a browned dome enveloping layers of goodness. It almost looked like a turkey. This could be the answer.

We struggled to remember the preparation from the movie, but the details eluded us. I looked through all our Italian cookbooks. There was only one vague reference to a *timpano*. Then we took a life-imitates-art approach and rented the movie, replaying the frames that included the dish. One scene showed a sheet of pasta lining a bowl and being filled with sautéed mushrooms, cooked pasta, other vegetables; another shot showed an unmolded *timpano* with compressed individual pieces of pasta making up the outside layer. We would have to experiment, preferably before our big night.

The enclosing outside layer generated the most discussion. Individual pieces of pasta seemed too risky; the whole thing might come tumbling down. A sheet of pasta was one idea; thinly rolled puff pastry another. We decided to make one of each, and knowing that there would be ample food, invited another couple for dinner to help us finalize the recipe.

The Ferry Plaza Farmers' Market provided ingredients: a sheet of egg pasta, red pepper rigatoni and garlic pasta spirals, shiitake and chanterelle mushrooms, kale and chard, leeks, carrots, oregano, sage, and parsley. I had chestnuts from the Twenty-Second and Irving Market that I roasted and peeled, and puff pastry from the Downtown Bakery. We chopped and sautéed the vegetables, cooked the individual pastas, and hard-boiled some eggs. Sidney, the resident saucier, made béchamel and tomato sauces.

Timpano #1 was the pasta version. First we brushed a stainless bowl with olive oil and draped the sheet of pasta inside. Then we layered in the ingredients, all four of us in the action. This one held kale, shiitakes, rigatoni moistened with tomato sauce, leeks, and sliced cooked eggs, with freshly chopped parsley and oregano as seasonings. When the bowl was full, we folded the excess pasta over the filling and drizzled on more olive oil. A piece of foil covered the pasta.

Timpano #2 had a puff pastry lining. Butter replaced the olive oil to brush the bowl. The filling was different—chard, chanterelles, chestnuts, the spiral pastas in béchamel, carrots, a few leeks, parsley, and sage. As with the first *timpano,* the pastry covered the filling and foil covered the pastry.

While our creations baked, we made a green salad and opened another bottle of wine. Since all the ingredients except the outside layers were already cooked, we decided that a piping-hot internal temperature of 160 degrees would be sufficient. Sidney took the hot bowls from the oven and removed the foil. Then with a quick flick of the wrist he overturned each one onto a platter. We all held our breath. Were the linings fused to the bowls? What luck—they came off easily. Both *timpanos* were a rich brown. If I squinted, they almost looked like roasted turkey breasts.

A lively discussion of the merits of each took place over the dinner table, as we tasted back and forth. The pasta lining of *timpano* #1 was a little brittle; everyone preferred the puff pastry. The filling of the puff pastry version seemed more balanced, the sweetness of the chestnuts and carrots and the earthiness of the chanterelles a good counterpoint to the creamy pasta. We declared *timpano* #2 the winner.

When I told Casey and Claire that we had found something special for Thanksgiving dinner, they were skeptical. Efforts to keep them out of the kitchen during *timpano* preparations were futile. They peeked at every chance and withheld judgment. But when the bowl was lifted from the steaming piece de resistance, it caught their attention. Sidney had toyed with the idea of adding balls of fried tofu to the platter to simulate drumsticks, but we didn't have any in the house. The vegetarians' fears faded when they tasted the *timpano*. They all ate seconds, as well as large helpings of watercress and apple salad and pumpkin bread, but left room for small slivers of apple pie and quince tart.

I loved the *timpano*. It will be the centerpiece of future Thanksgiving dinners, as long as vegetarians join us at the table. But I also liked the small turkey that we smoked in our new barbecue.

Dinner for 7: What Could Be Easier?

by William Grimes
from *The New York Times*

As chief restaurant reviewer for *The New York Times*, William Grimes dines out often and well, shaping restaurants' destinies as he bestows stars or takes them away. He found himself in the hot seat, for a change, when he and his wife decided to put together a dinner party for a few friends.

The urge to entertain can strike suddenly, without warning, in unexpected ways. In my case, it was a tarte flambée that did it.

It was an Alsatian classic, encountered at L'Actuel, wafer-thin and crunchy, spread with a layer of smooth crème fraîche and fromage blanc, and topped with thin loops of browned onion and tiny chunks of smoky bacon. It reminded me of a similar tart that my wife, Nancy, had made on a whim one weekend years ago. "You know, we should make that again," I said. "Better yet," she said, "we could do a whole Alsatian meal and have people over."

The dinner-party instinct is irrational. More often than not, entertaining involves blood, sweat and tears. It can be a one-way ticket to recrimination and regret. For the guests, of course, it's a sweet deal. They bring a bottle of wine or a bouquet and, presto!, they're inside the velvet rope, ready for a stress-free evening of food and wine. For the hosts, the point can seem more obscure, especially an hour before the guests arrive, and more especially, an hour after they leave.

But still the urge strikes, again and again.

This time it struck hard. After nearly a year of eating out day and night, I was dying to make food instead of ordering it from a menu. I wanted to eat in my own home, with a few friends, liberated from the rituals of a restaurant. I wanted an excuse to splurge on wine. I wanted to show off a little. In short, I wanted to entertain.

Easy to say, not so easy to do. Especially for me. When I give a dinner party, I set the bar high. I don't want simply to please my guests, I want to dazzle them. I want to explore new culinary territory, to learn something from the dinner. If truth be told, I also want admiration and applause. Add it all up, and the result is a high-pressure occasion, ratcheted up several notches these days because of my job. If guests leave the table unhappy, it's not just embarrassing, it's a professional disaster.

I have five principles of entertaining. First, the food must be superior. No one can lay on a meal to equal the work of a professional chef supported by a kitchen staff, of course, and some of my worst dinners have been the ones when I tried to do just that. (I dimly recall an Indian feast so elaborate that the guests became sodden with drink by the time we managed to get the chapatis on the table.) But I despise the notion that if the company is agreeable, guests will be happy with roast chicken, a glass of pinot grigio and a scoop of ice cream surrounded by Pepperidge Farm Milanos. I become seriously depressed when it turns out that the host cannot cook.

Second, I like the evening to have a theme or organizing principle. It should educate guest and host alike, in a subtle way. Alsace, one of the few parts of France I've never visited, offered the opportunity to study up a bit, try some different dishes and ingredients, and explore great, underappreciated wines.

Third, I believe that good dinner parties entail risk. It's boring to serve old standbys, no matter how delicious. Fail-safe food does not energize an evening. To bring out the unexpected and pull it off with flair—that's the challenge.

Principle No. 4: A successful evening begins at the beginning and ends at the end. In other words, you don't welcome guests by waving them vaguely toward the liquor cabinet when they hold their hands out for a drink. (I once scored a hit by serving a tray of Bamboo cocktails, an American classic of the 1890's.) And you don't let the meal trail off weakly with coffee. Serve those chocolates and liqueurs. Extract the last possible ooh and aah.

My fifth principle amounts to life insurance. Buy excellent wines. They disarm criticism of the food. Serve a good Champagne at the beginning of the evening, and the battle is half won.

Our Alsatian evening began, as all dinner parties do, with that enchanted couple of days when anything seems possible. Like travelers fantasizing about a trip, or scholars drawing up a reading list for a long-term project, we floated in a dreamlike state, surrounded by cookbooks. I was tempted by the foie gras au torchon in Thomas Keller's "French Laundry Cookbook." It involves the deveining, membrane-stripping, marinating and squeezing of a duck liver in cheesecloth until it becomes a compact, heart-stopping mass of fat and flavor, served cold with pickled cherries. What a coup it would be to set that on the table. Too fussy and complex, I decided. It sounded more like microsurgery than cooking.

We both leaned heavily toward a dish from Le Crocodile in Strasbourg: lamb fillets wrapped in leaves of Swiss chard spread with chicken mousseline. But history, a stern teacher, has shown that one sure-fire way to botch a dinner is to crowd the menu with too many dishes that have to be finished at the last minute. Guests do not want to spend the evening watching the hosts run back and forth to the kitchen.

In the end, our menu looked like this: tarte flambée followed by warm rabbit salad with truffle vinaigrette, and, for the main course, venison stew with hedgehog mushrooms, fettucine and steamed green and white asparagus. Dessert would be an Alsatian farmhouse cheesecake surrounded by a mixed-berry coulis. Naturally, after-dinner confections would follow.

It looked good. Not too frou-frou, but several notches above everyday fare. Even after a year of reviewing restaurants, I found, my approach to constructing a meal has remained more or less unchanged. My standards have risen, though, and thanks to constant exposure to highly talented chefs, I have looked within and discovered untapped reserves of humility.

With the menu drafted, the real work began. By Internet, I ordered venison and rabbit from D'Artagnan. Over the telephone, I ordered a black winter truffle and mushrooms from Urbani. The dinner was scheduled for a Thursday night. The Sunday before, I made a concentrated beef stock for the stew. A quick check of glassware and table settings turned up gaps. I drew up a list.

On Monday and Tuesday I hit the wine stores, checking out the selection of Alsatian wines. I bought wine glasses and a pizza stone for the tarte. On Wednesday I gathered the first round of raw ingredients: assorted lettuces and fruits from Grace's Marketplace, as well as fresh fettucine, although not without a twinge of guilt; in an ideal world, the fettucine would have been homemade spätzle, but I foresaw precious moments spent pushing dough through a colander. (My sixth, hidden, principle of entertaining is that strategic shortcuts must be taken to ensure the greater good.)

I procured both slab bacon and double-smoked bacon from Astoria Meat Products. Crème fraîche we'd make ourselves, adding a little buttermilk to cream and letting it ripen overnight, but Nancy and I both worried about whether the starter for the fromage blanc would take properly. As insurance, I bought back-up cheese, along with heavy cream, eggs and butter, from Ronnybrook Farm in the Grand Central Terminal market. Then it was uptown to Le Pain Quotidien for an old-fashioned crusty baguette and to the Payard Patisserie for fruit jellies and chocolates. Finally, I stopped at a couple of florists to fill one vase with daffodils and another with an assortment of parrot tulips and sweet pea.

Thursday dawned all too soon. The day was given over to an all-out assault in the kitchen, with the usual division of labor. I did most of the knifework, prep work and heavy lifting. Nancy did the finesse stuff. Unusually, the campaign seemed to move forward according to plan. The worst had already happened. We had survived a meat crisis when D'Artagnan ran out of venison shoulder. Urbani turned out to carry it as well. Overnight, the meat, cut into cubes, had bathed in a simple marinade. Now it glistened tantalizingly. Inevitably, the fromage blanc failed to thicken properly, but we had that back-up. Now it was simply a matter of following the timetable.

Nancy made the cheesecake and a bright, piquant coulis of raspberries, strawberries and blueberries. We braised the rabbit, then made a mustardy vinaigrette from the braising liquid. Its sweetly piquant aroma rose like an offering to the gods. I browned the venison, covered it in stock and wine, and set it in the oven to bubble away. Another heady scent filled the kitchen.

"This is going to be good," Nancy said.

Several hours later, as the dinner hour loomed and she began rolling out the tart dough, she was singing a different tune. "My back is killing me," she groaned.

Our guest list, in living form, materialized at the doorstep. In sketching out the preparations for the meal, I omitted the drafting of this list, although it is as important to the evening as organizing the menu. The fine art of shaping the human material for a dinner party has always stumped me, perhaps because human beings are far less reliable than food. Invite people who know each other too well, and you risk a dull evening. Spice things up with fresh faces, and personality clashes can arise, or the group, like our fromage blanc, can fail to coalesce. Matchmaking is definitely out. I learned that the hard way, setting up two people who instantly developed the kind of mutual hatred that normally takes many years of married life to achieve.

This evening, the guests were carefully selected from a pool of unwitting candidates, most of them artists with whom Nancy had shared studio space at one time or another. Artists make good dinner guests in one respect, unreliable ones in another. They tend to have a keen appreciation of the finer things. Too keen, in some cases. I well remember one guest who would slump forward, as the evening wore on, a cigarette in one hand and a drained wineglass in the other. Like a mechanical figure in the town clock, he would signal dessert time by bumping his nose softly on the table.

The other downside of an artistic gathering is the ever-present threat of disputation. Abstract painters, in their heart of hearts, have nothing but contempt for figurative artists, who, they believe, belong on the ashheap of history. Figurative painters bristle at being lumped with the likes of Andrew Wyeth. Both groups detest installation artists, conceptual artists and performance artists, but five minutes into a spirited attack on the common enemy, they can turn on each other without warning.

Our group of seven, all well-mannered bon vivants, looked just a little dicey. In addition to three figurative painters—Nancy, Patrick Webb and Anne Schaumburger (her mosaic bears appear on the walls of the BMT Fifth Avenue subway station)—there was one abstract painter, Nancy Olivier; one artist with possible conceptual leanings, Joseph Karoly; a choreographer, Brian Kloppenberg; and myself, the soul of reason. If I could just keep them away from the topic of art, everything would go smoothly.

And so it did. The wine flowed freely, and the talk did too. The rieslings, juicy and concentrated, elevated minds and turned the conversation to loftier themes.

True, there were a couple of gaffes along the way. The films of Peter Greenaway popped up, for reasons I cannot recall. My wife snorted. "Has he ever made one good film?" she asked. Mr. Karoly reared up indignantly. Greenaway, it turned out, ranks above John Ford and Alfred Hitchcock in his personal pantheon. Whoops. "Can you believe it?" Ms. Schaumburger asked about an acquaintance. "He's actually a Republican." She made it sound like a neo-Nazi snakehandling cult. Mr. Karoly bristled. "I'm a Republican," he announced. Oh.

It seemed like a good moment to bring out the cheesecake.

And the food? In the cold light of morning, Nancy and I performed the traditional post mortem. She is ruthless and unsentimental when it comes to her own cooking. The tart she pronounced a major disappointment; the dough had not been rolled out thinly enough, so it seemed like a cross between true Alsatian tarts and American thin-crust pizza. The rabbit salad was excellent in most respects, but we failed to get the servings arranged on the plates quickly enough, and what was supposed to be a warm salad ended up cool. Also, we were too stingy with the truffle. On the other hand, the venison stew, voluptuous and deeply flavored, could not have been better, underlining the truth that time spent making stock pays off in rich dividends.

The cheesecake, too, was beyond criticism, although Nancy insisted that a previous version, made with cottage cheese, was lighter and better. I liked the denser texture of the fromage blanc. It had a sour tang to it that played off nicely against the berry coulis. The wines made a major statement, except for the late-harvest riesling, which seemed awfully thin. Later I discovered why. In a mixup, I had poured a dry riesling instead of the intended dessert wine.

But all in all, a good meal.

Two stars.

The Breath of a Wok

by Grace Young
from *The Wisdom of the Chinese Kitchen*

In her brisk and lively cookbook, food professional Grace Young revisits the Chinese home cooking she was raised on, along with its inextricable set of cultural associations. To most Western cooks, stir-frying is a relatively straightforward technique. As Young describes it, however, her parents' approach to wok cooking had a gestalt all its own.

All my life I have heard Baba speak about *wok hay,* the *breath* of a wok. No matter whether he is in a restaurant or his own home, when a stir-fried dish comes to the table, the sight of the heat rising from the food always causes him to smile and say, "Ahhh, *wok hay.*" I know that many people dislike piping-hot food and prefer their food to cool before eating it, but most Chinese are just the opposite—the hotter, the better.

Wok hay is not simply hot food; it's that elusive seared taste that only lasts for a minute or two. It reminds me of the difference between food just off the grill and grilled food that has been left to sit. *Wok hay* occurs in that special moment when a great chef achieves food that nearly, but not quite, burns in the mouth. For the Chinese, if the dish doesn't have the prized taste of the wok's aroma, it isn't an authentic stir-fry.

As a child, I clearly understood that when dinner was announced there was no excuse for tardiness. It was totally unacceptable to explain that you wanted to see the last five minutes of a television show, finish a phone conversation, or even do a few more minutes of homework. Hot food was serious business, and the idea of missing the *wok hay* was unthinkable, The dishes were choreographed for completion at the moment we sat at the table and the piping-hot rice arrived. I always imagined wok hay as a special life force that, when consumed, provided us with extra energy, *hay*. Some readers may be familiar with the Mandarin word for *hay,* which is *qi,* as in *qigong. Qi* (pronounced "chee") is the Chinese concept of vital energy that flows through the body.

When my parents entertained, they cooked in tandem, bringing out each dish as it was stir-fried. Douglas and I were left to "entertain" the guests, and I recall thinking how uncomfortable we and our American friends felt. Our guests seemed more intent on socializing and, although they enjoyed the food, they couldn't comprehend my parents' refusal to eat one morsel until all the food was on the table. It puzzled them to see my parents cook one dish at a time, disappearing into the kitchen and not sitting until everything was done. When Chinese friends came over, however, they would agree, after politely refusing to eat, that sacrificing the *wok hay* was inappropriate and they would gladly eat dish by dish with gusto. Forgoing their own enjoyment of *wok hay* was my parents' gift to their guests.

Even today, whenever my family attends a Chinese banquet, I can guarantee that shortly after the dinner my parents will comment first on the crispness of the Peking duck, then on the amount of shark's fin in the shark's fin soup (versus the filler ingredients), and, finally, on the *wok hay* of the stir-fried dishes. Later the same evening, the critique will continue by telephone with a few of my uncles and aunts. The discussion will be brief, but no one in the family can resist commenting on the quality of the food. If the dishes were outstanding, then the evening was memorable. I have heard my family fondly recall meals from years ago where the shark's fin was extra thick or abalone was prepared particularly well. Baba likes to sit closest to the kitchen when we go to a restaurant, especially for dim sum. This way, he can get the freshest food the moment it leaves the kitchen. If there is no table available near the kitchen, Mama will occasionally ask one of us to go to the dim sum cart as it emerges to retrieve the piping-hot food ourselves. Why wait for the lifeless food that arrives by the time the waitress makes her way to us? My Uncle Sam reminds me that the family still laments the change in what was once a favorite restaurant. The establishment was so successful that it expanded to three floors, moving the kitchen to the basement. Same chefs, same cooking technique, but now the *wok hay* had disappeared, because the distance between the kitchen and the dining area was too far for the "breath" to last.

To achieve *wok hay*, it is necessary to learn a few secrets of successful stir-frying. Stir-frying, like sautéing, is cooking bite-sized pieces of meat or vegetables in a small amount of oil over high heat for a brief period of time. Stir-frying, especially, requires keeping the food in constant motion, tossing it with a metal spatula, to ensure that everything cooks evenly and quickly, preserving the vitamins and vibrancy of the ingredients. The wok must be sufficiently hot for the food to sizzle vigorously the moment it hits the oil. The ingredients must be dry, especially the vegetables. If there is any water left clinging to them after washing, the oil will splatter when the vegetables are added, and then they will steam, rather than stir-fry. For this reason, Mama washes vegetables early in the day to allow time for them to dry. It's best to have all the ingredients at room temperature and everything cut into uniform pieces to ensure the same cooking time. Some dishes . . . must cook in very small quantities because the home stove cannot produce the same amount of heat as a restaurant wok. Crowding food in the wok requires more heat and longer cooking time and results in braised food rather than stir-fried food.

My parents do not use a wok for stir-frying. They use an old fourteen-inch Farberware skillet or an eight-inch-wide, four-inch-deep metal pot that protects them from oil splatters. The traditional wok used in China was cast-iron, preferred because it adds iron to food and conducts heat well. Chinese cast-iron woks can be purchased in some cookware shops in Chinatown; they are thinner and lighter in weight than Western cast-iron pans. Today carbon-steel woks are more common; each time food is stir-fried the wok becomes seasoned, as the ingredients and oil leave a delicate varnish on the wok's surface. Unlike a cast-iron skillet that simply becomes black with use, a carbon-steel wok develops a rich mahogany patina after about six months of regular use. A well-seasoned cast-iron or carbon-steel wok is a Chinese chef's most treasured utensil, for the more you use it, the more it becomes like a nonstick pan, requiring less and less oil for stir-frying. Be sure never to use a well-seasoned wok for steaming, as the water will strip the wok of its seasoning. The important advice here is that fancy equipment is not necessary to stir-fry. Choose a twelve- to fourteen-inch skillet that conducts heat evenly on high heat, or a fourteen-inch flat-bottomed cast-iron, carbon-steel, or stainless-steel wok. Never use a nonstick or an electric wok. It's dangerous to heat most nonstick pans on high heat, and electric woks do not generate enough heat; without adequate heat the food cannot properly stir-fry. Also avoid the traditional round-bottomed wok popular in restaurants, because it is impossible to heat sufficiently on a household stove. A gas stove is always preferable to an electric one because the heat level can be regulated instantaneously; however, for years, my parents successfully cooked on an electric stove.

The time-honored way of seasoning a new cast-iron wok is to

wash it with mild soap, rinse, and let dry. Warm the wok and lightly grease it with vegetable oil. Place in a 300-degree oven and season 40 minutes. To season a carbon-steel wok, wash it in mild, soapy, hot water to remove the protective coating of oil from the factory. Dry the wok thoroughly before heating it over high heat until hot but not smoking. Add two tablespoons of vegetable oil and stir-fry a bunch of Chinese chives, *gul choy,* and discard the vegetables after cooking. This onionlike vegetable miraculously removes the metallic taste from the wok. Wash the wok in hot water and never use soap again. Be sure to dry it thoroughly. To wash a cast-iron or carbon-steel wok after cooking, soak the wok in hot water or rice water, then wash with a soft bristle brush. Scrub it well, as any excess food or oil left in the wok will become rancid with time.

In my own family, the level of cooking tension escalates as the stir-frying begins. I always think of the Cantonese as the Italians of the Far East, and cooking certainly brings out their "Mediterranean" emotions. Voices rise as the drama of the cooking performance commences. My parents cook with a high degree of difficulty, ranked for Olympic competition. Sometimes I will cringe at the possible dangers. Their Chinese slippers offer no protection from hot spills, and Baba, who always wears a sports jacket, is equally formally attired when he cooks. One parent will precariously carry the steamer of boiling water from the stove to the sink, while the other stir-fries, often leaning over the front gas burner to tame a pot on the back burner. Their voices rise with urgency as they react to the demands of each moment, against the backdrop of the exhaust fan and the sound of a reporter discussing some world crisis on the *CBS Evening News.* Suddenly, Mama climbs the kitchen ladder to reach into the cabinet for a platter and Baba matches her exploit by pouring boiling water over the platter to heat it. (Hot food can never be served on a cold platter.) Miraculously, my parents arrive at the table unscathed, along with the stir-fried dish, rice, the steamed dish, and a piping-hot saucepan of soup. Within seconds, it seems, everything is on the table, masterfully executed. If more than one dish is to be stir-fried, the second is cooked after we have sampled these first dishes.

Timing is the most essential technique to master for stir-frying. Prepare carefully, and never try to chop or measure anything at the last minute, especially while you are stir-frying. The moment the wok is hot, turn on the exhaust fan, swirl in the oil, and immediately add the food. One of the secrets for preventing food from sticking in the wok is to have the wok hot, but the oil cool. Do not heat the oil but heat the wok. Stay calm as the first crackle is heard as the food touches the oil. Sometimes the oil smokes or sputters. If you feel anxious, simply pull the wok off the heat and regroup.

Stir-frying is full of life and energy, and requires quick reactions. Garlic, ginger, and vegetables require immediate stir-frying; but poultry, meat, and seafood should cook undisturbed for a minute or two, so that the ingredient sears slightly before stir-frying. If you immediately start stirring, the meat will surely stick and tear, yet too much hesitation will result in food that is overcooked. Always swirl sauce ingredients down the sides of the wok to prevent the temperature of the pan from dropping. Stay focused, pay attention, follow these tips, and you will master the art of stir-frying. Eventually, too, you will achieve *wok hay* and understand why the Chinese have for centuries revered the experience of food that still breathes its life force.

The Cook, Her Son, and a Secret

by Maya Angelou

from *Gourmet*

Poet, professor, and all-around woman of letters, Maya Angelou (*I Know Why the Caged Bird Sings*) has become a cultural icon, her dignified, resonant voice recognizable to millions. But even cultural icons look forward to a good home-cooked meal with friends — and that's not always a simple proposition.

The host said we were eating braised beef and potatoes. We knew false modesty was a daily familiar with her and that in fact she had served us a cryingly good *daube de boeuf* with potatoes Annette. Her dessert almost knocked us back from the dining table: Like fried ice cream, it was oxymoronic. She ended her splendid dinner by serving a cold lemon mousse with a baked meringue topping. We were floored.

Everyone knew that I should be the next host, but I hesitated. How does one follow Escoffier? I rolled my trepidation into a pill and swallowed it. "Come to me next month. I'll be ready."

My friends looked at me pityingly.

Once swallowed, the fear remained buried, and I tamped it further down with the knowledge that after all I was a good cook and after all I was in New York City and anything I thought I needed could be found in the Apple. I toyed with duck galantine and sautéed veal with Sherry and macadamia nuts. I considered a ten-boy lamb curry, placing ten relishes in my mind's eye—grated coconut, golden raisins, Major Grey's chutney, diced avocado, diced onion, tomatoes, fried onions, banana, cucumbers vinaigrette, and plain yogurt.

Although no award was at stake, the competitive spirit among the circle of cooking friends was virulent. I did not dare risk those dishes I thought of against the dinner we had just finished.

When the group came to my house, I gave them a black-eyed-pea soup and southern fried chicken with homemade biscuits. For dessert I offered New Orleans pecan pie with a bourbon sauce. I obviously fell back on my own Arkansas upbringing. The food was a knockout; I had held on to my reputation.

Bebe was a single parent who bragged in her heavy Uruguayan accent that she couldn't cook and wouldn't cook. She said she was raising her tall, strapping teenage son, Bo, on dry cereal and milk in the morning, pizza and a salad for lunch, and the same thing for dinner. She was a businesswoman whose presence in our circle of writers who were also gourmet cooks was inexplicable, but she did belong. We were an eclectic assemblage who had, without planning, developed a habit of cooking for each other once a month. At the end of every incredible meal (each host tried to outdo the last), the next cook would volunteer.

Two years passed in which we ate, drank, laughed, and talked together before Bebe invited us to her home. We had just enjoyed another magnificent culinary feat when she shocked us by saying, "Come to my apartment for dinner next month." We almost choked on our profiteroles and crème fraîche.

"No, no. We know you don't know how to . . . "

"Really, I had planned to be in Bangkok that . . . "

"Okay, no, you shouldn't have to do this."

"Okay. We'll come and eat pizza, and salad."

"I like a good pizza . . . a good pizza is a work of art . . ."

Bebe said, "No, we won't eat pizza. I will cook."

When the evening was almost over, a date was chosen, and everybody left laughing in their hands. Would we really be given take-out pizza for dinner and did she at least make the salad dressing at home?

Four weeks later we met in the lobby of Bebe's building, still snickering.

"What do you think?"

"I brought my Tums. "

"I brought Alka-Seltzer for everybody."

When we emerged from the elevator at her floor, the hall was redolent with mouthwatering aromas.

"At least somebody on her floor knows how to cook."

"Or maybe just someone in the building."

We laughed as Bebe opened the door, but our laughter ended when we entered her apartment. As we followed her to the living room, we knew that the aromas emanated from her kitchen. We were stunned.

Her son, Bo, brought out a tray of drinks with a filled ice bucket, tongs, olives, and slices of lemon. We were invited to make our own drinks as Bebe disappeared into the kitchen. We could find nothing to say, so we offered blank faces to each other as we helped ourselves to libations.

Bo emerged from the kitchen again with a larger tray, which held oversize cups. He said, "Gazpacho. Please take one." The Spanish tomato soup was as cold as it should have been and rich with biteable sizes of cucumber and finely chopped onion.

Many would-be cooks have attempted to make gazpacho but concluded with horrific nonedible, nonpotable results. This was as perfect a blend as any I had ever read of or heard of or tasted. Bebe stayed in the kitchen as we chewed the crunchy vegetables and drank the beautifully flavored liquor.

Bo collected the empty cups and asked if we would sit to table. There were place cards. We knew she hadn't been brought up in a barn, but nothing about Bebe had prepared us for this sophistication. After we were seated, she stepped into the dining room and announced, "Dinner is served." When she turned back into the kitchen, the smile on her face was sweet enough to rot teeth.

She and Bo returned, placing on the table petits pois with pearl onions in a cream sauce, *haricots verts* in vinaigrette, twice-baked mashed potatoes and mushroom sauce, and the pièce de résistance—beef Wellington. We stood and applauded, and she joined in the admiring laughter. Each of us knew the complexity of building a beef Wellington. How the *duxelles* must be prepared while the loin is in the oven. How the loin must be cooling as the short pastry rests in the refrigerator. How the pâté must be at a spreadable consistency before the *duxelles* is patted in place.

Bebe said she would love to tell us how a noncook had managed to bring off a four-star dinner. As we sat with small bowls of good commercial ice cream, she described her day.

At 10 a.m. she telephoned *The New York Times* and asked to speak to the food editor, Craig Claiborne. She would not be pacified by his assistant. When Mr. Claiborne answered, Bebe—in her heavy accent and with her flair for dramatics—began to cry.

"Mr. Claiborne, I am the wife of the Uruguay ambassador and I have invited eight diplomats and two foreign vice presidents with their wives for dinner. This morning [here a loud outburst of sobs] my cook and his staff walked out in a huff. Oh my, Mr. Claiborne, I fear an international incident. I had the cook send out the menu, and I cannot possibly deliver."

According to Bebe, Craig Claiborne asked, "What is your menu?"

She replied, "Gazpacho, beef Wellington, petits pois, twice-baked mashed potatoes, *haricots verts.*"

She told him she had all the necessary ingredients. He assured her that he would keep the telephone open all day and would walk her through each dish. All she had to do was follow his instructions to the letter.

According to her, he did keep the telephone open. And from the success of the dinner, she certainly followed his instructions.

As we left her apartment, she said, "I did this to prove to you unbearable egotists that cooking is no big thing. After we eat up all the leftovers, Bo and I will be back to pizza and salad. I'm not a cook, and look what I was able to do."

I think Bebe is a great cook, although no one knew it then.

I believe one is born a great cook, one achieves the status of a cook, or one has the greatness of cooking thrust upon them.

Bebe is probably head chef at New York City's Four Seasons today.

Weekend Lunch

by Nigella Lawson
from *How to Eat*

British cookbook writer Nigella Lawson urges her readers to re-train their appetites, to think about what they like to eat before getting caught up in how to cook it. Her exuberant, sensual, often languid prose invites us to dwell on the tastes, aromas, and textures of what we're eating and the scene we set for eating it.

Although the dinner party remains the symbol of social eating, most eating in company among my friends actually takes place at weekend lunch. After a long day at work, many of us are, frankly, too tired to go out and eat dinner, let alone cook it. And there is, as well, the baby factor. For many people of my generation, having to get food ready after the children have gone to bed explains the popularity of the takeout menu. And even those who haven't got children are affected by the baby-sitting arrangements of their friends who have. When I was younger we stayed in bed on weekends until two in the afternoon; now that most of us are awakened at six in the morning, there is a gap in the day where lunch can go. We have got into the habit of filling it.

Lunch is more forgiving than dinner, there isn't the dread engendered by perceived but not-quite-formulated expectations; there's no agenda, no aspirational model to follow, no socioculinary challenge to which to rise—in short, no pressure. Lunch is just lunch.

And if you don't want to cook it, you don't have to. A weekend lunch can be at its most relaxed and pleasurable when it is just an indoor picnic. What matters, then, is what you buy. These days shopping is nobly recast as "sourcing"—and clever you for finding the best chili-marinated olives, French sourdough bread, or air-dried beef; there's certainly no shame in not clattering about with your own pots and pans instead.

Shopping is not necessarily the easy option. It's certainly not the cheap one. But discerning extravagance (rather than mere feckless vulgarity) can be immensely pleasurable. Indeed, I can find it positively uplifting—not for nothing is shopping known as retail therapy. Shopping for food is better than any other form of shopping. There's no trying-on, for a start. Choosing the right cheese, the best and ripest tomato, the pinkest, sweetest ham can be intensely gratifying. And in shopping for food that you are then going to prepare (even if that preparation involves no more than debagging and unwrapping) there is also the glorious, self-indulgence of knowing that you are giving pleasure to others.

Shopping is not a quick activity—you need to be prepared to proceed slowly, haltingly. Compromise can be ruinous. Of course, some of the time we all eat food that is less than perfect, less than enjoyable even, but you can't set out to buy inferior produce—what would be the point?

Good food doesn't have to be difficult to cook, and it certainly doesn't need to be difficult to buy. But you must know what you're after. The important thing is to be greedy enough to get what's good but not so restlessly greedy that you get too much of it. Restrict your choices, so that you provide lots of a few things rather than small amounts of many. This is partly an aesthetic dictate, partly a practical one. If you buy 4-ounce pieces of six different cheeses, everyone is going to feel inhibited about cutting some off; however generous you have been, it is, only the meagerness of each portion that will be apparent. Provide, instead, a semblance—indeed the reality—of voluptuous abundance. You don't need to buy more than three different cheeses, but get great big fat wedges of each. You want munificence, you want plenty, you want people to feel they can eat as much as they want and there'll still be some left over afterwards. Start by thinking along the lines of one hard cheese, one soft cheese, and maybe a blue cheese or chèvre. You needn't stick to this rigidly; sometimes it's good just to be seduced by the particular cheeses spread out in front of you on a cheese counter. Keep your head, though; without ruling out whim entirely, don't be immoderately ensnared by fanciful names or the provocatively unfamiliar. One type of cheese no one has heard of might well be interesting, but not three. Anyway, the desire to be interesting is possibly the most damaging impulse in cooking. Never worry about what your guests will think of you. Just think of the food. What will taste good?

And you don't have to go through the ridiculous pantomime of pretending everything is homespun. If you're still getting your shopping out and unwrapping your packages when everyone arrives, who cares? Your kitchen doesn't have to look like a set from a 1950s sitcom. It is curiously relaxing to be slowly creating the canvas—arranging the table, putting flowers in a vase, chopping up herbs, and putting water on for potatoes—while talking and drinking unhurriedly with friends.

The shops nearest you will probably govern what sort of food you buy for your indoor picnic. I stick to the plainest basics: meat, cheese, bread, with tomatoes, a green salad, maybe some robustly salted, herb-speckled potatoes, the waxy-fleshed, puce-skinned ones, cooked till sweet and soft then doused in oil, scarcely dribbled with vinegar or spritzed with lemon, and with a few feathery pieces of chopped zest on them, left to sit around to be eaten at room temperature.

If you're buying ham, get enough to cover a huge great plate with densely meaty pink slices. Choose baked ham and the cured Italian stuff. I like imported prosciutto di San Daniele better than prosciutto di Parma (the glorious, requisite, honeyed saltiness is more intense), but as long as it's well cut—and obviously freshly cut—so that each white-rimmed silky slice can be removed without sticking or tearing, that's fine—more than fine.

There is internal pressure in my home to buy bresaola—dried, salted, and aged beef fillet—but although I like eating it well enough, I never mind if I don't. I'd rather buy a big terrine en croûte. Salami, too, is good. I don't think you need both salami and the terrine, so choose which you prefer. If you buy a whole little salami, as with the large terrine, you can introduce an all-important Do-It-Yourself element into the proceedings. Put the salami on a wooden board with a sharp knife and let people carve off for themselves thick, fat-pearled slices of spicy sausage. This way, the individual act of cutting, slicing, serving yourself, becomes almost a conversational tool. It makes people feel at home when they're around your kitchen table. Allow yourself a few saucer-sized plates of extras—maybe some fresh, marinated anchovies, olives steeped with shards of garlic and crumbled red chilies, astringent little cornichons, those ones that look like cartoon crocodiles in embryo, a soft, moussy slab of pâté—but, again, don't go overboard. I sometimes succumb to those Italian olive-oil-soused blackened globes of chargrilled onion, sometimes available at Italian delis, sweet and smoky and wonderful with meat or cheese or a plain plate of bitter leaves.

If you prefer fish to meat, go for the old-fashioned traditional option: a huge plate of smoked salmon—mild, satiny, and softly fleshy—with cornichons, lemon, and maybe a pile of blinis or potato pancakes, thinly sliced bagels with cream cheese and/or already buttered black bread. If you have a shop or fish seller near you that sells a good-enough version of the stuff, then maybe you should get a tentacled mess of Italianish seafood salad. I quite like, too, that old-fashioned pairing of tuna and beans. My great-aunt Myra, who was a wonderful cook, always used lima beans (just out of the can, as was, of course, the olive-oil-preserved tuna) and would gently mix the two, squeeze lemon over, and cover with a fine net of wafer-thin onion rings. Yes, proper dried then soaked and cooked and drained real beans are always better, but there's something comforting and familiar for me in that quick and effort-free assembly. It tastes of my childhood.

Smoked salmon calls for black bread, but there's something reassuring about a thick wedge of white bread, heavy with cold unsalted butter and curved over a tranche of quickly grabbed ham to make a casual sandwich. But all that matters is that the bread is good: sliced chewy sourdough, a crusty peasant loaf, or French bread—which could be a just-bought baguette or, my favorite, the slender ficelle. I sometimes think if I see another ciabatta I'll scream.

Frankly, if you can get good enough tomatoes, I'd just leave them as they are, whole, with a knife nearby (a good, sharp, serrated one, suitable for the job) so that people can eat them in juicy red wedges with their bread and cheese, or cut them thinly and sprinkle with oil and salt to make their own private pools of tomato salad.

A green salad needn't comprise anything other than lettuce. All you need for dressing is good oil, a quick squeeze of lemon, and a confident hand with the salt, tossed with your own bare hands. You can, of course, supplement the torn leaves (and let's be frank, most of us will be opening one of those cellophane packets) with some thin tongues of zucchini (the slivers stripped off with the vegetable peeler), chopped scallions, or a handful of not-even-blanched sugar snap peas or whatever you want. There's one proviso: keep it green. There is something depressingly institutional about cheerfully mixed salads. I was brought up like this. My mother was fanatical, and her aesthetic has seeped into my bloodstream; my father takes the same line. Do not even think of adding your tomatoes—keep them separate. Cucumber tends to make the salad weepy. Give it its own plate, and dress it with peppery, mint-thick, or dill-soused yogurt or an old-fashioned sweet-sour vinaigrette.

In the same way, I am fanatical about keeping fruit separate. There is, for me, something so boarding-housey about the capacious bowl filled with waxy, dusty bananas, a few oranges, some pears and the odd shrunken apple. I want a plate of oranges, another of bananas, of apples, of pears. I even put black and white grapes on separate plates.

An unfussy, sprawled-out weekend lunch definitely doesn't demand culinary highjinks. Don't worry about dessert. You just need some tubs of good ice cream—Ben and Jerry's or whichever make you like most, or buy a tart from a good French pâtisserie.

Bragging Rites

by Rick Bragg
from *Food & Wine*

You *can* go home again, as Pulitzer Prize–winning *New York Times* Miami bureau chief Rick Bragg demonstrates here, his journalistic prose lapsing into a down-home drawl. Bragg, who previously mined this territory in his memoir, *All Over But the Shoutin'*, takes his place at the family table for a feast he can truly appreciate.

The meal we all live for, the one we gather for in my momma's house after the first frost and gentle fall have faded the splendid green from the foothills of the Appalachians, is really born months before in the damp, thick hot of an Alabama summer. People here still call that time of late summer the dog days, a time when the sun glares white, like an old man's blind eye, on the pine barrens and frame houses, until the afternoon thunderstorms come down like a fist and then blow themselves out, quick, leaving the ground to steam.

Thanksgiving is just a cool dream, then, for most of us, except for the man in the garden, a hoe in his hand, planning ahead.

It all begins, that wonderful November meal, with that tall, thin man, his silver hair hidden by a straw hat, moving slowly between rows of sweet corn and tomatoes and beans, being careful with his feet because any fool knows that the copperheads like to rest there, among the stalks, waiting on a field mouse. The man, my uncle John, is not afraid of snakes, but they can flat spoil an otherwise uneventful day. Besides, as I have heard men say here, in summer it's just too damn hot to get bit.

Corn is a science, maybe even an art. Pick it too soon and you waste it because there will not be enough on the cob to shave off even with the sharpest, oldest butcher knife, and people who grew up poor cannot live with themselves if they waste food. Pick it too late and all it's fit for is hogs. But pick it just right, Lord God Almighty, and it is a reason to live. My aunt Jo will boil it until it turns creamy, from the starch in it, and put it in the freezer to keep.

Uncle John Couch and my aunt Jo, who helped raise me, along with my uncle Ed Fair and my aunt Juanita and my aunt Edna, know the garden the way their mommas and daddies knew it, by feel, by smell, by something almost like magic. To say this is a simple life is a city person's ignorance. There is nothing simple about working a shift at Goodyear and then toiling bent over until the heat and the sweat bees run you into the house. But it is a rich life—rich because the food that will line the countertops in my momma's kitchen on Thanksgiving Day comes from the red dirt just outside the door, which beats the bald hell out of anything else. The tomatoes, the beans, the peppers will all be canned in kitchens where the air is spiced with salt and vinegar and set in a cool, dry place until November. Everyone knows it will be the turkey, swimming in pale yellow butter, that will steal the show, but without those steaming pots of vegetables crowding around it, the main attraction would be, well, nekkid.

Like I said, my uncle John knows gardens. He also knows turkeys. Uncle John, on the fourth Thursday in November, is a valuable man.

The women usually rule the kitchens in the houses that perch on the hills and inside the valleys that make up the counties of Calhoun, Cleburne, Clay, Cherokee, St. Clair and Talladega here in the northeastern part of Alabama, not far from the Georgia line. But one day a year, many of them grudgingly allow their men to enter that sacred, mysterious domain to help with the turkey, just the turkey. I do not really know why this is, why these pipe fitters, steelworkers, rubber workers, farmers, cotton-mill workers and shade-tree mechanics are brought into the kitchen on this one particular day. I have asked and been told simply, "Well, they just are. Go sit down."

Men do cook here, but outside. They are allowed to flip the hamburgers, turn the ribs and spin the pig but are usually not trusted with anything, as we say, "lectric." "Your aunt Jo says I can mess up a kitchen boiling water," says Uncle John, in explanation. Aunt Jo is a small woman, but it is best not to mess with her.

I asked Aunt Jo, before I asked Uncle John for the recipe, if there was any secret to the turkey, anything he might not share with me, out of cussedness. There was one thing, she said. "Your pan has to be at least 30 years old. We won ours at Coleman's Service Station. Every time you bought gas, you put your name in. And we won." The pan, once a shiny stainless steel, has been burned gold by four decades of Thanksgivings and Christmases. "Twice a year. That's all we use it. That's why it's lasted."

Funny to think that that pan will outlive me, will be passed down and down. It's nice, thinking that.

It is a covered pan with a small opening in the lid to let steam in and out, and that is one tiny secret to the turkey's tenderness. The important thing, Aunt Jo said, is not to care what it looks like when it comes out of the oven. "The legs always fall off," she said, because it is so tender.

In our house, presentation doesn't count for a real whole lot.

It is the cooking that matters, and Uncle John has done exactly the same thing for 40 years. Listen to him: "The first thing I do is slide a whole pound of butter inside the turkey, which is laying back-down. Then I coat the whole thing all over with poultry seasoning. That's black pepper, garlic powder, onion salt, some paprika and a little bit of sage."

I am beginning to taste it now.

The bird is a beautiful gold, specked with sage and black pepper, and when he raises the lid, the steam billows out and permeates the kitchen, the dining room, everything. And you hope, hard, that the pre-meal prayer will be a short one.

The dressing is my aunt Jo's job, and she does not cook it so much as she creates it. Listen to her: "Start the night before with a big pan of corn bread cooked in an iron skillet. The day of Thanksgiving, mix in some chicken juice—broth, but I call it chicken juice. Dice up an onion, a big onion, and mix in the sage and some salt, because we're salt eaters. Edna said last year I used too much sage, but I didn't hear nobody else complaining."

She bakes it in the oven in a shallow pan until the top is crispy, gold-brown, and the inside is pale yellow, creamy. "Some people go to the store and buy dried bread cubes and call that stuffing," she says, and I get the feeling she would rather eat a bug.

My momma handles it from there. She makes biscuits, called catheads, that are too good to be described by mere words, and though she is never satisfied with them—"Lord," she will say, "I sure did let y'all down on them biscuits"—I cannot remember a single time in my life when there was one left.

She makes the best mashed potatoes I have ever tasted, just butter, milk, salt, black pepper and—for reasons I have never understood but know better than to argue with—a teaspoon of mayonnaise. Every Thanksgiving, I scrape the pan.

The legacy of the garden, and that hot summer, sits steaming on a side table. There are the green beans, cooked to death, with pork, and the corn, simmered with butter. The tomatoes my

uncle John threaded his way through months ago are now pickled in quart jars, bright green and heavy with dill. They look
down from a high counter, waiting for someone with strong
hands to pry them open.

And we will have macaroni and cheese, which is a vegetable
in the South, and, one of the best things on earth, a big pot of
pinto beans, a massive ham bone swimming in the middle for
seasoning. The only fresh vegetable, the only cold thing except
for the cranberry sauce, which is chilled, can and all, in the
refrigerator, is cabbage slaw.

"Thank you, Lord, for this food for the nourishment of our
bodies," my uncle John will say, and every head is bowed.

Plates overflow. We drink sweet tea—this is a Protestant
house, and the only alcohol is in the medicine cabinet. Dessert is
pumpkin pies, pecan pies, coconut cake and a chilled strawberry
shortcake. I almost never eat dessert, because I am never able. I
live in big cities, in New York, Los Angeles, Boston, Atlanta,
Miami, so I do not see this food the rest of the year. I eat until it
hurts, and my brother Sam will grin at me, because he lives here,
works at the cotton mill, and can eat it all the time.

Kinfolks stop by, seldom the same ones every year. Everybody
eats. Everyone says it was better than last year, and, because of
the gray I see in their hair, in mine, I suppose it is. This is not
magazine-cover food. It is the food of my youth, my life. I guess
I would live longer if I didn't eat it, but the life would be so
bland. I would rather eat the pages of the magazines.

We sit and tell stories then, because it is all we are able to do.
Some of the people we talk about have passed on, like Grandma
Bundrum, who I still miss terrible, and my uncle John's daddy,
Homer Couch, who was a live wire of a man, a storyteller who
could make you feel good just standing in his shadow.

"Daddy used to tell this story," my uncle John says, "about
this man who wanted a turkey for Thanksgiving, and every day
the man would say, 'Lord, please send me a turkey.' And as the
weeks went by, no turkey came. So finally, it was a week before

Thanksgiving, and the man had to change his prayer. 'Lord,' he said, 'please let me go and get my own self a turkey.' And the Lord did. That might not be funny, unless you knew Daddy."

I would like to be the man trusted with the turkey some day, and maybe some day I will be. For now, I'll just have to be the man praying for one.

The Chef Challenge

by Tom Sietsema
from *The Washington Post*

The notion is simple but intriguing: How would a fancy restaurant chef cope with turning out a meal under the same limitations a home cook deals with every day? As *Washington Post* restaurant reviewer Tom Sietsema watches keenly, notebook in hand, the chef rises to the challenge, nervously eyeing the cash register, the clock, and a mere four-burner stove.

A rmed with professional equipment, well-stocked larders and more than two hands helping out in the kitchen, any chef worth his whites should be able to turn out a meal of distinction. Have a horn of plenty, can dazzle. But take away the fancy gas range, the pedigreed ingredients and a dish washer with benefits and what do you get? We hoped to find out. Could a trained toque tackle the real-life drill faced by the home cook?

Fresh from having run 26 miles in the Marine Corps Marathon only a day earlier, chef John Cochran—co-owner of Rupperts restaurant in Washington and a glutton for punishment—agreed to take on the Food section's challenge and prepare a meal for four for $30 or less.

Oh, we threw in a few hurdles. Except for pantry staples such as salt, flour and oil, all the ingredients had to be purchased from a neighborhood grocery store. There was a time limit of an hour to cook—generous by any civilian's standards, we thought. And just to up the heat, dinner had to be prepared in a home kitchen; thanks to two years of nonstop restaurant-hopping, my bachelor setup had been barely touched. Perfect!

As it turns out, Cochran raids the refrigerator of his restaurant more often than he shops at his local Giant, in the Shaw neighborhood, where the exercise begins at 6 p.m. "I don't eat at home much," the 33-year-old chef says, explaining that he puts in 12-hour days at his contemporary American restaurant, located at 1017 Seventh St. NW, just minutes away from the town house he shares with his wife and co-chef, Sidra, and 6-month-old daughter, Martin Lane. Who wants to drink coffee at home when there's a $10,000 espresso-maker at work, he figures. Diapers and frozen sorbet are his family's usual reasons for a trip to the market.

With a slight nip in the air and a display of root vegetables just begging to be turned into something satisfying, inspiration for dinner comes easily to the chef. The meal will be vegetarian and include lots of different tastes, he decides. "I want to hit all the bases," he adds, painting a picture where chunky meets creamy, crisp rides with smooth and sweet blends with savory. His eyes first catch a $3 container of shiitake mushrooms, but he decides that's too expensive. Some button mushrooms fill the role instead. Besides, "I'm leery of stuff that's prepackaged and already sliced. I can't see the quality." But he can and does warm to sweet potatoes from a nearby mound, massaging each tuber to identify skin that's not hard and selecting only those spuds with a welcome red sheen. At 69 cents a pound, the price is right, too. Into the cart they go.

Looking around, Cochran is also thinking of parsnips, which

he likes to serve as french fries, and brussels sprouts, which are "good if they're grilled or roasted but not boiled to death." They're local, too, which appeals to the man who tries to buy nothing for his restaurant menu that's grown farther away than Pennsylvania. A humble head of cauliflower stirs his creative juices. "Pureed, it's like butter, man," Cochran offers. A white and a red onion are added to the cart, along with a fistful of collard greens, while spaghetti squash is ruled out because it would take too long to cook. An orchard's worth of apples beckons; Golden Delicious are available only in 3-pound bags, but the Rome variety, winking from an open stack, allows Cochran to select the fruit by the piece—but not before each apple is sniffed for flavor. If the nearby dates suggest indulgence at $3.99 a pound, they'll also play sweetly in a dessert. Cochran grabs a few, mentally tallying his choices to see how much more his budget might allow.

The purchases thus far spell rabbit food. "We need some grains, we need some protein," Cochran thinks aloud. On his way to Aisle 3 and some rice and legumes, he spies a pat of fresh yeast and yelps. "Fresh yeast! Brilliant!" Images of bread sticks suddenly dance in his head. "This makes better bread," he says of the small, foil-wrapped square in his hand. "It works faster."

Standing before a wall of canned vegetables, Cochran, whose expansive home garden overflows with sorrel, arugula, fig trees and more, shakes his head and jokes, "We could do this in a couple of minutes if we used Jolly Green Giant." Instead, he reaches for a bag of brown rice and some dried lentils, grabs some walnuts, thinks to pick up some vinegars for bolstering the flavor of his mainstays, returns to the produce section for a piece of ginger and a tiny green chili pepper and heads to a checkout line. When the register flashes his total, he's relieved to see "$26.55" brighten the screen. So far, so good.

Cochran is no more than a minute into an unfamiliar kitchen than he turns on all four electric burners to "high" and the oven to a toasty 500 degrees. After organizing his bounty on the counter, he quickly surveys the contents of my cupboards and the state of my equipment. It is 7:45 and he has 60 minutes to transform the groceries into a dinner that any of us could—and would want to—make. The game plan: vegetable soup and a centerpiece of rice and lentils fleshed out with side dishes of roasted sweet potatoes, rutabagas partnered with onions, grilled Brussels sprouts with fresh ginger, bread sticks and "a free-form apple pie"—apple compote sheathed in a crackery walnut crust.

Dishes that will take the longest are started first. Cochran sprinkles some sugar over the fresh yeast, dissolving in some warm water, and decides to cook the rice with the lentils to save time. Water, grain and legumes are added to a pot and placed on a red-glowing burner. Mushrooms and onion tops, the beginning of a stock for vegetable soup, are tossed into another pot. And the sweet potatoes and parsnips are whittled into finger-length slices for faster cooking before getting shoved into the oven. "This is harder than a marathon," Cochran says as he juggles against time. He asks if there's any cheesecloth, a staple in his kitchen (but not mine, alas). And while he praises the edge on my blades, he gives my flimsy vegetable grater no stars. "This is going to kill me," he whines as the dull utensil disses a hunk of fresh ginger and a sturdy rutabaga. Switching back to the knife, he makes short work of both ingredients. A cutting board the size of a Hallmark card gets a disapproving glance and my choice of a pungent, extra-virgin olive oil wouldn't be his. (Cochran prefers the neutral flavor of grapeseed oil, which has the advantage of a higher burn point.)

My entire batterie de cuisine is being pressed into service. "Make sure your pans are large enough" for the food to fit in, the chef advises. "The temptation is to use things that are too small." Unexpectedly, the knife slips from his grasp and soars through the air, landing with a clank on the floor. "Rule No. 2: Don't ever try to catch a knife!"

Another close call follows: When he removes from the oven a

super-heated pan of sweet potatoes to check for doneness, the paper towel he's got in his free hand bursts into flames. Fortunately, he's standing over a sink. Unfortunately, the smoke alarm directly above the torch bleats for three ear-splitting minutes. The scene is not unlike rush hour in any home kitchen.

Forty-five minutes have flown by. "You know what?" Cochran announces. "Things have got to change. At this point, it's called survival." Surveying the scene, he decides that the soup is going to become a stew thick with unpureed cauliflower and parsnips. Chop, chop, chop. The heap of greens is washed and reduced to a fluffy and quick-to-cook chiffonade and added to the stock pot. The bread sticks and apple tart? Suddenly, they're being rethought as flatbread and walnut flatbread, respectively. The latter will be paired with dates and slices of apple—raw as opposed to cooked. To minimize mess, Cochran uses his hands to crush the nuts in the bag. Without benefit of an apron or rolling pin (a bottle of vinegar is substituted), the dough is pressed out to the edges of two olive oil-slick cake pans and shoved in the oven.

"I need two more minutes for stress!" the chef playfully begs. But the clock slows down for no one. Besides, Cochran is making the most of the minutes he has left. Halved Brussels sprouts sizzle to a light golden turn on the stove; they are but a sprinkle of minced ginger and a few tablespoons of rice wine vinegar away from readiness. The gently caramelized rutabagas and softened onions are pulled from the oven and given a splash of balsamic vinegar. The craggy breads, now filling the air with their perfume, are flipped over for an even tan. They're as good as done.

Touch, sight, hearing—no sense is left out of the ballet. As he moves from dish to dish, Cochran also tastes and tastes some more. Partial to kosher salt, he is settling for regular tonight, but not without imparting that the difference between the two is "the difference between a tuba and a trumpet." Chock full of vegetables, the stew is missing something. Tang? Sass? That minute chili pepper, inadvertently tossed into the trash, is fished out from a plastic bag. Thrown into the simmering liquid, it adds a welcome piquancy.

Tick, tick, tick. Sliding into a few seconds of overtime, Cochran's efforts are transferred to serving plates and put on display on the counter: half a dozen dishes that could convince any home cook that he could do the same. Warm-from-the-oven bread is dipped into the soup. Sublime. Our fingers return again and again to the nouvelle Brussels sprouts as well as the batons of sweet potato, gussied up at the last moment with cider vinegar. Pieces of walnut bread are mated with crisp apple and sweet dates. A rustic finale.

It's a meal that celebrates autumn and serves up a moral, says the champ of his workout: "You've got to be flexible!"

Someone's in the Kitchen

The Objects of Our Culinary Affections

by Greg Atkinson

from *Seattle Times Pacific Northwest Magazine*

A rare combination of skilled chef and gifted writer, Greg Atkinson heads the kitchen at Seattle's top-ranked Canlis restaurant and is the author of *The Northwest Essentials Cookbook,* as well as a frequent contributor to the *Seattle Times Pacific Northwest Magazine.*

Writers typically have someone to whom they write. Beyond our actual readers, almost subconsciously, we imagine a certain ideal reader, and our voice on the page is for that enigmatic someone who will fathom our every intention. Jamaica Kincaid, author of *Annie John* and *Autobiography of My Mother,* says she writes for her first editor at *The New Yorker* magazine. He could detect every nuance of meaning, and even though he no longer serves as her editor, she still writes for him, imagining that he will read every word.

Just as writers have their audience, so cooks have theirs. Naturally, we cook to feed the people who will eat our food, but the most passionate cooks also cook for someone else, someone who may never taste their food. We cook for a kind of imaginary connoisseur who will focus intently on even our simplest efforts, someone who will notice if the pastry was handled lightly or if the sauce was made from bouillon cube or a reduction of pan juices. Our ideal consumer will deconstruct our dish, without failing to simultaneously enjoy it with abandon.

More often than not, the people whose palates we aim to please are family members. Sometimes, they are the ones who taught us to cook; other times they are simply the people we live with. We cook to please our children, our mates, our customers. Even when we cook to please ourselves, we cook to please the abstract standards that were set by others. After all, what pleases us is what others cooked for us, or told us was good.

Sometimes, I cook for my grandfather who ran the Hotel San Carlos in the early part of the last century in Pensacola, Florida. He died when I was barely eating, let alone cooking, but his palate was legendary. He knew exactly what was good and why, they say.

Though I never cooked anything for him while he was alive, my grandfather's presence loomed larger than life over the kitchen where I learned to boil eggs and butter my bread. His potato slicer and nutmeg grater hung in our kitchen. And when I earned the right to chop onions and pickles for potato salad, I stood on a chair and used Grandpa's double-bladed halfmoon cutter in his big maple salad bowl, inherited by my mother. I tried to make the salad just as I imagined he would make it, even following his formula for homemade mayonnaise to dress it. Today his tools are gone, but his presence is in my kitchen, influencing my decisions, measuring along with me the judicious pinch of that, the generous sprinkling of that.

I also cook to please my grandmother, who was less a mentor than an object of my culinary affections. I often cooked for her, and I continue to use her standards as my own. Born when

Teddy Roosevelt was president and King Edward was the newly crowned successor to Queen Victoria, she grew up in a world very different from the one she shared with me. It was her preference for unprocessed foods that led me to bake my first whole wheat bread, and sent me as a teenager to farmer's markets and natural food stores looking for the kinds of vegetables and cheeses that she extolled from her childhood. She was always grateful when I cooked for her, and I was grateful that she taught me what was good. Oddly, she was a woman who seldom cooked herself. "I don't cook," she claimed. "I'd rather do dishes any day." But she could often be found stirring up a little pot of cheese grits or stewed okra for a quiet lunch.

Other people I know cook to please their family mentors too. My friend Kate Stone, who runs a wild and wonderful little lunch place in Friday Harbor called Katrina's, cooks for her Grandma Cora Kelly who once owned and operated a restaurant on Hood Canal.

"She had all sorts of people coming around every day because of the kind of person she was," says Kate of her grandmother. "She had millions of friends." And everyone who came by seemed to bring something interesting to eat. "People would come in with oysters and clams. They would bring big buckets of smelts in from the ocean and my grandmother would fry them up. They had such a distinctive smell," recalls Kate. "A very good smell," she hastens to add.

Kate remembers too the crisp and delicate oatmeal cookies her grandmother made, and so does everyone who has an opportunity to try them today at Katrina's. Thin as the skin of a smelt, they break like porcelain plates and melt into a wonderful buttered-toast kind of flavor on the tongue.

Sometimes we feel the presence of our culinary mentors in subtle ways. Some of the things I cook and eat now are unlike anything my grandparents ever tasted. But even if I'm shopping for peppers for a Thai-style curry, I use Grandma's standards for choosing the peppers. And if I'm tossing fingerling potatoes from the Farmer's Market with Nicoise olives for a simple summer side dish that's a world away from Grandfather's potato salad, I still test the potatoes for doneness according to his standards that my mother passed on to me.

At other times, when we actually try to recreate the dishes that were made by the cooks who preceded us, we feel their presence even more. And the spirit of those good cooks doesn't limit itself to their direct descendants. Even though I never knew Kate Stone's Grandma Cora Kelly, I think of her every time I make her oatmeal cookies, and I try to make them in a way that would please her.

Grandma Cora Kelly's Salty Oatmeal Cookies

The challenge of these cookies is pressing the dough thin enough to achieve a cookie of ethereal delicacy. Kate Stone and her Grandma Cora's secret is to flatten each cookie with a glass tumbler wrapped in cheesecloth and dipped in flour between every cookie. "It's really hard to get them as thin as they need to be," admits Kate. "But that's what Grandma recipes are all about, isn't it?"

(Makes 2 dozen large cookies)
1 cup butter
¾ cup sugar
1 ½ teaspoons vanilla extract
1 ⅔ cup flour
1 teaspoon soda
½ teaspoon salt
2 cups quick oats
kosher salt

Cream butter, sugar, and vanilla extract together. In a separate bowl, stir together flour, soda, and salt. Add the flour mixture to the butter mixture and stir just until blended. Stir in oats and chill for about an hour or until very firm. Preheat oven to 350°, and grease and flour cookie sheets or line them with bakers parchment. Shape walnut-sized balls from the chilled dough and arrange on cookie sheets. Cover the bottom of a glass with cheesecloth and dip it in flour. Use this cloth-covered glass to flatten the cookies into very thin rounds about 4 or 5 inches in diameter and about ⅛-inch thick, the thinner the better. The glass will need to be re-dipped in flour between each cookie. Just before baking, sprinkle the cookies with a light coat of salt. Bake 8-10 minutes (depending on thickness) or until the cookies become aromatic and begin to brown.

A Day in the Life

by Anthony Bourdain
from *Kitchen Confidential*

Another superb chef/writer, Anthony Bourdain made the best-seller lists with his eye-opening exposé, *Kitchen Confidential*. The author of two previous novels, Bourdain wields a gonzo narrative style to reveal what happens behind the scenes in a tony Manhattan restaurant's kitchen— and it ain't pretty.

Thanks to my Bigfoot training I wake up automatically at five minutes before six. It's still dark, and I lie in bed in the pitch-black for a while, smoking, the day's specials and prep lists already coming together in my head. It's Friday, so the weekend orders will be coming in: twenty-five cases of mesclun, eighteen cases of GPOD 70-count potatoes, four whole forequarters of lamb, two cases of beef tenderloins, hundreds and hundreds of pounds of meat, bones, produce, seafood, dry goods and dairy. I know what's coming, and the general order in which it will probably arrive, so I'm thinking triage—sorting out in my head what gets done first, and by whom, and what gets left until later.

As I brush my teeth, turn on the shower, swallow my first couple of aspirin of the day, I'm reviewing what's still kicking around in my walk-in from previous days, what I have to unload, use in specials, merchandize. I hear the coffee grinder going, so Nancy is awake, which leaves me only a few more minutes of undisturbed reflection on food deployment before I have to behave like a civilian for a few minutes.

I watch the local news and weather with my wife, noting, for professional reasons, any major sporting events, commuter traffic and, most important, the weekend weather forecast. Nice crisp weather and no big games? That means we're going to get slammed tonight. That means I won't come crawling home until close to midnight. By now, half-watching the tube, and half-listening to Nancy, I'm fine-tuning the specials in my head: grill station will be too busy for any elaborate presentations or a special with too many pans involved, so I need something quick, simple and easily plated—and something that will be popular with the weekend rubes. The people coming to dinner tonight and Saturday night are different from the ones who eat at my restaurant during the week, and I have to take this into account. Saddle of wild hare stuffed with foie gras is *not* a good weekend special, for instance. Fish with names unrecognizable to the greater part of the general public won't sell. The weekend is a time for buzzwords: items like shrimp, lobster, T-bone, crabmeat, tuna and swordfish. Fortunately, I've got some hamachi tuna coming in, always a crowd-pleaser.

As I walk up to Broadway and climb into a taxi, I'm thinking grilled tuna livornaise with roasted potatoes and grilled asparagus for fish special. My overworked grill man can heat the already cooked-off spuds and the pre-blanched asparagus on a sizzle-platter during service, the tuna will get a quick walk across the grill, so all he has to do is heat the sauce to order. That takes care of fish special. Appetizer special will be cockles steamed with chorizo, leek, tomato and white wine—a one-pan wonder; my garde-manger man can plate salads, rillettes, ravioli, confits de canard while the cockle special steams happily away on a back burner. Meat special is problematic. I ran the ever-popular T-bone last week—two weeks in row would threaten the French theme, and I run about a 50 percent food cost on the massive hunks of expensive beef. Tuna is already coming off the grill, so the meat special has got to go to the sauté station. My sous-chef, who's working sauté tonight, will already have an enormous amount of mise-en-place to contend with, struggling to retrieve all the garnishes and prep from an already crowded low-boy reach-in—just to keep up with the requirements of the regular menu. At any one time, he has to expect and be ready for orders for moules marinières, boudin noir with caramelized apples, navarin of lamb (with an appalling array of garnishes: baby carrots, pearled onions, niçoise olives, garlic confit, tomato concassée, fava beans and chopped fresh herbs), filet au poivre, steak au poivre, steak tartare, calves' liver persillé, cassoulet toulousaine, magret de moulard with quince and sauce miel, the ridiculously popular mignon de porc, pieds du cochon—and tonight's special, whatever that's going to be.

I've got some play here: both leg of venison and some whole pheasants are coming in, so I opt for the pheasant. It's a roasted dish, meaning I can par-roast it ahead of time, requiring my sous-chef simply to take it off the bone and sling it into the oven to finish, then heat the garnishes and sauce before serving. Easy special. A lay-up. That should help matters somewhat.

By the time I arrive at Les Halles, I have my ducks pretty much in a row.

I'm the first to arrive, as usual—though sometimes my pastry chef surprises me with an early appearance—and the restaurant is dark. Salsa music is playing loudly over the stereo behind the bar, for the night porter. I check the reservation book for tonight, see that we already have eighty or so res on the book, then check the previous night's numbers (the maître d' has already totaled up reservations and walk-ins) and see that we did a very respectable 280 meals—a good portent for my food cost. The more steak-frites I sell, the better the numbers will be. I flip through the manager's log, the notebook where the night manager communicates with the day management, noting customer complaints, repair requirements, employee misbehavior, important phone calls. I see from the log that my grill man called one of the waiters a "cocksucker" and pounded his fist on his cutting board in a "menacing way" when five diners waddled into the restaurant at three minutes of midnight closing and ordered five côtes du boeuf, medium-well (cooking time forty-five minutes). I sip my cardboard-tasting take-out coffee from the deli next door and walk through the kitchen, taking notice of the clean-up job the night porter has done. It looks good. Jaime grins at me from the stairwell. He's dragging down a bag full of sodden linen, says, "Hola, chef." He's covered with grime, his whites almost black from handling dirty, food-smeared kitchen floor mats, and hauling hundreds of pounds of garbage out to the street. I follow him down, walk through the still wet cellar to the office, plop down at my desk and light my tenth cigarette of the day while I rummage around in my drawer for a meat inventory sheet/order form. First thing to do is find out exactly how much cut, fabricated meat I have on hand. If I'm low, I'll need to get the butcher on it early. If I have enough stuff on hand to make it through tonight, I'll still have to get tomorrow's order in soon. The boucherie is very busy at Les Halles, cutting meat not just for the Park Avenue store, but for our outposts in DC, Miami and Tokyo.

I kick off my shoes and change into checks, chef's jacket, clogs and apron. I find my knife kit, jam a thick stack of side-towels into it, clip a pen into my jacket sideways (so it doesn't fall out when I bend over) and, taking a ring of keys from my desk, pop the locks on the dry-goods room, walk-in, reach-ins, pastry box and freezers. I push back the plastic curtains to the refrigerated boucherie, a cool room where the butchers do their cutting, and grab the assistant butcher's boom-box from the work-table. Knives, towels, radio, clipboards and keys in hand, I climb the Stairmaster back up to the kitchen.

I've assembled a pretty good collection of mid-'70s New York punk classics on tape: Dead Boys, Richard Hell and the Voidoids, Heartbreakers, Ramones, Television and so on, which my Mexican grill man enjoys as well (he's a young headbanger fond of Rob Zombie, Marilyn Manson, Rage Against the Machine, so my musical selections don't offend him). I'm emptying the sauté station reach-in when he arrives. Carlos has got a pierced eyebrow, a body by Michelangelo, and considers himself a master soup-maker. The first thing he asks me is if I've got snapper bones coming in. I nod. Carlos dearly loves any soup he can jack with Ricard or Pernod, so today's soupe de poisson with rouille is a favorite of his. Omar, the garde-manger man, who sports a thick, barbed-wire tattoo around his upper arm arrives next, followed quickly by the rest of the Queens residents; Segundo the *vato loco* prep centurion, Ramón the dishwasher, and Janine the pastry chef. Camelia, the general manager, is last—she walks to work—and we exchange *"Bonjour!"* and *"Comment ça va?"*

Soon everyone is working: Carlos roasting bones for stock, me heating sauces and portioning pavées, filet mignons, porc mignons, duck breasts and liver. Before twelve, I've got to cut and pepper pavées and filets, skin and slice the calves' liver, lug up cassoulet, caramelize apples, blanch baby carrots, make garlic confit, reload grated cheese, onion soup, sea salt, crushed pepper, breadcrumbs, oils. I've got to come up with a pasta special using what's on hand, make livornaise sauce for Carlos, make a sauce for the pheasant—and, most annoying, make a new batch of navarin, which will monopolize most of my range-top for much of the morning. Somewhere in the middle of this, I have to write up the specials for Camelia to input into the computer and set the prices (at nine-thirty sharp, she's going to start buzzing me on the intercom, asking me in her thick French accent if I have "le muh-NEW").

Delivery guys keep interrupting me for signatures, and I don't have nearly as much time as I'd like to check over the stuff. As much as I'd like to push my snout into every fish gill and fondle every vegetable that comes in the door, I can't—there's just not enough time. Fortunately, my purveyors know me as a dangerously unstable and profane rat-bastard, so if I don't like what I receive, they know I'll be on the phone later, screaming at them to come and "Pick this shit up!" Generally, I get very good product. It's in my purveyors' interests to make me happy. Produce, however, is unusually late. I look at the kitchen clock nervously—not much time left. I have a tasting to conduct at eleventhirty, a sampler of the day's specials for the floor staff, accompanied by detailed explanation, so they won't describe the pheasant as "kinda like chicken."

The butcher arrives, looking like he woke up under a bridge. I rush downstairs, hot on his heels, to pick up my meat order: a towering stack of milk crates, loaded with plastic-wrapped côtes du boeuf, entrecôtes, rumpsteaks, racks of lamb, lamb stewmeat, merguez, saucisson de Toulouse, rosette, pork belly, onglets, scraps, meat for tartare, pork tenderloins larded with bacon and garlic, pâtés, rillettes, galantines and chickens. I sign for it and push the stack around the corner for Segundo to rotate into my stock. Still downstairs, I start loading up milk crates of my own. I try to get everything I need for the day into as few loads as possible, limiting my trips up and down the Stairmaster as much as I can. I have a feeling I'm going to get hit on lunch today and I'll be up and down those stairs like a jack-in-the-box tonight, so those extra trips make a difference. Into my crates go the pork, the liver, the pavées, filets, some duck breasts, a bag of fava beans, herbs and vinegar for sauce. I give Ramón, the dishwasher, a list of additional supplies for him to haul up—the sauces to be reduced, the grated cheese—easily recognizable stuff he won't need a translator or a search party to locate.

On my station (sauté), I've got only a six-burner Garland to work with. There's another range next to it which is taken up with a bain-marie for sauces and onion soup, the rest of it with stocks—veal, chicken, lamb and pork—which will be reducing at a slow simmer all day and into the night. One of my burners during service will be occupied permanently by a pot of water for Omar to dunk ravioli in, leaving me five with which to work. Another burner, my front right, will be used mostly by him as well, to sauté lardons for frisée salads, to sear tidbits of hanger steak for onglet salad, for sautéing diced potatoes in duck fat for the confit de canard, and the cockles—which will leave me, most likely, with three full-time burners with which to prepare a wide range of dishes, any one of which alone could require two burners for a single plate. Soon, there'll be a choo-choo train of sauté pans lined up waiting for heat, requiring constant prioritizing. If I get a six-top, for instance, with an order for, say, two orders of magret de moulard, a porc mignon, a cassoulet, a boudin noir and a pasta, that's *nine* sauté pans needed for that table alone.

Reducing gastrite (sugar and vinegar) for duck sauce while the Dead Boys play "Sonic Reducer" on the boom-box, I have to squeeze over for Janine, who melts chocolate over the simmering pasta water. I'm not annoyed much, as she's pretty good about staying out of my way, and I like her. She's an ex-waitress from Queens, and though right out of school, she's hung tough. Already she's endured a leering, pricky French sous-chef before my arrival, the usual women-friendly Mexicans, and a manager who seems to take personal delight in making her life miserable. She's never called in sick, never been late, and is learning on the job very nicely. She inventories her own supplies on Saturdays, and as I hate sticky, goopy, sweet-tasting, fruity stuff, this is a great help to me. As I've said before, I greatly admire tough women in busy kitchens. They have, as you might imagine from accounts in this book, a lot to put up with in our deliberately dumb little corner of Hell's Locker-room, and women who can survive and prosper in such a high-testosterone universe are all too rare. Janine has dug in well. She's already managed to infuriate the whole floor staff by claiming she inventories the free madeleines we give away with coffee. I'm pleased with her work, making an exception in my usual dim view of pâtissiers.

Next to me, Omar, my garde-manger man, is on automatic. I don't even have to look over at his station because I know exactly what he's doing: loading crocks, making dressing, rubbing down duck legs with sea salt for confit, slowly braising pork bellies for cassoulet, whipping mushroom sabayon for the ravioli de royan. I rarely have any worries about his end. I smell Pernod, so I know without looking what Carlos is up to: soupe de poisson.

Segundo is downstairs receiving orders from the front delivery ramp. I hear the bell every few minutes, as a few more tons of stuff arrive. He'll have my walk-in opened up like a cardiac patient by now, rotating in the new, winnowing out the old, the ugly and the "science experiments" that sometimes lurk, forgotten and fuzzy, in dark corners, tucked behind the sauces and stocks. He's a mean-looking bastard. The other Mexicans claim he carries a gun, insist that he sniffs "thinner" and "pintura," that he's done a lot of prison time. I don't care if he killed Kennedy, the man is the greatest prep cook I've ever had. How he finds the time and the strength to keep up with deliveries, the nuts and bolts of deep prep, like cleaning squid, washing mussels and spinach, dicing tomato, julienning leek, filleting fish, wrapping and deboning pigs' feet, crushing peppercorns and so on, and yet still finds time to make me beautiful, filament-thin chiffonaded parsley (which he cuts with a full-sized butcher's scimitar) is beyond me.

The last cook to arrive is our French fry guy. This is a full-time job at Les Halles, where we are justifiably famous for our frites. Miguel, who looks like a direct descendant of some Aztec king, spends his entire day doing nothing but peeling potatoes, cutting potatoes, blanching potatoes, and then, during service, dropping them into 375-degree peanut oil, tossing them with salt, and stacking the sizzling hot spuds onto plates with his bare hands. I've had to do this a few times, and it requires *serious* calluses.

I hold the waiters' meeting and tasting at eleven-thirty. The new waiter doesn't know what prosciutto is, and my heart sinks. I run down the specials, speaking slowly and enunciating each syllable as best I can for the slower, stupider ones. The soup is soupe de poisson with rouille—that's a garlic pepper mayonnaise garnish, for the newbies. Pasta is linguine with roasted vegetables, garlic, baby artichokes, basil and extra virgin olive oil. The whole roasted fish of the day is black sea bass—that's not *striped* bass, for our slower students—and crusted with sel de Bretagne. The fish of the day is grilled tuna livornaise, asparagus and roasted potatoes. Does anyone need "livornaise" explained . . . *again?* The meat special is roast pheasant with port wine sauce and braised red cabbage. There *are* faux filets for two available (that's the big, hip-end piece off the sirloin, strip-carved tableside for fifty bucks). Dessert special is tarte Tatin. It's not *too* bad a line-up on the floor today: Doogie Howser, "Morgan the part-time underwear model," Ken the veteran (who has a maniacal laugh you can hear out on the street; he's everyone's first choice for Waiter Most Likely to Snap, Shave His Head, Climb a Tower and Start Shooting Strangers); and some new waiter, the one who doesn't know what prosciutto is. I haven't bothered to learn his name, as I suspect he will not remain with us for long. There are two busboys, a taciturn workaholic from Portugal and a lazy-ass Bengali; they should balance out, as usual.

My runner today is the awesome Mohammed, nicknamed Cachundo by the kitchen—the best we have. I'm lucky to have him, as it looks like it's going to be busy, and the other runner, let's call him Osman, tends to lose it when things get hectic and has an annoyingly sibilant way of pronouncing the letter "s," making his calls for "musssselss," "meat sspesssiall" and "Calvesss leever" particularly painful to hear when you're under fire. Cachundo immediately begins picking chervil tops, arranging garnishes, filling small crocks with grated Parmesan, harissa sauce, rosemary and thyme, gaufrette potato chips, and picking out my favorite saucing spoons from the silver bins. . . .

. . . Twelve noon and already customers are pouring in. I get a quick kick in the crotch right away: an order for porc mignon, two boudins, a liver and a pheasant all on one table. The boudins take the longest, so they have to go in the oven right away. First, I prick their skins with a cocktail fork so they don't explode, grab a fistful of caramelized apple sections and throw them in a sauté pan with some whole butter for finishing later. I heat a pan with butter and oil for the pork, fling a thick slab of calves' liver into a pan of flour after salting and peppering it, heat another sauté pan with butter and oil for that. While the pans are heating, I take half a pheasant off the bone and lay it on a sizzle-platter for the oven, spinning around to fill a small saucepan with the port sauce to reduce. Pans ready, I sear the pork, sauté the liver—the pork goes straight into the oven on another sizzler—the hot pan I degrease, deglaze with wine and stock, add pork sauce, a few garlic confit, then put aside to finish reducing and mounting later. The liver half-cooked, I put aside on another sizzler. I sauté some chopped shallots, deglaze the pan with red wine vinegar, give it a shot of demiglace, season it and put that aside too. An order for mussels comes in, with a breast of duck order right after. I throw on another pan for the duck, load a cold pan with mussels, tomato coulis, garlic, shallots, white wine and seasoning. The mussels will get cooked à la minute and finished with butter and parsley.

More orders come in. It's getting to be full-tilt boogie time: another pheasant, more pork, another liver, and *ouch!* a navarin—a one-pot wonder but requiring a lot of digging around in my low-boy for all the garnishes. The key to staying ahead on a busy station is moving on a dish as soon as its name is out of Cachundo's mouth—setting up the pan, doing the pre-searing, getting it into the oven quickly, making the initial moves—so that later, when the whole board is fluttering with dupes, I can still tell what I have working and what I have waiting without having to read the actual tickets again.

"Ready on twelve!" says Carlos, who's already got a load of steaks and chops and a few tunas coming up. He wants to know if I'm close on my end. "Let's go on twelve!" I say. Miguel starts dunking spuds. I call for mashed potatoes for the boudins from Omar, give the apples a few tosses over flame, heat and mount my liver sauce, pull the pork mignons from the oven and clip off the strings that hold them together, heat potatoes and veg for the pheasant, squeeze the sauce for the pheasant between pots on to a back burner, move the mussels off the heat and into a ready bowl, calling, *"Papas fritas para conchas negras"* to Miguel as I spin and bend to check my duck breasts. Sauce pot with duck sauce and quince, I'll heat those right in the sauce, no room now, the orders are really coming in, the printer chattering away nonstop. I'm sneaking peeks at the dupes while they're still coming off the printer, trying to pick out what I'll be needing, like a base runner stealing signals. The intercom buzzes and I pick up, annoyed.

"Line one for the chef," says the hostess.

I push the blinking green light. It's a salesman, wanting to sell me smoked fish. I answer all sweetness and light, lulling him into the bear trap in the Bigfoot style: "So let me get this straight," I say, after he's jabbered away about his full line of delicacies, me trying to sound a little slow and confused, "you want to sell me food, right?" "Yes!" comes the reply, the salesman sounding encouraged by my interest and apparent stupidity. "And in general, you'd say," I continue, "you have like, a *lot* of restaurant accounts—in fact, you'd probably say that, like, you are in the business of servicing restaurants . . . and *chefs* in particular?" "Oh, yes!" says the witless salesman, beginning a litany of the usual prestigious accounts, the names of other chefs who buy his fine smoked sturgeon, salmon, trout and fish eggs. I have had enough and cut him off cold. "So . . . WHAT THE FUCK ARE YOU DOING CALLING ME IN THE MIDDLE OF THE FUCKING LUNCH RUSH?!" I scream into the phone, smashing it abruptly into the cradle.

I catch the duck just in time, roll it over skin-side down again and pull it out of the oven. I've got a filet poivre on order—not on the regular lunch menu—but it's a steady customer, says Cachundo, and I'm set up for it anyway, so I start searing one off. Another pasta. I pour extra virgin into a pan and sauté some paper-thin garlic slices with some crushed red pepper, add the artichoke hearts, roasted vegetables, some olives. I don't know why, but I always start humming Tony Bennett or Dino—today it's "Ain't That a Kick in the Head"—when I'm cooking pasta. I *like* cooking pasta. Maybe it's that I always wanted to be Italian American in some dark part of my soul; maybe I get off on that final squirt of emulsifying extra virgin, just after the basil goes in, I don't know. More porc mignons, the runner calls down to Janine, who's making clafoutis batter at her work station in the cellar, and she comes running up to plate desserts . . .

We're doing well, so far. I'm keeping up with the grill, which is a faster station (unless a table orders a côte du boeuf or a faux filet for two or a whole roasted fish, which slows the order down). Omar is up to date with the appetizers, and I'm actually feeling pretty good, right in the zone. No matter what comes in, or how much of it, my hands are landing in the right places, my moves are still sharp and my station still looks clean and organized. I'm feeling fine, putting a little English on the plates when I spin them into the window, exchanging cracks with Carlos, finding time to chide Doogie Howser for slipping that filet poivre by me without checking first.

"Doogie, you syphilitic, whitebread, mayonnaise-eating, Jimmy Sear-ass wannabe—next time you slip a special order in without checking with me first? Me and Carlos gonna punch two holes in your neck and bump dicks in the middle!"

Doogie cringes, laughs nervously and scurries out on to the floor, trailing muttered apologies.

"Chef," says Omar, looking guilty, "no más tomates. . ."

My jaw drops, and I see white.

I *ordered* tomatoes. I had thought that tomatoes had arrived then remember I broke up the order between three companies. I call Segundo on the intercom, tell him to come up *horita*. I'm also furious with Omar for waiting until we're out of tomatoes to tell me there are no more.

"What the fuck is going on?" I ask Segundo, who slouches in the doorway like a convict in the exercise yard. "No Baldor," he says, causing me to erupt in a blind, smoking rage. Baldor, though a superb produce purveyor, has been late twice in recent weeks, prompting me to make some very uncivil telephone calls to their people—and worse, forcing me to do business with another, lesser company until they got the message and began delivering earlier. Now, with no tomatoes, and no delivery, and the rush building, I'm furious. I call Baldor and start screaming right away: "What kind of glue-sniffing, crackhead mesomorphs you got working for you? You don't *have* an order for me? *What?!* I called the shit in *myself*. . . I spoke to a *human!* I didn't even leave it on the tape! And you're telling me you *don't have my order?* I got three fucking produce companies! THREE! AND IT'S ALWAYS YOU THAT FUCKS ME IN THE ASS!" I hang up, pull a few pans off the flame, load up some more mussels, sauce a duck, arrange a few pheasants, and check my clipboard. I'm in the middle of telling Cachundo to run across the street to Park

Bistro and ask the chef there if we can borrow some tomatoes when I see, from my neat columns of checked-off items on my clipboard, that in fact I ordered the tomatoes from another company, that I didn't order anything from Baldor. I have no time to feel bad about my mistake—that'll come later. After screaming at the blameless Baldor, my anger is gone, so when I call the guilty company, I can barely summon a serious tone. It turns out that my order has been routed to another restaurant—Layla, instead of Les Halles. I make a mental note to refer to my restaurant as "Less Halluss" in the future. The dispatcher at the guilty company apologizes for the mixup, promises my order within the hour and gives me a hundred dollars in credit.

More ducks, more pheasant, lots of mussels, the relentless tidal wave of pork mignons . . . finally lunch begins to wind down. I enjoy a cigarette in the stairwell while Carlos continues drilling out steaks, chops and paillards, nothing for my station. D'Artagnan arrives, my specialty purveyor, bearing foie gras, duck legs, and an unexpected treat—a 200-pound free-range pig, whole, which José, one of my masters, has ordered for use in pâtés and tête du porc by the charcutier. Now, I can lift a 200-pound, living breathing human—for a few seconds anyway—but dragging 200 pounds of ungainly dead weight by the legs through the restaurant and down the stairs to the boucherie requires four strong men. The boucher, charcutier, dishwasher and I wrestle the beast down the stairs, its head bouncing gruesomely on each step. I now know what it must be like to dispose of a body, I mutter. I do not envy the Gambino crime family—this is *work!*

The general manager sits down to lunch with the hostess. Two calamari, no oil, no garlic, a fish special no sauce, a céleri remoulade. Frank, my new French sous-chef, arrives. I have a list for him: dinner specials, mise-en-place, things to do, things to look out for. When he takes over the sauté station later, relieving me, I am grateful . . . my knees are hurting and the familiar pain in my feet is worse than usual. . . .

• • •

. . . Dinner service. Overbooked as usual—with two whopping twelve-tops booked for prime time. I remain in the kitchen to expedite, hoping that maybe, just maybe, things'll slow down enough by ten for me to have a couple of cocktails and get home by eleven. But I know full well that the two big tables will hold up seatings by at least an hour; more than likely, I'll be here for the full tour.

By eight-thirty, the board is full. Entree tickets flutter in the pull from the exhaust fans. To my right, below the window, plated appetizers are lined up, waiting to get delivered to the tables, the window is full of sauté dishes, the work table in front of the fry station a panorama of steaks of different donenesses. It's still Cachundo—he's working a double too—and he ferries the plates out by hand, four or five at a time. Still, I have to press-gang the occasional busboy or empty-handed waiter, separating them out from the herd at the coffee and bread stations and returning dirty plates and glasses, into delivering desserts. I don't want ice cream melting over the clafoutis, or the whipped cream on the chocolate mousse to start falling. Food's getting cold, and my voice is already blown out from calling out orders over the noise from the dishwasher, the hum of the exhaust, the whine of the Paco-Jet machine and the growing roar from the dining room. I make a hand gesture to a friendly waiter, who knows what I want, and he soon arrives with an "Industrial," a beer stein filled with margarita, for me. The drink manages to take the edge off my raging adrenaline buzz and goes down nicely after the three double espressos, two beers, three cranberry juices, eight aspirins, two ephedrine drinks, and a hastily gobbled hunk of merguez, which I managed to squeeze into a heel of bread before swallowing in two bites. By now, my stomach is a roiling hell broth of suppressed frustration, nervous energy, caffeine and alcohol. The night garde-manger man, Angel, who looks like he's twelve but sports a tattoo of a skull impaled with a dagger on his chest (future wife-beater, I think) is falling behind; he's got three raviolis, two duck confits, five green salads, two escargots, two Belgian endive and Stilton salads, two cockles, a smoked salmon and blini, two foie gras and a pâté, working—*and* the sauté and grill stations are calling for urgent vegetable sides and mashed potatoes. I swing the pastry commis over to Angel's station to help out, but there's so little room, they just bump into each, getting in each other's way.

Tim, a veteran waiter, is dry-humping Cachundo—to Cachundo's apparent displeasure. He's blocking the lane and impeding traffic in the narrow kitchen with his thrusting. I have to ask Tim nicely not to sexually harass my runners *during* service . . . after work, please. An order comes back for refire and Isidoro is *not* happy about it; it's cooked perfectly. I peer out into the dark dining room and see nothing except the dark silhouettes of customers waiting for tables at the bar, hear, even over the noise in the kitchen, the ambient chatter, the constant roar of diners as they shout over the music, the waiters describing specials over that noise, then fighting each other to get at the limited number of computer terminals to place orders, print out checks. "Fire table *fourteen!* Catorsayy! . . . That's *six, seven, fourteen* and *one* on *fire!*" I shout "Isidoro! You time it!" "I ready fourteen," says Isidoro, the grill man, as he slaps the refire back on a plate. Cachundo reaches around me and loads up with food, picking out plates seemingly at random, as if he's plucking daisies. I dry-swallow some more aspirins, and duck back into the stairwell for a few puffs of a cigarette.

A whole roasted fish comes back. "The customer wants it deboned," says an apologetic waiter. "I told them it comes on the bone," he whines, anticipating decapitation himself. Isidoro growls and works on the returned fish, slipping off the fillets by hand and then replating it. The printer is going nonstop now. My left hand grabs tickets, separates out white copy for grill, yellow copy for sauté, pink copy for me, coffee orders for the busboys. My right hand wipes plates, jams gaufrette potatoes and rosemary sprigs into mashed potatoes, moves tickets from the order to the fire positions, appetizers on order to appetizers out, I'm yelling full-time now, trying to hold it together, keep an even pace. My radar screen is filled with incoming bogeys and I'm shooting them down as fast as I can. One mistake, where a whole table comes back because of a prematurely fired dupe, or a bad combination of special requests ties up a station for a few critical seconds, or a whole roasted fish or a côte du boeuf has been forgotten? The whole line could come grinding to a dead stop, like someone dropping a wrench into a GM assembly line—utter meltdown, what every chef fears most. If something like that happens it could blow the whole pace of the evening, screw up everybody's heads, and create a deep, dark hole that could be very hard to climb out of.

"I gotta hot nut for table six!" I yell. There's a rapidly cooling boudin in the window, waiting for a tuna special to join it.

"Two minutes," says Isidoro.

"Where's that fucking *confit?*" I hiss at poor Angel, who's struggling valiantly to make blini for smoked salmon, brown ravioli under the salamander, lay out pâtés and do five endive salads at once. A hot escargot explodes in the window, spattering me with boiling garlic butter and snail guts. "Shit!" I say, dabbing my eye with a side-towel. *"Peenchayy* escargots!"

Frank's doing well, very well, keeping up. He did his apprenticeship with Robuchon, making food somewhat more elegant and delicately arranged than our Les Halles' humble workingman's fare, so it's a nice surprise that he's turned out to be such a line stud, cheerfully cranking out simple brasserie chow with speed and efficiency. He doesn't over-rely on the salamander, which I like (a lot of his French predecessors insist on cooking everything stone-rare, slicing and then coloring the slices under the salamander—something I hate to see); he makes minimal use of the microwave, which the cholo contingent has come to refer to contemptuously as "cooking French-style," and I've only seen him throw one steak in the fry-o-lator. All-in-all, he's worked out well so far.

"Platos!" screams Isidoro. The dishwasher is buried up to his

shoulders in the pot sink, his pre-wash area stacked with plates of unscraped leftovers and haphazardly dumped silver. I snarl and grab a Bengali busboy, shove his snout into a plate heaped with gnawed bones and half-eaten vegetables. "Scrape!" I hiss menacingly, referring to the mess of unscraped plates. "Busy, chef," complains the busboy who, from what I've seen, has been wandering around with his thumb up his ass, taking out the occasional coffee, for hours. "I don't give a fuck if you're saving the world," I say. "Scrape the plates *now,* or I'll tear your booga off and hurl it across the street at Park Bistro!"

David the Portuguese busboy is making espressos and cappuccinos behind me, but he moves pretty gracefully back there, not bumping me or spilling. We're used to each other's movements in the narrow space we share, knowing when to move laterally, when to make way for incoming dishes, outgoing food, the fry guy returning from downstairs with another 100-pound load of freshly cut spuds. I feel only the occasional light tap on the shoulder as he squeezes through with another tray of coffee and petit-fours, maybe a whispered, "Behind you" or *"Bajando."* Fred and Ginger time.

Finally the printer starts slowing down, and I can see by the thinning crowd at the bar that the last seating is under way: white spaces opening up in the dining room, stripped tables waiting for customers. We've got 280 dinners under our belts already. I turn the expediting over to Cachundo, drag my ass down the Stairmaster for a final walk-through. I check the stocks cooling in plastic buckets outside the walk-in, the gauze-wrapped pigs' feet which will have to be painstakingly deboned tomorrow, the soaking tarbais beans which have to be blanched, the salt-rubbed duck legs which will have to be confited in duck fat and herb, and I notice the produce that José and I bought earlier at the market.

I make a final swing through the dry-goods room, note that I'll be needing more peanut oil soon, more peppercorns, more sherry wine vinegar. I'm already working on an early draft of tomorrow's Things To Do list, tomorrow's order list. I've got striped bass already ordered, and baby octopus, I remind myself. José's got a boner for black mission figs—he saw some at the market—so I'll have to tell Janine to start thinking about figs for a special. I have weekly inventory tomorrow morning, which means I'll have to weigh every scrap of meat and fish and cheese in the store and record it, count every can, bottle, case and box. There will be payroll tomorrow, making sense of the punch-ins and punch-outs of my not very computer-wise cooks and porters and dishwashers, all fourteen of them—and there's that extra shift for Carlos who worked extra for me last week, and the extra half for Isidoro the night he covered Omar and Omar doubled twice to cover the vacationing Angel—and shit!—there's the overtime for that event at Beard House, and a promo party for what was it? A Taste of NoHo? Burgundy Night? A benefit for prickly heat? I have to record all the transfers of food from my stores to our outposts: the smoked salmon I shipped off to Washington, the flageolets I sent to Miami, the rosette and jambon de Paris I sent to Tokyo. I have to record all the stuff I gave to the butcher counter up front, and Philippe, my other boss, wants a list of suggestions for specials for the Tokyo chef. I peel off my fetid whites, groaning like 2,000-year-old man as I struggle into my jeans and pullover.

I'm on the way out the door but Isidoro wants to talk to me. My blood runs cold. When a cook wants to talk to you, it's seldom good news: problem with another cook, minor feud, paycheck problem, request for time off. In Isidoro's case, he wants a raise. I gave Carlos a raise last week so I'll have a rash of greedy line cooks jumping me for money for the next few weeks. Another note to self: Frank needs the 16th off so I have to call Steven. I'm still buzzed with adrenaline when I finally push through the last waiting customers by the hostess stand and out the door, and wave for a taxi.

I'm thinking about going home but I know I'll just lie there, grinding my teeth and smoking. I tell the cabbie to take me to the corner of 50th and Broadway, where I walk downstairs to the subway arcade and the Siberia Bar, a grungy little underground rumpus room where the drinks are served in plastic cups and the jukebox suits my taste. There are a few cookies from the Hilton at the bar, as well as a couple of saggy, bruised-looking strippers from a club up the street. Tracy, the owner of the joint, is there, which means I won't be paying for drinks tonight. It's 1 a.m., and I have to be in at seven-thirty mañana, but the Cramps are playing on the jukebox, Tracy immediately fiddles with the machine so there's twenty free credits and that first beer tastes mighty good. The Hilton cookies are arguing about mise-en-place. One of them is bitching about another cook nicking salt off his station, and the other cook doesn't see why that's such a big deal—so I'm gonna be involved in *this* conversation. The Cramps tune is followed by the Velvets singing "Pale Blue Eyes," and Tracy suggests a shot of Georgian vodka he's got stashed in the freezer . . .

The Chef of the Future

by Phyllis Richman
from *Gourmet*

Suddenly last summer, everyone in the culinary world seemed to be talking about this chef in some tiny place in Spain who does these amazing things with foam. *Washington Post* food critic Phyllis Richman tracked him down and, resisting all the hype, gave us a balanced assessment of his gifts.

A cluster of orange bubbles, small enough that dozens fit in the porcelain spoon, glisten within a sheath of glass. No, not glass, a membrane of sugar, thin as film and hard as ice. Once your teeth break through the sweet crackle, you can feel the bubbles burst into oily, saline juices. So simple, so startling, so exquisite: salmon roe shrink-wrapped in caramel.

But how do you tackle it? It's no longer enough to know which fork to use. Not after chef Ferran Adrià, the Salvador Dalí of the kitchen, has declared, "Tradition is dead." If Adrià is the chef of the future, diners have a lot to learn.

But there is help for the uninitiated. At Adrià's three-star restaurant, El Bulli, on Spain's Costa Brava, nearly every dish is accompanied by instructions. "Eat it all at once," directs the waiter as he delivers a crisp puff of bread the size of a quarter. That's because when the dough shatters, it spurts warm olive oil that runs down the throat and fills the sinuses with its perfume. The secret? A hypodermic needle.

"We demand that you drink slowly but continuously until the end. Don't stop, please." Those are the orders for a tall glass of green-pea soup, steamy at first but gradually dropping in temperature until the last sip chills your tongue and makes you aware that a warm soup tastes and smells different from a cold one. Here Adrià has used temperature almost as a seasoning. This gradation has been made possible by dripping the hot soup onto the cold with a contraption designed to layer liqueurs for a pousse-café.

Sometimes you're beseeched to play with your food. A small bowl holds a lake of warm white Parmesan custard with glistening black eddies of truffle oil. The sandy-looking bulwark at its shore turns out to be fresh-corn polenta frozen and pulverized into a powder, its aroma as strong as newly turned earth. The game is to taste each part separately, then together, and in every permutation of temperature, texture, and flavor. The goal is to note how the ingredients strike a different pose with each variation.

Nothing is just what it seems at El Bulli. What looks like whipped cream might be a foam of cod or of potato or simply aerated smoke. That odd mousse? Just seawater. And those noodles are probably made not of flour but of gelatin. Warm gelatin, somehow not melted. The only constant of a meal at El Bulli is surprise. Liquid-filled one-bite "ravioli" of coconut milk are encased in pasta-thin cuttlefish. How is the seafood shaved so finely? No knife could accomplish this; Adrià's tool is the kind of slicer every deli uses for salami plus a freezer that not only firms the cuttlefish for slicing but solidifies the coconut milk before it's wrapped.

I approach my first visit with skepticism. Is Adrià a chef or a mechanic? By the end, I've joined the apostles. This dinner of high-tech gimmicks is exquisite. It has toyed with my senses, tickled me with surprises, and left me longing to taste each dish again.

But it's not easy to eat at El Bulli. This is possibly the world's most inaccessible restaurant. It's open as few as five days a week for seven months of the year, from March to the end of September. And the mountain road to the tiny Cala Montjoi cove— coincidentally, a half hour's drive south of the home of Salvador Dali—is so rutted that one wonders whether it was intended to keep away outsiders. It winds from the seaside resort of Roses through the mountains, only to deposit you unexpectedly at the edge of a bay.

Adrià's path to celebrity was equally rocky and unexpected. He started cooking as a teenager, working in Ibiza during a summer vacation. At age 21, right from economics studies and military service, and without any formal kitchen training, he landed a temporary job as a *stagiaire* at the two-star El Bulli. That was 1984. Within a year, Julio Soler, who was managing the small restaurant, suddenly found himself in need of a chef. He promoted Adrià then undertook his education.

First there was the grand tour of top kitchens in France, with introductions to their chefs, then came apprenticeships at Georges Blanc and Pic. Back in his own kitchen, Adrià began reproducing what he'd learned, copying the masters, as a young painter would. El Bulli lost one of its *Michelin* stars and gained a new owner, Soler. Then in 1990, Adrià was born again as an inventor, committed to cooking food that nobody had ever seen before. The second star returned, and a mere half dozen years after Adrià set out on his own road, El Bulli was awarded a third *Michelin* star. With characteristic reticence, Adrià took the occasion to announce, "French cooking is over."

A compact man whose fine features are set in a taut, serious look that makes him appear older than 37, Adrià is driven to innovate. "It's my strength," he boasts, "that I had no mentor." He did, however, have an important advocate. About seven years ago, Joël Robuchon, the now-retired legendary Paris chef, was persuaded by a friend to make a detour to El Bulli for lunch, though he planned to hurry afterward to the auto-train. The meal changed his mind. He stayed on, returning to dine at El Bulli several times. Then he proclaimed Adrià the most important chef in the world and repeated his praise on television and in print. Thus Adrià was launched. The decrepit road was no deterrent once the honors piled on.

Adrià saw as his goal to break down the barrier between the savory kitchen and the pastry kitchen. His techniques, his textures, and his contrasts of temperature came from the world of the ice-cream sandwich, the hot-fudge sundae, and the baked Alaska. His plates began to look like desserts, arrangements of foams, mousses, ice creams, and sorbets fashioned from savory ingredients such as vegetables, meat, and seafood.

Foam was the medium that started people talking. Adrià had become obsessed with the gas-cartridge cream whipper—called a siphon or "charge"—and began aerating everything in sight. With a little gelatin to stabilize it, he discovered, any liquid could be transformed into a fluff—an *espuma,* as he called it. Truffle juice, asparagus, saffron, cheese, foie gras, mushroom: The list was endless. He could serve the resulting foam hot or cold.

Foam provided a new perspective on old flavors. Stripped of its normal texture and puffed into a cloud, the pure taste of that asparagus or codfish could reach every part of a diner's tasting and smelling faculties. That's why Adrià boasts, "My basil jelly has more taste than basil does. My philosophy is to make with a carrot something more than a carrot."

Adrià's foams became the butt of jokes and the source of inspiration for other, more adventurous chefs. Their fame has led Adrià to license the sale of siphons with his logo. Even in the U.S., his foams are making their mark.

Charlie Trotter of Chicago and Ken Oringer of Boston have arranged to send cooks to Adrià for training. At the James Beard Foundation's showcase for rising star chefs in New York last spring, foie gras foam was on the menu. One of the chefs, José Andres, of Café Atlantico, in Washington, DC, worked for four years at El Bulli and has been introducing his diners to creations in the El Bulli style. Young chefs in Spain see Adrià as a model. His second book, *The Secrets of El Bulli*—a dense 333 pages of lists, charts, and philosophy—has sold some 70,000 copies in Spain, and foams can be spotted in both tapas bars and elegant dining rooms. Adrià sees El Bulli as having "two significances": "It's a restaurant with three stars, and it's a professional disseminator of new ideas, new concepts, techniques, and philosophy. It's a spiritual thing."

In winter, when El Bulli is closed, Adrià spends his time thinking and traveling, often to the U.S. He's always looking for new techniques, and one year he brought back the squeeze bottle from U.S. kitchens. Even so, he says, "In the past five years, I have seen nothing new. For this reason El Bulli is important." There are people who love his work, he says, and people who don't like it. But they all understand that it's new. This November he's coming to cook for the first time in America. He will join an international lineup of chefs for the Vinaffair benefit at the Four Seasons Hotel Chicago, organized by Charlie Trotter.

Last winter Adrià showed his techniques to a packed crowd at the Slow Food Salone del Gusto, in Turin. "We made a revolution in Spanish cuisine. Sixty to seventy Spanish restaurants are following me," Adrià announced at a press conference there. "You can like it or not, but it's revolutionary." At the same time, he showed off the new pastry book by his younger brother, Albert. For sweets and pastries, said Adrià without the faintest blush of modesty, "it is the most important book in history."

Those are the words that drive some chefs up the wall and others to put El Bulli on their itinerary. The latter join gastronomic pilgrims from around the world for lunches that stretch up to six hours and dinners well beyond midnight. The sunny terrace, with arches overlooking the Mediterranean, is in stark contrast to the not-quite-beautiful white stucco dining rooms with high-backed chairs, dark beams, and heavy upholstery. In similar contrast, diners are as likely to be wearing T-shirts as jackets and ties. While waiters are dressed in monastic high-neck black tunics, Julio Soler, now Adrià's partner as well as director, often sheds his proper tucked-in shirt and tie in favor of a flapping unbuttoned plaid shirt.

Nearly everyone who dines at El Bulli stops in to see the kitchen, so there's no hiding the fact that it is more handsome than the dining rooms. The newest part of the restaurant is built into the hillside, with expansive windows framing rock faces and greenery, a black stone floor, a sculpture of a bull's head centered on the stainless-steel serving counter, and the all-electric stoves Adrià favors.

A kitchen visit also affords the diner an appreciation of what those foams and gelatins involve: as many as 40 cooks racing around double-time to feed a maximum of 55 guests per meal. Cooking times are counted in seconds: five seconds for the clams, ten seconds for the poached pear ravioli skins. Four cooks hover over each dish. Every tasting menu requires at least three dozen pieces of silverware for the two dozen dishes.

Adrià fears that the more publicity his dishes get, the harder it will be to surprise diners. Thus, even though one faithful customer sent him a list of 290 dishes he'd tried at El Bulli, Adrià is ever more driven to come up with new ones. The foams are playing a minor role nowadays; Adrià's current style is to gather several techniques on one plate. And he spends each winter inventing more. Adrià claims he's come up with 30 new concepts in recent years.

Take the noodles in carbonara: They're consommé-flavored gelatin, though their sauce of Parmesan cream transforms them into pasta in your mind. The secret of their staying firm even when hot is that they are made from agar-agar. Tomato ravioli are also glistening and transparent: Those wrappers, too, are seaweed gelatin. Gelatin forms a refreshing aspic surrounding near-raw clams. The runny poached quail egg is sparkling not with aspic but with a sheet of caramelized sugar melted under the salamander to enclose it, as is the porcelain spoonful of salmon-trout roe. The flash of sweetness at first bite heightens the taste to follow. Adrià's hope is that diners will first look at a dish, then smell it before they consume it. And that afterward they will think about it.

They usually do. People don't simply eat Adrià's food. They react to it, visibly. They examine it with a puzzled knotting of eyebrows, take a bite with a look of expectation. Then their eyebrows leap upward. An expression of surprise, often of delight, suffuses their faces. They look like children encountering their first helium balloon. A few, of course, don't like such fiddling with their ingredients. They order something traditional from the à la carte menu or go elsewhere.

The meal begins with an apéritif—last season, blood-orange juice with Campari foam. Then comes a parade of "snacks," first perhaps a bite of pork crackling topped with a dab of pine-nut foam. Five dishes offer futuristic sweet-salty bar food the likes of airy codfish-flavored rice-flour strips, wispy slices of fried lotus root, and crumpled little mango crunches.

The *Alice in Wonderland* tapas arrive one by one: the oil-filled bread puff, a salty and foamy tomato-water sorbet, or a cube of potato filled with a few drops of coffee and *mascarpone*. The most memorable is a chicken croquette, its center of chicken essence pouring down your throat so richly that it could be liquefied ortolan.

You're barely started. There's the hot-cold pea soup or the almond broth with milk foam and vanilla oil, a cold glazed clam with hot diced vegetables in a lemon-chicken stock, the deconstructed carbonara with gelatin noodles, and more vegetable novelties, such as a foamy Parmesan and tomato tart, asparagus with caramelized grapefruit, pineapple as thin and supple as a crêpe wrapped around unsweetened herbed coconut sorbet. Last of the tapas might be the wonder of all, a legume pie. That means a green strip of warm basil-flower gelatin, painstakingly paved with tiny peas and favas, bits of white asparagus, and a punctuation of tomato, decorated with foam. Here Adrià teaches the excitement of bitterness, using it the way a Texan chef uses chiles.

The parade goes on to seafood—cuttlefish displayed in myriad textures ranging from inky jelly to a small solid chunk hollowed out for a crater of oil, or butter-soft fresh scampi wrapped in a skin of shaved *porcini* with pine-nut vinaigrette. Spain's delicate white sea cucumbers—a world away from China's slithery gelatinous ones—are wrapped in grilled mango with black-olive paste and balsamic vinegar, one of those uncanny marriages that works against all odds.

Once you're into the seafood and meat dishes—ducks' tongues with chopped oysters and ravioli of lichees, calf's brains in seaweed sauce with sesame-crusted turnips and knots of flashcooked spinach and seaweed, veal-tripe ravioli and sweet tomato essence with hot pepper oil and a minted chick-pea purse—you're faced with the Spanish passion for salt. Main courses, particularly grilled ones, can leave American palates gasping. You might also have noted that while Adrià carefully yet boldly contrasts sweet, sour, bitter, and salty tastes within each dish, his menu as a whole shows no such ideal. Three dishes in a row might feature Parmesan and several taste of mint, blood orange, or pine nuts. Why? Adrià says he has a reason, but he can't explain it.

Desserts echo the themes and techniques of the savory courses, showing yet new aspects. Warm and cold are contrasted in layers of pineapple, one caramelized, one crunchy, and one a thin layer of ice. A gelatin of red fruit is encrusted with tiny wild strawberries and red currants; the waiter instructs you to eat the one large strawberry at the end. Sure enough, it's a shock, a powerful and mysterious flavor mingling anise, pine, menthol, and balsa wood. It turns out to have been macerated in Fisherman's Friend, that potent old-fashioned throat lozenge, which shows up again in chocolate candies. And the last dessert often brings the meal full circle. Mango ravioli with basil and tomato, a savory earlier in the meal, is now a sweet, filled with ginger pudding and just-squeezed orange juice.

Visually, at least, the best comes last. El Bulli's version of petits fours is a tray of silver sculptures, each holding a separate edible toy. The lollipop is a jolt of lemon and coffee rimmed with white chocolate. Fruit kebabs are encased in jiggly sheets of gelatin as malleable as plastic wrap. Disks of white chocolate are flavored with pink peppercorns and dill.

In Europe, El Bulli has become a gastronomic mecca, particularly after its third star. In the U.S., Adrià's influence has only slowly gathered force. But the chefs here are starting to notice. Spanish-born Julian Serrano, longtime chef of Masa's, in San Francisco, and now running Picasso, at Bellagio, in Las Vegas, observed, "Everybody is watching this guy right now. Nobody else does what he does. He's opened my mind. I left saying that with cooking, anything is possible."

Natural-Born Keller

by Michael Ruhlman
from *Gourmet*

Author of two books—*The Making of a Chef* and *The Soul of a Chef*—Michael Ruhlman has given a lot of thought to the mystery of how genius operates in the kitchen. Who better, then, to explicate the surprising career of California-based wunderkind Thomas Keller, star chef of The French Laundry.

You arrive for dinner at The French Laundry in a mood of grave purpose. The restaurant, in the tiny Napa Valley town of Yountville, is in a turn-of-the-century home built of timbers and fieldstone. You are seated at a table dressed with a crisp white cloth, wineglasses sparkling, the ivory walls bare. The restaurant is library quiet. Expectations are not just high, they demand a certain sobriety because you know that the proprietor, Thomas Keller, has been called the best chef in America. You expect to have one serious meal here.

And then the waiter brings you tapioca pudding with an oyster in it.

"Oysters and pearls," as Keller calls the dish, is both ridiculous and sublime. And the tension of these opposing effects in the severely elegant French Laundry is enough to make some people laugh. Here is a chef with a sense of humor.

Once, Keller froze tomato water, shaved the ice into tiny paper cups with an Italian ice machine, and added grilled shrimp, red onion, cucumber, and bell peppers. But Keller's gazpacho snow cone may have been an idea ahead of its time. "People didn't get it," he says sadly.

In the kitchen one night, I stop Keller to ask him where the notion for oysters and pearls came from.

"Certain things you just know," he says. "It's all just logical."

"Putting an oyster in tapioca is not a logical thing to do," I say.

"For me it was. Tapioca, pearls. Where do pearls come from? Oysters, right? So to me it's completely logical. How does it taste to you?"

"What do you think?" I ask him.

"I've never tasted it," he says.

"Excuse me?"

"I know that's not a good thing for me to say. But I know it tastes good. You don't have to stick your hand in fire to know it's hot."

I am in Yountville to find stories for Keller's first cookbook, ones that illuminate the philosophy behind the chef's recipes and his restaurant. If he had his way, Keller's book would resemble Fernand Point's *Ma Gastronomie,* his favorite cookbook, which he loves more for its stories about the chef than for its recipes.

"A recipe has no soul," Keller says. "That's why there's such a contradiction between a cookbook and a cook. A cookbook is a document; a cook's life is a constant evolution. I want the stories to be as important as the food."

And so I look for stories, roaming the kitchen, watching the preparations, tasting, interviewing the cooks, the servers. I travel from Sonoma County to Maine interviewing key purveyors in their homes and on their farms. I live as a guest in an upstairs room of Keller's house for a month and spend countless hours talking about food and cooking with the chef. I am given unlimited, unqualified access to an extraordinary restaurant for two years. And what compels me at every step is this: the mystery, maybe accident, of Thomas Keller himself.

The facts have been well reported: Keller's early New York years, including work at Polo under chef Patrice Boely (and a *sous-chef* named Daniel Boulud); his *stages* at *Michelin*-starred restaurants in France; his critical acclaim at Rakel in Manhattan in the late 1980s, at Checkers in Los Angeles. And then, after purchasing The French Laundry in 1994, a Niagara of accolades, including the James Beard Award for Outstanding American Chef in 1997.

The lesser-known details of this chef's life, though, are odd and alluring: Keller had no formal training, nor did he have any interest in food or cooking until he was an adult (for a vocation, he tended toward carpentry). Born in 1955, the youngest of five boys raised by a single mom in a chaotic household, he absorbed no sublime taste memories or any kind of appreciation for food. As a high school graduate not considering college, he found himself washing dishes at The Palm Beach Yacht Club in West Palm Beach, one of several restaurants managed by his mother, Elizabeth Keller. When the chef there quit, Elizabeth told her son he was the chef.

"I called up my friend Przemko and asked him if he wanted a job," Keller recalled. "We went out that night and partied. We were going to become *chefs*." At the time, age 19, he did not know how to sauté a piece of meat, cook an omelet, or clarify butter; he did not know how to make a stock, and he knew only that sauces came in jars.

Twenty years later, Washington, DC, chef Michel Richard, as chauvinistic about his native France and its food as a chef can be—and quick to claim there is no such thing as a great American chef—says of Keller, softly, "He's one of the best French chefs anywhere."

Jean-Louis Palladin, who shuttles between restaurants in Las Vegas and New York, says, "He has the mind of a French guy, you know? He's thinking like a French cook."

The question rings in my head like a fire alarm. How on earth did this youth—emerging with no apparent ambition and no particular food knowledge from the parched landscape of 1970s South Florida—become not just one of the best American cooks working today but, more, the country's best French chef?

Hollandaise sauce. It began there. Egg yolks and butter. That fundamental emulsion created in the 17th century.

The Palm Beach Yacht Club served burgers and fries as well as prime rib, lobster tail, and eggs Benedict. When Keller didn't know how to broil a lobster tail, he called his brother Joseph, a cook in neighboring Palm Beach. It was Joseph who walked Keller through his first yolk-based emulsion, and Keller was so excited by the result, he ran out of the harborside restaurant to show the dock manager what he'd done. Looking back, Keller says the high point of every morning for the next two years, after sweeping the dining room and scrubbing the bathrooms until they shone, was making hollandaise. For him, it was not a chore but a quest. He made it in order to perfect it.

The French Laundry kitchen is all white tile and stainless steel, and everything shines as brightly as the surfaces he left behind at The Palm Beach Yacht Club. Sometimes the staff must throw away what appear to be brand-new sauté pans, beautiful, heavy-gauge pieces, because the pot washers have scrubbed so much steel off them, they no longer rest flat.

In virtually every professional kitchen, inch-thick black

rubber mats, with holes to allow slopped food to spill through, cover the floor. Keller uses carpeted mats: His *brigade* cooks on *carpet*.

The kitchen leads to the butchery-stock room: a screened porch beneath an ancient Chinese hackberry tree with views of the Mayacamas Mountains beyond the grassy courtyard and walls of honeysuckle.

"The first thing I noticed when I walked in here," says one French Laundry cook, "was that it didn't smell like a kitchen. It smelled like someone's home."

At 5:30 each evening, the kitchen is spacious and quiet. The four hot-line cooks wipe down their stations. Keller is at the pass, a small bank of steel tables covered in thick white cloth, checking his *mise en place*—containers of fresh herbs on ice, a dozen powders, a half dozen oils—an arsenal of finishing garnishes. Before 6:00, Keller will leave the pass, stride across the gravel parking lot to his house behind the restaurant, shower, sit for a moment by himself with an espresso, then return in a fresh jacket. In a normal week, Keller oversees nine of the ten services in the 62-seat restaurant's seven-day week, spends most of each day in the kitchen prepping, and also tries to maintain some control over Bouchon, his nearby French bistro, where his brother Joseph is the managing partner.

By 8:00, the kitchen is in full roar and will produce between 90 and 100 five- to twenty-course meals in the next seven hours, as many as 1,000 courses.

A husky, baby-faced waiter, David Mason, returns from the dining room with four sets of dishes in his arms for Keller's inspection before they disappear to be cleaned. "Chef, this is table seven," he says.

Keller, a skinny tower in clogs and immaculate jacket, his eyes so dark they seem almost solid black, regards the plates, then snaps his gaze back on David. "They said it was wonderful," David pleads. "They're just full."

Keller looks again at the plates, mostly empty but for a few unfinished pieces of meat. He reaches into one and lifts something out between his thumb and index finger. He exhales.

Four hot-line cooks are hustling, fifth gear, no time to pause even for an instant: turning . . . plating . . . cooking . . . stooping at their lowboys . . . turning . . . firing . . . plating. Keller appears to have all the time in the world. "Mark," he calls casually to the cook on the meat station.

"Yes, Chef," Mark answers. The cook doesn't look up—he's pulling pans from the oven, has several sauté pans working on the flattop, and is ready to plate several dishes.

"Mark."

"Yes, Chef!" But still Mark does not stop moving. He can't. There's too much to do, too much to keep organized. A cook in full swing can't afford to lose his momentum or chain of thought.

"Mark."

"Yes, what?" Mark says angrily and at last stops to look at the chef.

Keller tosses a brown circle of string to the cook, then turns back to his work. Mark bobbles the string and catches it. For a moment he doesn't know what it is. Then he recognizes it and seems visibly to deflate. He has sent a veal fillet to a table without removing the butcher's string that had kept it uniform as it cooked.

Ultimately, the kitchen hits a groove and the effect is extraordinary. The chefs actually move more slowly, more fluidly but produce more finished plates. The dishes, sculptures two inches wide, three inches high, are beautiful. The kitchen is silent except for the measured voice of the chef ordering and picking up.

"You have to have enormous respect for food," Keller says later. "It's why I killed the rabbits." It is after midnight, and Keller has stretched out on a couch in his living room to tell me a story.

In 1980 Keller began cooking at La Rive, in upstate New York. He lived in a cabin behind the small restaurant. He cooked classical French cuisine six days a week, his only staff the owner's

80-year-old mother, who would mince shallots and snip beans. La Rive proved to be an ideal self-teaching ground for a chef not yet 25 years old. He could experiment without fear. In rural New York, offal was in abundance, and he learned how to cook tripe and other innards, as well as cocks' combs, ducks' testicles, and other unusual items. He built his own smokehouse. He developed relationships with growers in the area, and when his rabbit purveyor arrived with the weekly delivery, Keller said, "Next time, bring them alive." He'd never butchered a rabbit, and he figured this would be the best way to learn.

The following week, the purveyor appeared with 12 live rabbits. "He knocked one out, slit its throat, pinned it to a board, skinned it, gutted it, the whole bit," Keller remembers. "Then he left." Alone in the grass behind the restaurant with 11 little bunnies, he lurched for the first victim. "Rabbits scream," Keller says. "And this one screamed really loud." Keller tried to kill it, but the rabbit struggled to get away. The rabbit nearly broke free, but Keller gripped it by the leg, and the leg snapped in his hand. Terrified and now likely in great pain, the rabbit could no longer run, and Keller managed to kill it.

Thus did Keller learn how to butcher a rabbit, and it had been an unhappy experience. He had by this age worked in a half dozen kitchens and knew the dynamics, how easy it was, in the heat of a Saturday-night service, to take a lamb chop or a saddle of rabbit too far, throw it in the garbage, and fire another. But killing these rabbits had been so horrible for him, had so humbled him, he would not squander their lives. He determined to use all his powers as a cook to ensure that these were the best rabbits ever.

Respect all food, and avoid its waste, Keller says, "because it is life itself."

When The Palm Beach Yacht Club closed for the summer, Keller, then 21 years old, headed to Rhode Island for the summer and found a job at a beachside restaurant in Narragansett. Roland Hénin, a classically trained chef from Lyons, needed a staff-meal cook at the Dunes Club.

"He taught me how to peel a tomato and other things that nobody took the time to show me before," Keller says. Hénin taught Keller how to make stocks, how to cook a green vegetable, how to utilize scraps for staff meals of beef *bourguignonne, coq au vin,* and lamb stew. Again Keller took the idea of the family meal and made an important intellectual jump. "The question was," Keller says, "Can you be passionate about cooking staff meals? Only the staff sees it. If you can do that for these people, create that passion, that drive, that sincerity, and take it to another level, then someday you'll be a great chef. Maybe."

When writers attempt to define Keller, they almost invariably use the word *perfectionist,* to which Keller responds, "I've been called a perfectionist for so long, I don't really know what it means anymore."' Observers will note that Keller's walk-in coolers are almost neurotically organized—painters' tape labels each plastic container (name of item, date, initials of the cook who stored it, the label itself adhering perfectly straight, "because why would you put it on crooked?" asks Keller). Fish are stored on ice "in the same position they swim," Keller says, to avoid stressing the fish.

I speak with a former cook who spent all morning shucking and peeling pounds of fava beans as Keller asked. But when this cook put them in the pot of water to blanch, the water lost its boil for a moment; Keller spotted it and told the cook to throw out the favas and start again. When you boil a green vegetable in heavily salted water, the water should not lose its boil.

I ask Keller: What is the single most important skill he values in a cook? "Salt," he says. "The ability to season food properly."

Keller says none of these basic cooking techniques are difficult. They are decisions based on knowledge about how food behaves. No single ingredient is particularly special. But when you combine thousands of small, proper decisions, and you do so with great feeling and imagination in pursuit of perfection, the result can be extraordinary.

"It goes back to the rabbit story," Keller says finally. "At some point you either have to learn or be taught the importance of the food that we eat. It's not about thanking God or anybody; that's an individual thing. But it is about understanding the relationship between you and the food. And how that relationship has to be nurtured."

In fact, it goes back to the hollandaise. And the ultimate question becomes this: Where, in a 19-year-old boy, did that urge to perfect hollandaise come from? It came from somewhere outside himself, and it made all the difference.

On Burgundian Tables

by Anne Willan

from *From My Chateau Kitchen*

Director of the esteemed École de Cuisine La Varenne cooking school, Anne Willan celebrates the food of the Burgundian countryside near her restored château in her handsome cookbook, a collection of excellent recipes laced together with Willan's knowing appraisal of her French culinary colleagues.

Moving to Burgundy opened a whole new *pays* of restaurants and we soon marked every page of the red *Guide Michelin* listing the towns in our region. Other guides have challenged *Michelin*'s preeminence but none has such ancient authority (it was founded in 1898) and, conservative that I am, I've always found it the best place to start. Around Château du Feÿ there was an encouraging cluster of restaurants rated one, two, and three stars. Clearly there was food for investigation and I was eager to find out just what makes a restaurant outstanding, and what gives a chef the passion and dedication to reach the top. I'm still learning. Every restaurant has a different personal story, and in this small, warm world I've made many good friends.

We started at the top. Back then, in 1982, the Côte St. Jacques in Joigny had two stars ("worth a detour" in Michelinese) and it was soon to become one of some twenty restaurants in France that earn the highest three-star rating, meriting "a special trip." For us no special trip is needed as ten minutes brings us to the restaurant door. *"Bonjour, bonjour,"* greets Chef Michel Lorain, a cheerful, gap-toothed figure in impeccable chef's whites—no toque, though; this was the freewheeling eighties. We have a little chat about wild mushrooms, and then are ushered to our table by Madame, Parisian in approach and very much in charge. Looking back, I realize that Michel has always had a keen sense of style, of creating dishes with just that touch of novelty which compels attention, earning praise from restaurant critic Patricia Wells, for "thoroughly modern, classic French cuisine that displays a rare sense of equilibrium and sophistication."

After dinner Michel comes around for a chat. Socializing in the dining room now forms an important—often too important—part of a chef's public relations, and with his engaging manner and shock of gray hair (now almost white), Michel is very good at it. He told me he had ambitious plans for the property, which had been a posting inn but was now being ruined by the trucks thundering past on the *route nationale* outside. The chef hoped to tunnel under the road and gain access to the river Yonne, never mind the cost. "Then we will have a garden, a pool, suites of very elegant rooms, and of course a bar." One hitch was the trailer park just across the river. "One may need to buy it," says Michel, and later he does. Over the years we've seen Chef Lorain acquire a boat dock and launch to go with it, a helicopter pad, and a miniature golf course. He has planted 7 hectares/18 acres of vineyard high above Joigny, and is bravely making the best he can of its Pinot Gris, perhaps more as a gesture of solidarity with the town

than as a pleasure for his guests. He has also constructed an excru-
ciatingly modern budget hotel on the opposite side of the river,
the roof picked out in green neon. Michel's tastes in decoration
do not accord with mine, but otherwise we are the best of friends!

When our son, Simon, was sixteen, Chef Lorain kindly
offered him a summer job as *bagagiste*. Clad in prickly black reg-
ulation trousers and a white shirt, the tails invariably flopping,
Simon would hump suitcases through the tunnel and up to the
famous suites of rooms overlooking the river, each decorated in
a different, ever more eclectic style. When the regular bellman
took over during the more lucrative mornings and late afternoons, Simon was put to washing up, scoffing leftovers of the
remarkable petits fours. He did his best, but at a puppylike 6 feet
4 with hands to match, the damage to the house crystal was
scary. "I only broke three glasses and a window," Simon confided cheerfully one day and, seeing me wince, added, "It's all
right, Mum, they don't know who did it!"

Simon worked at the Côte in 1986, the banner year when the
restaurant received its third star. By then, young Jean-Michel
Lorain was thoroughly into his stride after ten years of culinary
training, first as an apprentice with his father, then as a commis
and sous-chef in the kitchens of Troisgros in Roanne, Girardet
near Lausanne, and finally at Taillevent in Paris, all legendary
kitchens, all rating three Michelin stars. Such initiation, almost
a pilgrimage, can be crucial in forming the taste and the techniques of a gifted young cook. It is the contemporary approach,
the little touches of presentation, and above all the philosophy
of a master chef that his young acolytes seek to discover. . . .

But an economic cloud dimmed the brilliance of the Côte St.
Jacques' third star. *"Etoile d'immobilier* (a real estate star),"
carped one critic. Some people blame the *Guide Michelin* for

sending the wrong signal to the three-star restaurants, and others think the chef-owners were too compliant. Either way, among the top restaurants in France during the glitzy 1980s there was a reckless over-investment in infrastructure—top-of-the-line Baccarat crystal, Limoges china, Porthault linens, flashy paintings, and decorator-distressed paint work—fun to look at but nothing to do with cuisine. "Great chefs have no taste," quips [my husband] Mark, looking around at some dining rooms of that period with their brassy chandeliers, purple felt on the walls, gazebos and grass cloth, knickknacks and nudes, financed essentially by piling up debt. Those like Michel Lorain who expanded early have survived, but the 1990s economic downturn has hurt more recent debutants and ruined a few.

Among the chefs who feel at risk in the fickle restaurant business is Bernard Loiseau at the Côte d'Or in Saulieu. Chef Loiseau (his name means "the bird") is a bit of a loudmouth who expounds his difficulties on television. "How can I create great food when I have to worry about finding 50,000 francs ($8,000 or more) every single day of the week to pay back the bank," he trumpeted just recently. He underestimates himself. Bernard Loiseau is a brilliant, creative chef who loves to push invention to the limit. "The table is a festival, every meal should offer a dream," he declares. Remembering that as a child he gathered snails among the stinging nettles, he put them together in the pan. For several years he banished butter, cream, and egg yolks from the kitchen. Well before the current phobia of animal fats, Loiseau was using nonstick pans and a minimum of oil. He abandoned the use of stock, regarded as the basis of much French cuisine (the French word for stock, *fond,* also means "foundation") and turned to water for extracting fresher, purer essences of taste. He thickened sauces with vegetable purées, for example replacing the usual garlic butter on frogs' legs with a jus of parsley. Lentils give body to mussel soup, testament to what can be done without a roux.

• • •

The third member of the triumvirate of top chefs in our area is Marc Meneau of L'Espérance at St. Père-sous-Vézelay. Like Lorain and Loiseau, Meneau has a strong sense of style as well as a keen nose for contemporary trends. Unusually for a top chef, he did not follow the usual path of apprenticeship and *stages* all over France, as he only started to cook professionally in his mid-twenties. Monsieur Meneau's natural talent was honed by talking and working with nearby chefs, and by study. "I learned to cook by reading books," he says. "Life has taught me discipline. From my mother I inherited the café-grocery of St. Père, a fine legacy, and the knowledge that money does not come easily." His cuisine displays a strong sense of place, of *terroir*. He loves dark, earthy flavors and each year gives a Fête du Saint-Cochon (Feast of the Sacred Pig) with long-forgotten dishes such as couée with pork lungs, liver, and heart seethed in red wine and thickened with blood. "My food is full of flavor; appearance, for me, has always come second to taste," he says.

Marc Meneau also has an exceptional hand with pastry. With Julia Child and Patricia Wells, I once took a group of culinary professionals on a gastronomic odyssey, visiting a trio of three-star restaurants in twenty-four hours. Knowing the chef's brilliance with desserts, we asked him to cover the sweet end of things. He protested—no chef likes to be restricted to pastry—then created an unforgettable repast. Each table was set in eighteenth-century style with a galaxy of pastries and petits fours, including homemade marshmallows, miniature pound cakes, almond tiles, fondant-coated fruits, little fruit tartlets, fruit bonbons, and filled chocolates.

Course followed course, first a bowl of hot drinking chocolate made with whole, unpasteurized milk and whisked, we were told, for two hours over the lowest possible heat. Ethereal toasted brioche came separately for dunking. Then came a tart of dark rose petals in fresh cheese, the perfume of rose harking back to the Renaissance. And the pièce de résistance, Chef Meneau's grandmother's apple gâteau, baked overnight to achieve the requisite essence of apple with a hint of orange and butter. . . .

Promotion and the development of ancillary activities are an essential part of today's restaurant game. Chefs are celebrities, appearing on television talk shows much like rock stars. Indeed, chefs are often more successful media personalities than managers—a great meal, after all, is theater, a concert performance that has an overture, a theme, and a grand finale. The kitchen *brigade* forms a closely knit team with the same camaraderie and sense of drama as a theatrical troupe led by the stars. Says Alain Ducasse, another three-star mogul: "Chefs need to emerge from their kitchens to be visible to the world at large so that French cuisine maintains its international reputation." When a star chef has a competent substitute, often a family member, to take over at home, this suits everyone. With Jean-Michel Lorain up to speed at the Côte St. Jacques, he or his father can take engagements elsewhere.

Chefs also get tied in knots over merchandising. Constantly looking for ways to expand the limited income from meals, they sell branded jams and chocolates and put their name to frozen and vacuum-packed dinners. Bernard Loiseau declares that the shop where he sells monogrammed chef's jackets for kids beside the house Champagne makes more money than the restaurant itself (I hope he's joking). Spin-offs need careful handling, easily diluting the focused, essentially luxury image of a top name.

Sheer physical strength is another limitation in the kitchen. After forty the long hours and tough conditions start to take their toll. By mid-fifties a chef can no longer stand the pace of twenty years earlier, no matter how fit he may be. Stars rise, but they also fall and the question of succession becomes key. The smooth transfer that has taken place within the Lorain family is rare. For example, in the 1960s on our local food scene the Frères

Godard were renowned, two brothers of a restaurant family, one in Sens, the other in Joigny, each with a Michelin star. Today the stars are gone but the brothers are still there, and so are their sons who are now in their mid-thirties and yearning for independence. In Sens, young Philippe Godard has found a steady tourist market for the poached fish and roasts that once formed the glory of the house, but each year his face is a little plumper and a little sadder as he follows his father around the dining room. In Joigny his cousin Claude has catered with success, but his father obstinately keeps a brigade of cooks for a half-abandoned dining room. This summer, Claude decided enough was enough and packed up his knives for a bistro in Manhattan.

The struggle to the top for one chef, in this case Bernard Loiseau, has been recounted in epic style by William Echikson in *Burgundy Stars*. For Echikson, "To aspire to three Michelin stars takes a special character: creative, durable, and, *mais oui,* a bit crazy." To find a chef who can inspire young, ambitious cooks and transfer great food to the plate reliably, year after year, is rare. At L'Espérance, Marc Meneau is inclined to philosophize, at least to judge by his dotty aphorisms ("In choosing a dish which allows us to run faster, higher, and stronger, we must activate our entire mind"), but when he puts knife to chopping board he becomes more practical. "We must take today's new products and show others how we make the most of them, following our classic traditions. We must pursue the *terroir,* which adds so much character and impact." How right he is! All too often, menus with their lobster, truffles, and chic allusions to the latest dining fad could play equally well in Los Angeles, New York, or Hong Kong. It was Escoffier who said, *"Faites simple* [keep it simple]," a lesson all cooks should take to heart.

So far we've looked at the top three chefs in our region, the success stories. It goes without saying that these restaurants are expensive. If I'm at each of them once a year, I consider myself lucky. It must be admitted that the overwhelming proportion of their customers are from Paris, or from overseas; the number of diners these restaurants attract locally is tiny. So where do our Burgundian neighbors go most of the time? For that matter, where do Mark and I like to eat out? My preference is always for establishments with a strong sense of place, which serve regional dishes, the best of them made with local ingredients in simple, comfortable surroundings that don't intrude. (You'd be surprised how much neon lighting has reached rural France.) When dining out, we test the terrain, assessing the number of cars parked outside and eyeballing the menu, which under French law must be displayed at the restaurant door. Our son Simon has a nose for good eating places. I've known him to grind to a halt outside a log cabin in the wilds of Russia. "The *gai* traffic police park here," he says, "that's a good sign." Sure enough, there was no electricity but the soup was delicious.

Take the Pavillon Bleu just down the hill in Villevallier, which was our first outing when we came to live at Le Feÿ. Madame extended a warm welcome (she recognized the car) and Monsieur stuck his head out of the kitchen to say hello. The cooking was respectable—a homemade pâté de campagne, ripe melon with country ham, and a remarkable coq au vin falling from the bone and clearly reheated several times so the sauce had mellowed to a rich nose-tingling bouquet. Monsieur's poached eggs in meurette red wine sauce, a featured specialty, were equally successful.

Le Pavillon Bleu, by the way, is next to a Relais Routier, part of the truckers' café network throughout France. Truckers everywhere are good trenchermen and French ones have their own guide, which lists such amenities as free showers and superior food, denoted by a little casserole. Our local Relais features "home cooking" with a three-course menu of such unbeatable classics as egg and tomato mayonnaise, pâté de campagne, or composed salad as appetizer, a choice of ten main courses including roast leg of lamb, beef with carrots, roast chicken, skate in cream sauce, or oven-roasted blood sausage, all followed by a cheese platter (help yourself) or dessert. It's an astonishing value for under $10. To my amusement, in between visits to carriage museums and underground grottoes, the guide urges truckers to seek out Ecole de Cuisine La Varenne at Château du Feÿ. So far we've had no takers!

The next direction our restaurant exploration took us was to Sens. La Madeleine was a disappointment at first: the chef, Patrick Gautier, seemed to try too hard; Madame Gautier was hesitant and shy. After a year or two the decor, installed on a shoestring budget (Chef Gautier was only twenty-six when the restaurant opened), began to wilt and I could see his face lengthening in defeat. Then Patrick struck gold. He opened a wine bar in the space next door, decorating at minimum expense and servicing it out of the main kitchen. The choice of a second Patrick as server (waiter is too polished a description) was brilliant. Gray-haired, slim as an eel, Patrick keeps thirty diners happy with a jocular word here, a free glass of wine there, turning tables two or three times, a feat almost unheard of in France where a table is yours for the night.

At first, Patrick Gautier had feared that the wine bar's success would undermine his main restaurant, but now he finds the contrary. Customers start out at the wine bar, then become regulars, graduating to the restaurant for more special meals and celebrations. La Madeleine is doing better each year, enough to finance a renovation of decor. For the chef, the pressure is relentless and Patrick has been known to fall asleep at the lunch table when he comes to give a class on his day off. But he looks five years younger than in quieter, less successful times and has no complaints: "Cooking is *la folie*—the restaurant business even worse. No leisure, no time for family, nothing. But we're not in it for that."

I asked Patrick if he wanted to enter the star circuit. "A Michelin star is a minimum," he says and then hesitates. "For me it is a personal thing, a recognition by my peers that I've arrived." When I mention the prospect of doing better financially with a star, he laughs. "Oh, that's double-edged. Yes, you get more customers, but they are the butterflies, the tourists that may never come again. By contrast, many chefs feel that when they gain a star, they lose their old clients who fear prices will go through the roof. If ever I am awarded a star, I won't make that mistake."

Now is his chance! Recently Patrick Gautier won that coveted first star. He can expect visitors from all over the world and a 20 percent increase in business during the first year; such is the power of the *Guide Michelin*. Both nationally and internationally, eyes are on him as one of the emerging young talents. By contrast, Marc Meneau, longtime leader in the region, has lost one of his three stars. He has been demoted from one of twenty master chefs at the top to relative obscurity among seventy-five others, a devastating blow.

Jacques Pépin's Safari

by Kate Sekules

from *Food & Wine*

Travel writer Kate Sekules gives us this fly-on-the-wall account of a "gourmet safari" with French cooking master Jacques Pépin. It's an adroit sketch of Pépin's insatiably curious personality as well as an evocative look at a land that falls off many travelers' culinary maps.

We call these Desert Pringles," Ralph Bousfield says, wielding a handful of salt grass. "Try one!" Jacques Pépin breaks off a spiky blade, tastes and frowns. Though spring hares crave it, salt grass turns out to be a less satisfying snack than the next item on the menu, harvester termites. "They're crunchy," Pépin says, chewing one. "Quite nutty, buttery."

Pépin is sampling bush food at Bousfield's San Camp, an outpost in the Kalahari Desert. It's the first stop on a seven-night safari that will take us through the southern part of Africa, from

Botswana to Zambia. Of course, seven years would be a more realistic time frame for exploring this vast terrain, but Pépin has a lot on his plate, with two TV series and his duties as a dean of the French Culinary Institute in New York City. On this tour, he is going to get a concentrated taste of the continent, even if it only serves to whet his appetite for a return visit. Africa does this. Nobody can shrug off the huge plains and rivers and skies, the wild beasts, the music and the people, even the shameful, beautiful remnants of colonialism. Nobody who has been here once is immune from wishing to come back.

African food, varied as it is, is not normally the draw. All too often, for the safari visitor at least, menus promise that dreaded noncuisine known as "international"—partly a legacy of the colonial era, partly the product of lowest-common-denominator tourism economics. The two camps on Pépin's itinerary, how-ever, are way more sophisticated than that. Here at San Camp, the chefs conjure up wonderful food in the middle of the desert; at Tongabezi, the resort in Zambia where we will spend three days at the end of the week, the chefs are skilled at incorporat-ing African ingredients into Western dishes. From working with the cooks in these places, Pépin is hoping to discover something of southern African food, both in its undiluted state and as it has been adapted for travelers.

The Kalahari itself is all about adaptation. Every living thing here has developed ingenious ways to survive, from the salt grass, which would pickle itself alive if it hadn't learned to pump salt out through its leaves, to the Sua Kwe Bushmen, who have figured out how to subsist on and around the Makgadik-gadi salt pans, an astonishing expanse that was once a vast salt-water lake roughly the size of Switzerland. The land appears barren of life, but the more we look, the more we see. Every few yards our handsome and logorrheic guide, biologist Chris Varco, whips out his binoculars. "Look! Impalas! That's so rare here. They're obviously on a day trip." (Little do they know they're on tonight's menu. Africa is harsh.) "See there! A secretary bird eating a snake. Those birds hate to fly. They hunt on foot." We see helicopter birds taking off vertically, and ostriches striding like Nureyev, and *mopane* trees folding their leaves like butterfly wings in the sun.

After our introduction to the Kalahari, we head back to San Camp. The most amazing desert adaptation of all may be the one performed here by Bousfield and his wife, Catherine Raphaely, who have created a fantastical outpost—with canvas tents, hardwood floors, Persian carpets, leather trunks and antiques—out of the only positive aspect of colonialism, its visual style. Each day a very basic kitchen produces three-course feasts, complete with fresh-baked breads, from a single weekly delivery of provisions. The men who accomplish this feat are Benson Mwenda, the head chef, and his sous-chef, Foster Bube. Raphaely, who taught them most of what they know about Western cooking, is keen for the two (plus the chefs from San's sister camp, Jack's) to spend time with Pépin. "By meeting you," she explains to him, "they'll see that being a chef is an international profession and a man's profession. I don't want them to think it's a white madam's thing."

Perhaps because they have been told of Pépin's exalted status, or perhaps because the white madam is hovering, Mwenda and Bube are a little shy at first. Pépin quickly breaks the ice with some sleight of hand from his apprentice days, creating butter roses and caramel cages, incongruous froufrou that the other chefs find hilarious and pick up instantly. In no time, the language of food has created a bond among the three men. For the remainder of his stay at San, Pépin is forever disappearing, only to be discovered rummaging in the freezer with Mwenda.

The truth is, Pépin is just as eager to learn from Mwenda and Bube as they are to learn from him. He wants to know about the privations and challenges of cooking in the bush, where opportunism in the use of ingredients is key, and he is even more interested in the real cuisine of the land, the dishes Mwenda's and Bube's mothers taught them. But this will have to wait for a special delivery of bush ingredients. So their first joint venture becomes a Franco-African dinner menu. They select impala, which Pépin proceeds to rub with rosemary and lemon zest. "Don't use the lemon juice," he explains to Mwenda and Bube. "The acid will cook the meat." For dessert, the chefs infuse milk with *rooibos* tea (which takes the place of coffee in half the continent) for a crème anglaise.

At dusk, before the actual cooking, we head out once more into the desert on special motorbikes with four fat tires. We chase the twilight deep into the Makgadikgadi, then park and recline on the salt plain to watch the night sky. This is the proverbial middle of nowhere, nothing but salt and stars, atmosphere and silence, from horizon to horizon. It's a place that shifts your axis forever.

Pépin dips a finger into the salt and pops it in his mouth. "Just like *fleur de sel*," he declares—the world's most expensive salt.

With difficulty we tear ourselves away to ride home. En route, we spot a fire up ahead. "Be careful," Varco says. "It's poachers. They could be armed." But in the best surprise the desert has yet yielded, the "poachers" turn out to be Mwenda and Bube, who are preparing a plum sauce and baking sweet potato gratins in a Dutch oven on the campfire. A huge table has been set for dinner and a full bar has miraculously appeared right on the salt flats. Pépin picks up a pan and joins the chefs as they sear the impala.

"Out here," he laughs, "I don't feel like a cook, I feel like a shaman."

The following day, when the bush ingredients arrive, Mwenda and Bube set to work teaching the teacher about their food. There are jars of *marula* fruit jam and sacks of *mielepap* meal, a ground maize very like polenta. There are dried melons; *morogo* (also known as wild spinach); dried *mopane* worms; and *buyu*, the fruit of the baobab tree, which yields the original version of cream of tartar. "It's sensational," Pépin says, chewing a piece of *buyu*, "powdery, white and tart."

"What do you do with dried melon?" he asks Mwenda.

"You can boil the melon for about three hours and eat it with sugar; and you can drink the liquid separately as a soup along-side *mielepap* meal."

"When would you eat that?" he asks. "For breakfast?"

"Yes, like a soft porridge, or else for dinner with relishes."

"What relishes?"

"*Mopane* worms, or *seswaa*, or *morogo*."

"What is *seswaa*? How do you prepare the *morogo*?"

Soon, Mwenda and Bube start answering Pépin's questions by preparing a meal, which they'll take out into the desert and sample at sunset. *Seswaa* is an economical long-cooked meat stew; the *mopane* worms and the *morogo* are rehydrated and cooked with onions and tomatoes.

The next morning, Pépin says his goodbyes to Mwenda and Bube and we set out for Zambia. At Victoria Falls on the border we meet up with Cherri Briggs, president of Explore, the custom safari outfit that designed our trip. Briggs knows every corner of Africa. Zambia, she thinks, is the most beautiful, unspoiled country on the continent; along the road to Tongabezi, it certainly looks green and promising. If the desert was about adaptation, Tongabezi, a cross between a Caribbean resort and the Swiss Family Robinson's tree house, is about relaxation. My room is shaped like an amphitheater, with one huge curved wall painted with murals and the Zambezi River where the audience should be. The bed could comfortably sleep six. Beneath my mosquito netting, I fall asleep to a hippo lullaby.

Pépin is clearly relieved that the kitchen at Tongabezi is professional, if a little eccentric, with battered aluminum pans where the All-Clad should be. One reason things are in good order here is the influence of the camp's Scottish chef, Craig Higgins. We were looking forward to meeting him, but there is some disappointing news. He tried to hang on for Pépin we are told, through a nasty case of malaria, only to succumb to a burst appendix. He has flown home to Scotland to recover. But we are in the capable hands of his African protégés, with George

Kalaluka at the helm and his sous-chefs, Zui, Rogers, Agnes and Albert, assisting him. They have inherited Higgins's inventive African-accented recipes: butternut and cassava leaf ravioli with sun-dried tomatoes; fritters of *kapenta,* the Zambian version of whitebait; crocodile marinated in yogurt; and guava torte.

After touring the kitchen, we all head to Livingstone Market where Kalaluka, a father of three, shops for his family. He and Pépin hit it off famously, poring over dried fish and live fowl, greens and oils and Kalahari salt. Pépin examines every fish, leaf, root and fruit; for him, this market is better than any museum. In close consultation with Kalaluka, he picks the freshest greens, some of the tiny eggplants called *impua,* cabbages and tomatoes. Pépin attracts a giggling crowd of shoppers—we are the only tourists here—especially when he makes a comedy act out of learning to pound groundnuts with a big stick. He also encourages Kalaluka to pose with a large and irritable chicken. "You know, when we were kids we'd kill the chicken by cutting under the tongue, and we'd keep the blood for the sauce," Pépin says. Kalaluka explains that at Tongabezi, they buy their chickens already dead. We taste a carton of Shake Shake 7 Days, a millet beer fermented for six days and drunk on the seventh. (Do not try this.) Finally, we repair to the nearby Mosioi-tunya Game Park to view, at last, some really big animals.

We start with warthogs (Pépin is fond of them, having made warthog prosciutto on a trip to Senegal a couple of years ago). Then come crowds of malevolent jackhammer baboons and herds of bouncing impalas and placid zebras. A pair of giraffes appear, elegant in slow motion, and, finally, the biggest thrill of all: elephants. "This is the way to see game," Briggs says. "Animals in the zoo are like human beings in a mental hospital."

Time at Tongabezi, filled with eating, lazing, game watching and (for the brave) white-water rafting, passes at cheetah speed. All too soon, it is time to make our way to Tongabezi's tiny downriver island outpost, Sindabezi, for our farewell lunch. We reach it by canoe. Never get between a hippo and the shore,

Briggs warns. They hate that. Despite their Beanie Baby looks and vegetarian diet, these creatures are the biggest killers of humans in Africa, more dangerous even than crocodiles. The lower Zambezi teems with both. We row very, very carefully.

At Sindabezi, Pépin enjoys a meal cooked entirely by Kalaluka, a simple salad of the youngest leaves (a rare commodity) and herbs from the Tongabezi garden, freshly baked rolls and spiced, marinated, wood-fired beef fillet en brochette. Pépin is amused to hear that beef fillet is cheap and plentiful here and the meat at the bone is prized.

"George's food," Pépin confides, as if grading one of his students at the French Culinary Institute, "is well balanced and substantive. He has a really good, solid sense of seasoning. A natural." Thus proving what we knew all along, but have found afresh in Africa—as Pépin puts it: "You don't have to torture yourself to express yourself. You are within the food you make whether you like it or not."

Rice: From "Ripe Lips" to "The Ultimate Act of Love in the Kitchen"

by Cherry Ripe

from *Ripe Enough?*

Peripatetic Australian food writer Cherry Ripe can be opinionated, but her passion for good food—wherever on the planet she finds it—is absolute. And when she does find it, she makes you want to eat, now.

Savory rice pudding?" The driver was incredulous. "We're driving *all the way to Italy* to learn how to make 'savory rice pudding'?" That Italian classic, risotto, had so far eluded the culinary education and tastebuds of this English fanner.

It wasn't quite as bad as it sounds. We were in France at the time—having crossed the Channel the night before—speeding down the autoroute heading for the Mont Blanc tunnel. Besides, this cousin of mine fancies a bit of a stir. We were off on a gastronomic foray into the Piedmont, to take in a cooking school, and the white truffle market held on autumn Saturday mornings at Alba. Grown men, we'd been told, conspiratorially open brown paper bags to sniff—and furtively finger—the earthy treasures inside. (The bags are to keep the lumps of "white gold" out of sight of the prying eyes of tax collectors who might want a share of the loot.)

Winding down the treacherous mountain curves of the Aosta Valley, you suddenly hit the vast flat plains of the Piedmont. That particular October, with the Po in a raging flood, it was more dramatic than usual with its rice fields for the most part harvested, blanketed in fog in a grey and golden twilight, as the sun poked in shafts through the clouds, dumping still more rain on the already sodden earth.

Risotto benefits from being understood in its cultural context. The Piedmont is risotto territory: rice was introduced there in the 1400s. Along with polenta, it is the main starch of the region: the only pasta here is *taglierini*.

Although risotto frequently and somewhat inappropriately turns up on Australian summer restaurant menus, and can even be found in Italian cookbooks made with summery zucchini flowers, it is quintessentially, and historically, a winter dish. In the Piedmont, when the freezing fog rolls in and settles for the winter around the fortified farmhouses which were—and some still are—home not just to a family, but to an entire farming community, church and all within their high walls—binding all indoors, something rib-stickingly warm and nourishing is needed to keep out the cold—and damp. Valentina Harris likens risotto to internal central heating.

In the farmhouse kitchen of La Camilla, formerly a monastery and now home to the Scavia family, Valentina was demonstrating five different ones on the last day of a week-long residential course, one of Tasting Italy's culinary holidays. The rice came from the nearby plains, the butter from the Scavia's dairy herd.

Run out of milk in the middle of class? It's out the back door to the dairy with a jug.

Although she learned to make risotto when she was three or four, standing on a chair in a farmhouse kitchen very like the one at La Camilla, the way Valentina tells it, making risotto is like a love affair: you have to make it with passion. A perhaps unintentional sexual metaphor runs right through her cooking instructions. (Luckily by then my farming cousin had gone for a siesta, or we might never have heard the end of it.)

While it is important, like sexual chemistry, that you get the two main ingredients right—the proper type of rice, and very good boiling stock—the next step, after sautéing the finely chopped onion in butter, is the crucial one. You have to wait until the nice grains are crying out, begging, for liquid.

"This is the most crucial moment of all," says Valentina. "The stock has to be boiling hot, but it is very important that you wait—and wait—until they are absolutely desperate for you to give them a drink. I want these grains of rice to be so desperate for liquid that they really let me know about it when I add it."

This produces a climactic moment—a big whoosh. "It's called *il sospiro*—the sigh of relief. When the first lot of liquid goes in, you get this wonderful hissing noise and a great column of steam. Then you know that you're in business." From this moment on, the heat is turned down, and it's a matter of stirring continuously for the next twenty minutes or so.

But as everyone who is serious about risotto insists, the rate at which you add the liquid is also important. "You are having an affair with your rice grains. You're teasing them and teasing them all the time. They've got to want more—they've got to be asking for more and then you add more. That way you keep it concentrated. You are not trying to evaporate the liquid, you're forcing the rice grains to drink it, so you don't add any more until it begins to go dry again. When it's nearly dried out, in goes a bit more liquid. It's constantly got to remind you of waves lapping on the surface just like the sea, and it's got to make that sea sound, and be bubbling on the surface, but sticky on the bottom," says Valentina.

"It's a labour of love—the ultimate act of love in the kitchen—because you are loving it and loving it, until it comes to this wonderfully creamy consistency, but [the grains are] bitey in the middle, with lots of flavour—a perfectly textured and perfectly flavored marvel.

"Once you've mastered the basic technique, you can put anything you like in it—game, fish, fruit. It's entirely up to you: just plain herb risotto, but I have eaten rose petal risotto and a wild strawberry risotto."

Certainly in England they do: no other dish appeared so frequently on modish "modern British" restaurant menus in the early 1990s, whether it was a saffron risotto at Canteen (Michael Caine and Marco Pierre White's collaboration) or with "courgettes" and their flowers at Alastair Little's—not to mention the more usual ones elsewhere, with radicchio, or prosciutto and rocket, or squid ink, champagne or nettle. They even ran to having gold leaf on them at Gualtiero Marchesi at L'Alberta outside Milan, or at the Halkin in London, which in the mid-1990s was running to a risotto with that and saffron. Oxymoronic for a dish which once sustained the peasantry of Lombardy.

Since 1995 we have been growing Arborio in Australia. But while it is the risotto variety with which we are most familiar, there are others. As Antonio Carluccio dictates in his wonderful *Complete Italian Food*—to date the most comprehensive tome on the subject—"the best rice for risotto is Arborio, Baldo, Vialone Nano or Roma." (And he also insists, before "starting the risotto, make the stock." That, of course, goes without saying.)

However, Valentina cites an old book in which every single risotto recipe calls for a different, specific, variety of rice. As with so many traditional foodstuffs, the diversity of rice varieties has been diminished by modern agricultural practices. There used to be many, many others. "There was one called *razza setanta sette*—variety 77—which I remember so well as a child, that you just can't get anywhere any more. Carnaroli has almost disappeared: most of it goes for export or is grown elsewhere, but here locally in Piemonte it is very difficult to get."

With the introduction of mechanization, dozens of distinct varieties have completely disappeared. Valentina believes that only somewhere between half a dozen and fifteen are left. "In the old days the rice picking in this area was done by the *mondine*—women who would come up from the south of Italy for a break from their normal routine. They wore wonderful big hats and colorful skirts and they would spend all day bending and picking. Since the harvesting machines have been trundling all over the rice fields of Lombardy and Piedmont, the result has been that we have lost lots and lots of different varieties of rice."

Risotto is the antithesis of fast food. It is a technique, a specific method, and there are no short cuts.

Contrast then Keith Floyd's risotto from his series, *Floyd on Italy*. Standing on a quayside of the Cipriani Hotel in Venice with what he called the "Droges" (rather than Doges') Palace over his shoulder, he starts by throwing a huge lump of butter into the pan. While the butter is still a large, solid lump, he heaves in the raw rice. Then—and this is still before the butter has melted!—he sloshes in some wine. So much for frying the grains first, let alone the *sospiro,* the sigh of relief that the by-then thirsty grains are meant to give off. Then—horrors—having added some cold chicken stock, Floyd advocated putting the lid on and letting it finish cooking by itself, uninterrupted. (Perhaps *he* was the thirsty one, itching to get to the pub.)

This method is anathema to anyone who knows anything about Italian cooking: it's not even a pilaf, but rather steamed rice. A risotto it's not.

Marcella Hazan is adamant on the subject. "Risotto is a uniquely Italian technique for cooking rice. The objective is to cause the rice to absorb, a little at a time, enough hot broth"—yes, "hot broth"—"until it swells and forms a creamy union of tender yet firm grains." At any one time, you only add as much liquid as the rice can absorb. "When the rice dries out, add simmering broth, stirring constantly."

Like Valentina, Marcella would no doubt be horrified by recipes which recommend short cuts such as "oven-baked risotto"—considered by purists to be more of a pilaf—or by the even more weird recommendation in one Australian cookbook, to first take "a cup of cooked brown rice." The result shouldn't be dignified with the name. A risotto it isn't. Savory rice pudding, maybe.

The Risotto Lesson

by Dorothy Kalins
from *Saveur*

In this profile of Marcella Hazan, doyenne of Italian cooking, *Saveur*'s editor in chief Dorothy Kalins not only transmits a great cook's techniques, but also profiles one of the culinary world's living legends.

R isotto has a reason," she says in that unmistakable voice, paved by a lifetime of Marlboros and of speaking her mind. Drawing us out of her tiny Venetian kitchen into a small study, Marcella Hazan, now not just a legendary cooking teacher and indispensable author, but also a scientist with two advanced degrees, commands us to inspect three single grains of carnaroli rice: "Look carefully. Each grain has two starches: The translucent outside is amylopectin, the inside is amylose. They react differently to heat and moisture. The inside expands while the outside dissolves. That's why you must keep stirring risotto."

This Marcella, who does not suffer fools gladly, has nonetheless welcomed students—six of them, nine times a year, for 15 years—into her cannily designed kitchen at the top of a 16th-century house, in the *sestiere* ("quarter") of Cannaregio. And—she cannot help herself—this is turning out to be her last class in Venice, though the three of us from *Saveur* have come ostensibly for lunch. Just as Craig Claiborne, the *New York Times* food critic, did some thirty years ago, when he went to lunch and discovered the young Italian housewife from a fishing village on the Adriatic, cooking only the food she knew, for her elegant and exigent husband, Victor.

"Carnaroli," she pronounces, "is the best rice for risotto. Look for carnaroli marked *ai pestelli* on the package, which means it was hulled with a mechanical mortar and pestle. This leaves the rice covered with a powdery starch. You never wash the rice first because you need that starch to make it creamy. Carnaroli doesn't go from undercooked to overcooked in a second; it is starchy—and it has more finesse than arborio, which caught on in America because it was more available."

She leads us back into the kitchen, past stacks of books and boxes packed for shipping. For Marcella and Victor Hazan (a celebrated wine expert; "Venetian life is lubricated by wine," he likes to say)—her partner in teaching, her translator, and still the man she cooks for—are about to begin the next chapter of their life together . . . in Florida.

Now, though, Marcella is making risotto. "I never wait until the fat is hot," she says, adding vegetable oil, butter, and chopped onions all at once to a deep saucepan on her Zanussi four-burner professional gas range. ("I sold all my copper pots," she remarks later without regret. "We have only electric in Florida.") "You can add broth—we don't have stock in Italy—water, anything," she continues (she uses bouillon cubes herself). "It doesn't matter. What matters is that you do it right. That television chef, Mario Batali, he makes risotto in a frying pan!" She rolls her eyes mischievously. "You cannot make risotto in a frying pan. There's too much floor. It goes too fast. My students are always asking when to add liquid. When it's *dry,* I tell them. And no salt yet. Butter is salty. Broth is salty. Enough. And you cook it over *high* heat. The broth is always simmering." It is chastening to discover I've been making risotto wrong all these years.

This risotto will be flavored with green beans and yellow peppers. She has earlier thrown several handfuls of the beans into a pot of boiling water with a generous handful of salt, declaring: "I am against crunchy vegetables. When they're cooked, they taste string beans. But before, they taste grass. In California they don't even cook vegetables; they just show them the water."

Preparing this last lunch, Marcella turns nostalgic. She and Victor reminisce about their students: about the surgeons—"lots of them"—whose taste buds they've awakened, watching them find unexpected pleasure in pitting peaches, "just like removing a tumor from the brain." Some students have become lifelong friends, and others, well, they just make good stories—like the anorexic who cut each piece of penne into four pieces before eating it, or the gentleman of 75 who fell hopelessly in love with a fellow student. "How long do you cook the pasta?" one woman would constantly whine. "Until it's done," Marcella finally shot back. "Most people are afraid to taste," she says. "If they don't know taste, how can they tell when it's done?"

How many times, I wonder (hundreds? thousands?), have the Hazans risen early to walk across the four bridges from their apartment to the Rialto market (as they did with us) and patiently reveal to students—jet-lagged or restless—that all radicchio is not round? How many times have they leaned across a restaurant table (as they did with us) and brightly explained that the lightly fried gray shrimp you are about to devour like popcorn is the only sea creature that stays gray after it's cooked? How many times have they enthusiastically enumerated (in three languages—the obvious two, plus Venetian) the glorious variety of octopi, squid, and cuttlefish? How many souls have they tried

to stir behind the wide-eyed stares of housewives sent by hopeful, hungry husbands back in Texas? How often have they
shared the subtle pleasures they find in the shopping, preparing,
cooking, and eating? And how many of their students have
really changed, really understood?

There's a resignation in some of the Hazans' tales. Do any of
them really *get* it, those people who've paid $3,000 for six days
in Venice? After all these years, Marcella seems genuinely puzzled by Americans' relationship with food. "Why do they always
ask me how I find time to cook?" she'll suddenly wonder. "It's like
asking how I find time to shower." Or she'll look up and ask,
"Why are Americans so in love with leftovers? How could they
take home these, these . . . what do you call them, Victor? . . . dog-
gie bags from restaurants. Italians would never do that." How, in
other words, could she have published four best-selling cookbooks in America—over a million copies—and how could she be
as recognized by her first name as Julia, and still believe that
"people think there's such a thing as Italian food—but there's
only *regional* food, from Bologna or Tuscany or Rome."

"What the risotto needs now," says Marcella in her kitchen,
bringing me back, "is tasting." Then comes the *manticare*, the
"beating in": Marcella pulls the pot off the fire and adds butter
and some grated parmigiano. "I put all the cheese in the cooking
and none at the table. People put too much cheese. They ruin my
dish." She gets cranky with the seriousness of it all; at once
impatient and generous. Very Marcella.

Risotto coi Fagiolini Verdi e il Peperone Giallo
(Risotto with Green Beans and Yellow Bell Pepper)

Serves 4–6
This recipe is from *Marcella Cucina* (HarperCollins, 1997).

> ½ lb. green beans, trimmed
> Salt

1 beef bouillon cube
3 tbsp. butter
1 tbsp. vegetable oil
1 small yellow onion, peeled and finely chopped
1 yellow bell pepper, cored, seeded, and diced into ½"
pieces
1 ⅔ cups carnaroli or other Italian risotto rice
⅔ cup freshly grated parmigiano-reggiano
Freshly ground black pepper

1. Cook beans in a medium pot of boiling salted water for 2 minutes, then drain. Cut cooled beans into ½" pieces, then set aside.
2. Meanwhile, bring 6 cups of water to a boil in a medium pot over high beat. Reduce heat to low, add bouillon cube, and stir until dissolved. Keep broth warm over low heat.
3. Heat 1 ½ tbsp. of the butter, the oil, and the onions in a medium-size heavy pot over medium-high heat. Cook, stirring often with a wooden spoon, until onions are pale gold, about 7 minutes. Add peppers, increase heat to high, and cook for about ½ minute, stirring constantly. Add reserved green beans and cook, stirring often, for 3–4 minutes.
4. Add rice to the beans and peppers, stirring to coat with the oil and butter and to combine it with the vegetables. Add ¾ cup of the simmering broth at a time, stirring the rice constantly; wait until almost all of the broth has been absorbed before adding more. Continue, cooking and adding broth (you may have some broth left over) until rice is tender but firm to the bite, about 15 minutes.
5. Remove pot from heat and vigorously stir in remaining 1 ½ tbsp. butter and the parmigiano-reggiano, then season liberally with salt and pepper. Transfer to a warm platter and serve at once.

Should Chefs Write Cookbooks?

by Anne Mendelson

from Gourmet

Ever buy a glossy cookbook by a "name" chef and discover it was, well . . . kind of hard to *cook* from? In this essay, food writer Anne Mendelson finally blows the whistle on the publishing world's infatuation with celebrity kitchens.

What do you do when you're invited to utter an honest opinion of something you've uneasily edged around for years? If you're me, you get psyched up to speak plain truth about expensive baloney, and then begin to squirm as you realize truthfulness also means acknowledging a snag or two in your own thinking.

The matter at issue is chefs' cookbooks. Not to waste time being polite, I believe that in the aggregate they're about as much use as Cognac in the gas tank. By "chefs' cookbooks" I mean not the deserving, workmanlike efforts that chefs once in a blue moon produce by knuckling down to a self-sufficient culinary topic without obtrusive parades of high art, but the enormously larger class of swanky volumes in which the only essential subject is a chef (or a bunch of them) seen as an emblem of restaurant glory.

Few of these grandiose productions show the minimal teaching competence most of us would demand from a manual on fly-fishing. The reason is no secret: Chefs don't cook from cookbooks. The job of shaping a restaurant's repertoire into orthodox recipes usually falls to a coauthor, ghostwriter, compiler, or editor. This party may or may not have got the picture straight at both the restaurant-kitchen and the home-kitchen ends. As an illustration of what can go wrong, take these gems from a blini recipe muzzily confided to the page in Karen Gantz Zahler's anthology *Superchefs: Signature Recipes from America's New Royalty.* (She attributes it to David Burke of New York City's Park Avenue Cafe, but I doubt that much of the original made it into print unscathed.)

> *"In a bowl, whisk the egg yolks and oil for several minutes, creating a mayonnaise."*

> *"Heat several 3-inch blini pans, melt the butter in them. . . ."*

> *"Pipe with a pastry bag 3 mounds of horseradish crème fraîche 1 ½ inch vertically in the center of the blini. . . ."*

Anyone who goes out and commits a cookbook should know that whisking egg yolks and oil for what is essentially a pancake batter will produce not mayonnaise but a loose mixture; that home cooks can't be expected to have or acquire "several 3-inch blini pans"; and that piping "3 mounds . . . 1 ½ inch vertically" doesn't make sense. Furthermore, Zahler's script has you using a quart of milk, 4 ¾ cups of flour, and—to cook all the resulting

3-inch blini—one tablespoon of butter. She has you planning for 12 pancakes, though, as she helpfully notes, "there will be extra blini." Yeah, like maybe 40.

Did anyone at the publisher, John Wiley & Sons, observe a few shingles missing from the roof here? Why, no—no more than the editors at Ten Speed Press noticed anything dumb about having recipe after recipe in *Charlie Trotter's Seafood* call for far-side-of-the-moon fish and seafood varieties (African pompano, *moi,* black pomfret, *gindai*), with only the vaguest mention of their qualities and no suggestion of how the common folk might find them.

I'll spare you more examples. The crucial fact is that making chefs' cookbooks usable requires extraordinary editorial efforts sometimes shirked or botched by those who should be trying the hardest. The path from restaurant cooking—especially among fusion virtuosos—to comprehensible home recipes is strewn with awful pitfalls. It amounts to taking swift and complex assembly-line fandangos performed with dazzling arrays of ingredients like lambs' tongues or *moi* and painstakingly reinventing them as hobbled exercises for amateurs to walk through in their own kitchens. Those involved in the translation must move carefully between the two spheres, weighing every detail, or the book will end up presenting no intelligible kind of cooking at all.

To be fair, the difficulties inherent in the genre never stopped a few hardy souls from turning cutting-edge restaurant acrobatics into solid, diligent instruction for home cooks. (*Alfred Portale's Gotham Bar and Grill Cookbook* is a prime example.) But, as far as I can see, genuinely conscientious guidance, with all the necessary groundwork in place—reliable number-crunching, notes on sources for exotica, decent attempts to verbalize the visual, and thoughtful explanations of variables—sells no better than muddled or unrealistic prattle that leaves the user clueless about vital information. Besides, following directions in even the finest cookbook will never, never in a million years remotely resemble "cooking with Hugo Wunderkind at your side," or whatever malarkey is on the dust jacket.

Case closed? Not at all. Whether I like it or not, there's another side to this question of restaurant-fantasy cookbooks: They point to profound changes taking place in the interests and underlying value systems of American cooks and diners.

It may be true that chefs' cookbooks, on the whole, would be useless boondoggles if anyone bought them expecting to go into the kitchen and cook. But here comes the profound-change part: Many or most buyers don't get them for any such purpose.

On both the publishing and the retail sides, there is uncanny agreement that not many meals get cooked from cookbooks—even (or especially) big-ticket items steeped in restaurant glamour. The reason is very simple: Not all that much is getting cooked at home, period. More and more of us do more and more of our eating outside the home or bring precooked food into it—frozen microwave dinners, a pie from the pizzeria, elegant goodies-to-go tailored to the loftier tax brackets. Anyone who tries to juggle a work schedule and daily cooking knows exactly why this is happening, and has no business moralizing about it.

Amazingly, books of recipes continue to pour forth, and the market hasn't dried up. Or maybe not so amazingly. To buy a $45 cookbook for the sake of one or two recipes or just for armchair enjoyment is no oddity these days. Thousands of people get their greatest pleasure from a cookbook by sitting down with it and floating into realms of imagination conjured up by clever graphics, opulent layouts, and, above all, color photographs.

Chefs' cookbooks are among the most striking examples of the trend. Small wonder. They promise to make the user—or, rather, the beholder—not just a citizen of some generic food-fantasyland but a sharer in the restaurant-theater energy generated by particular superstars. Eat at the shrine, buy the cookbook, belong to the enchanted circle.

We're talking about a major shift in food hobbyists' perspectives over a fairly short span of time. Thirty years ago, excited would-be learners used to spend hours or days busting their own personal chops to make venerable French or other European or maybe even American dishes that advanced their practical kitchen skills and knowledge—things like *boeuf en daube*, lasagne, cherry pie. In a development that I've become aware of somewhat after the fact, their counterparts today look more to restaurant meals for the elements of a culinary education.

Thus, throngs of cookbook buyers reveling in a big, ornate volume with some restaurant connection honestly think they've got their money's worth because, in a way, they *have*. Rightly or wrongly, the book stands for the restaurant in many admirers' estimation. I can't dismiss the equation as a mirage, because I probably subscribe to the reverse of it. Rightly or wrongly, I look at chefs' cookbooks and wish that other kinds of cooking still mattered more to food mavens than the last word in multi-star restaurant cooking.

Prejudice? Sure. In both my professional and my private lives I would much rather eat than have a Dining Experience. And I'm not the only food writer I know who thinks that the pursuit of the latter has been an awful influence on contemporary food. Some of us closet philistines reserve our deepest loyalty for home cooking or kinds of restaurant cooking that resemble it enough to represent values unaffectedly shared within a community. Hence, we are happier in luncheonettes and unsung ethnic neighborhood places than in restaurants where the food is busy proving something to somebody.

At bottom, the things that bother me about today's deliriously upscale-restaurant cookbooks are the same things I can't stand about today's stunning, fantastic upscale restaurants. A few of the standards I'd like to apply in both cases may be an antidote to frenzied hype; others are laughably irrelevant to what a far-from-stupid audience is getting from a new kind of theater.

I scramble away from the subject with two parting thoughts. One is from a bookseller pal who finds chefs' cookbooks a lively and, in general, valid part of the scene. Like me, he zeroes in on the photographs as being at the heart of the matter, but his take is about 180 degrees from mine. Noting that in the ordinary course of events a plate of food sent to table is chomped to smithereens in no time flat and never seen again in its glory, he points out that restaurant cookbooks constitute a kind of record. They allow a talented artist's fugitive achievement to live on *in perpetuo* for those who were or weren't there; they preserve some essentials for the sake of others who may be able to build on the idea, like artists drawing inspiration from colleagues.

The other bit of perspective comes from a genuine superchef whom I don't know but recently heard chatting with an acquaintance. (This chef is remarkable for not wanting to be remarkable, and I doubt he'd thank me for mentioning his name.) The friend inquired whether Mr. X had any thought of doing a cookbook. No, he said, and tried to explain why in his rudimentary English. To paraphrase: In his view, his kind of bravura cooking is more like a musical or dramatic performance than a permanent art form. When it's over, it's over—and that spontaneous, never-to-be recaptured electricity of the moment is just what's most rewarding about it.

Dining
Around

Restaurant Baby

by Karen Stabiner
from *Saveur*

Running a restaurant takes more than just putting a chef in a kitchen and waiters in the dining room. In this nostalgic glimpse of the 1950s Chicago restaurant business, L.A.–based Karen Stabiner shares her unique window onto dining out.

t is 11 a.m. The empty bar at this hour seems about 40 feet long, curved mahogany polished to a high sheen, like the shinbone of some extinct woodland giant. The mirror behind it reflects row upon row of bottles, the popularity of their contents revealed by the level of liquid in each one. The room smells of leather, cigarettes, and last night's perfume. My drink sits on a napkin in front of me. Down at the far end of the bar, the owner huddles with a friend over bottomless cups of coffee. On his way to refill their cups, he smiles and wordlessly plunks another maraschino cherry in my glass.

And then the door opens, letting in a thin, pale shaft of winter light and a rush of cold air. I jump off my stool to embrace Flower. She is the most exotic creature I know: false eyelashes and lots of eyeliner; a figure I will come to think of as voluptuous; ratted, brassy red hair piled high on her head; a laugh sanded by too many hours of inhaling smoke and speaking above the din. She smothers me in a hug and hustles me off to the waitresses' changing room with the promise of a present. There, in the private jumble of coats and mirrors and makeup and satiny black uniforms, Flower hands me a paper bag. Inside is an oversize picture-book edition of *Bambi*.

I am absolutely convinced that this is the best place on the face of the earth.

That was 1959, Sage's restaurant, downtown Chicago. I was 9, and the drink Gene Sage kept dropping cherries into was a shirley temple. His friend was my father, Ira Stabiner of the Ira China Company, a restaurant-supply business whose slogan, embossed on blue pencils, read, "Don't settle for less—get the best—at Ira China Company."

Whenever I was invited, I spent the weekend accompanying my father on his rounds while he sold thick Shenango or Carr china, a mysterious assortment of utensils never seen in our convenience-food home kitchen, and stockpots big enough to hide in. Sometimes our calls would overlap the restaurants' dinner hour, and I'd get a glimpse of the clientele: glamorous women and sharp-suited men wrapped in smoke and intrigue at Sage's; local guys in Bermuda shorts learning the fine art of flirtation from Hy at Sam & Hy's Delicatessen; and oh, the elegant couples who held court at the Red Carpet, the only restaurant I knew that had a canopy covering the distance from front door to curbside.

Restaurants were everything our suburb, Evanston, was not: unpredictable, seductive, a sophisticated nod to at least one of the seven deadlies. They had a secret life, in the hours before they opened, and then a public one. I was the only kid I knew who was allowed backstage.

We did not travel much, so restaurants were my introduction to the outside world. They were my United Nations, full of people from somewhere else who were obsessed with creating not just a dish, but a universe. I still recall one of the fancier restaurants we frequented (though I no longer remember its name), a place where "Continental cuisine" meant anything from shish kebabs to crêpes suzette. It employed a Russian waiter, a man so big and heavy that the floorboards vibrated as he stomped towards your table, who had perfected a magical trick: He wielded a large silver coffeepot from shoulder level, somehow managing to refill my father's cup from three feet up without spilling a single drop.

My father, who was exceptionally good at finding reasons to like his life, offered me these dining experiences as a writer might offer his child a treasured book. When I graduated from junior high school he took me to lunch at Chez Louis, a French restaurant, with an express purpose in mind. My coming-of-age, he felt, should involve learning how to eat raw oysters. That day is as clear to me now as if it were a movie I'd seen—the platter full of ice, the little gray blobs nestled in their half shells, the octagonal crackers, the lemon slices, the cocktail sauce. And then the luscious, briny shock of that first oyster: another successful venture into the unknown.

The restaurateurs who could not afford to pay my dad invited us back during business hours, preferring to feed their creditors for free rather than give up in favor of a more profitable line of work. Every year, we celebrated my birthday at Capri Pizza, an indebted Italian dive near the el tracks. My mom never understood why I failed to pick a more upscale spot, but I still remember the couple who owned the place. They produced what I considered at the time to be perfect lasagne and always seemed to have a birthday cake with my name on it stashed in the kitchen.

I was never a picky eater. Simple economics demanded that I consume the meals set before me; they were the currency of much of my father's business. But there was something else at work. We ate what was presented to us out of respect for the people who made it. I obeyed my family's cardinal rule—you have to taste one bite, and if you don't like it you don't have to finish it—not because I was a particularly obedient child, but because I knew the people who put the food on my plate. The young guy at Capri who was serving me mushrooms had eaten them himself when he was my age, and now he and his wife were doing their best to transform a dimly lit, empty room into a theater of happiness. Memory on a plate. How could I refuse? And of course, once the food got past my preconceptions and hit my palate, I was fine. My mind, now, plays a kind trick: There must have been food I did not care for, but I cannot remember a bite of it.

I know my father had customers I never met—entrepreneurs who talked about themes and concepts instead of celebrating food itself. Our outings were supposed to be fun, so he spared me the restaurateurs who were in it to be the next big success story. Which is why I still value being a regular customer far more than being the first to visit a new restaurant; a sense of belonging matters to me almost as much as the food does.

When I can, now, I take my 10-year-old daughter, Sarah, with me to restaurants—to the dining room, because I want her to enjoy the show, but more important, in the quiet hours, to the kitchen, so she can see how the place lives. I have an image of her, half her life ago, suspended over a pot of minestrone by a chef who held her in one arm and waved the steam towards her with his free hand, imploring, "Can you smell how good it is?" We could not leave until we had sampled that soup alongside yesterday's, to see how the flavor changed.

Today she is sitting at the back of the kitchen at Valentino in Santa Monica because I am writing a cookbook with its owner. She balances a plate of prosciutto and bread on her knees and is trying to read—but she is distracted, her eyes darting around the room. A moment later she defects to visit the pastry chef and returns clutching a vanilla bean and a sprig of mint with the same reverence I must have felt for that copy of *Bambi*.

I watch her; my father watched me. My friends tease me for having raised a food snob. They are right: She wants risotto with zucchini flowers—and she doesn't want McDonald's. But they are also wrong. She isn't out to trump anyone. She is after romance, just like her mom was.

. . . And $300 Fed a Crowd?

by Eric Asimov

from The New York Times

When a restaurant charges stratospheric prices, who can tell us whether it's all hype or worth every penny? A restaurant reviewer on an expense account, that's who. Eric Asimov, whose usual beat for the *New York Times* food section is restaurants in the $25-and-under range, drew the plum assignment of sampling one of America's most expensive restaurants.

As I pulled my rental Pontiac into a parking garage under Rodeo Drive, I felt uncomfortable. A Ferrari was in front of me, a Bentley behind me, and a glowering specimen of Parkingattendus southerncalifornius awaited, ready to confirm my lowly status with a sneer.

Instead, the attendant held the door for me and greeted me politely. I stepped out, straightened my back and headed to the elevator for Ginza Sushiko. The Zagat Survey for Los Angeles says Ginza may be the Most Expensive Restaurant in America—$300 a person for dinner, I was told, not including wine, tax or tip—but its site, on the second floor of Two Rodeo, a small shopping center with all the charm of an office building, is far more Pontiac than Bentley.

As I stepped out of the elevator, though, I didn't see any restaurant. I turned left, passed a shoe store and headed down a shabby corridor with a peeling linoleum wall covering. I got to an emergency door propped open by a cinder block before deciding I'd better turn back. I walked past the men's and ladies' rooms this time, and there it was, behind a lattice wood door, Ginza Sushiko.

This was the most expensive restaurant in America? A modest sushi bar with nine seats and two tables on the second floor of a unprepossessing building? What's more, even though the restaurant is a favorite of the film and fashion industries, nobody else was there, other than the chef and an assistant. Admittedly, it was only 6:30 and shoppers in the plaza below still wore their Guccis in the sunshine, but I had a plane to catch and so was eating early.

I was beginning to feel odd again. I don't ordinarily spend a lot of money at restaurants, and when I had made a reservation several days before, the fellow on the phone made sure that I understood the $300 prix fixe. Even with the broader trend toward higher prices, this is an extreme example, and I got the sense that more than a few first-time customers had bugged out with sticker shock at Ginza. The restaurant took my credit card number and explained that if I canceled my reservation it would still cost me $100. I was dismissive, with the inner calm of one who has been blessed by the expense account gods.

Now, I wasn't so sure of myself. I took a seat at the sushi bar, a smooth wooden chair with a brass plate bearing the name S. Snukal on the backrest. All the chairs had names on them, in fact. The assistant told me the nameplates were for the members of a club. I silently apologized to S. Snukal for sitting in his or her chair (and to R. Snukal, whose chair was being used by my bag), and looked up at Masa Takayama, the chef and owner, who stood expectantly behind the bar. "Omakase," I said, indicating I was putting myself into Mr. Takayama's hands.

Not that I had any choice. Ginza does not offer a menu, which was fine by me. I prefer that the chef serve what he likes, depending on what's freshest and how he's inspired. As Mr. Takayama got to work, I looked around at the sleek counter of unadorned blond wood, at the slate floor and at a large triangular niche behind Mr. Takayama, where a half-moon pool of water was adorned with flowers. The work area held the usual assortment of knives and graters, along with a small charcoal brazier, a tub of rice and a bowl of fresh ginger, wasabi root, small limes and other flavorings and garnishes. No fish was visible.

Ginza has no wine list, but feeling bold, I asked for "your best sake," and the assistant returned with a ceramic carafe, which he placed in a lacquered bamboo bowl with ice and flowers. "Dry but a little sweet," he said as he poured a thimbleful of the clear, icy liquid into an etched glass.

By this time Mr. Takayama had placed a small bowl in front of me with okra, cooked in seaweed broth and topped with grated lime zest, a light, refreshing way of inaugurating the meal. "Anything you don't eat?" he asked me. I shook my head, and the procession of small dishes began.

Mr. Takayama pulled out a pink, well-marbled block of meat. "Toro," he said, the prized fatty part of the tuna belly. Cutting swiftly, he fanned out shreds of the toro in a small bowl, topping it with gray beads. "Caviar," he said as he maneuvered small rectangles of bread over the brazier with his chopsticks and placed it all in front of me. "Toro tartare," he said. With chopsticks, I made a neat hillock of tuna and caviar on the bread and ate, the salty, bracing flavor of the roe melding with the buttery toro and the smokiness of the soft grilled bread. Mr. Takayama seemed pleased by my sighs.

Then came a small bowl of Spanish mackerel blended with lime zest, scallions and tiny lavender shiso flowers, which have the anise flavor of the shiso green without any of the harshness. They were mild and pleasing, leaving a glow in the mouth.

Mr. Takayama worked smoothly and easily, as his assistant, unprompted, brought out precisely the ingredient or tool he required. As the assistant grated fresh wasabi, Mr. Takayama prepared freshwater eel, lightly broiling the fillet over the coals, then topping it with small green kinome leaves, an herb that gave the perfectly delicate eel the mildest scent of vanilla.

It is easy, when splurging, to be overly price-conscious, as if the mental abacus cannot help but continually reassess whether you're getting your money's worth. But all I could think about as I ate was how wonderfully fresh and clean everything tasted, and how graceful and imaginative Mr. Takayama's combinations were. The artistic bowls and plates, selected specifically to complement each course, were beautiful, but the ultimate appeal was the sublime purity of the ingredients, which I later found out are flown in from Japan several times a week. Freed from budgetary constraints, liberated from the assembly-line compromises of cooking for a crowd, Mr. Takayama has created a dream sushi bar where each ingredient is an ideal.

For the next course, Mr. Takayama withdrew from a cabinet a beige mass the size of a small cauliflower—foie gras, I realized in a double take—and sliced off several good-size pieces. Then he made fine slices in a piece of cream-colored fish resembling yellowtail and put both on a plate in front of me, as his assistant placed a dish of ponzu sauce and a bowl of bubbling hot seaweed broth beside it.

"Look," he said. He picked up a slice of foie gras with his chopsticks, swirled it in the broth and put it on my plate. As I dipped it in ponzu and ate, the liver seemed to melt in my mouth. Then Mr. Takayama picked up a slice of fish, dipped it ever so briefly in the broth, and magically, it seemed to blossom into a beautiful rose, its brininess playing counterpoint to the rich foie gras. I cooked the next slices myself and drank the broth.

Now, the preliminaries were over. The assistant replaced my

chopsticks with a fresh pair, and it was time for sushi. Mr. Takayama began, again, with toro, supremely tender and luxurious, on perfectly prepared rice. Too often, rice is the ignored half of the sushi partnership, taken for granted, but Mr. Takayama's rice was soft and lightly vinegared, each grain independent, yet part of an indivisible unit.

Next came cool, clean aji, or horse mackerel, its shiny skin shimmering, and then ika, or squid. In front of me I had a dish of soy sauce, freshly grated wasabi and ginger, but Mr. Takayama looked pained as I picked up the ika with my fingers and moved toward the soy sauce. "No, don't dip," he interjected, and I pulled back just in time. He was right: the squid was perfect with no more than his signature lime zest and a pinch of salt over the top.

As the sushi dishes came one after the other, I was still the only diner there. Sweet clam, bright, delightful and a little chewy; red clam, with a lovely crosshatched design, tangy and a little sharper than the sweet clam; small, silvery gizzard shad, which tasted like pickled herring; and then wonderfully tender maguro tuna, broiled ever so briefly and painted with fresh wasabi.

Mr. Takayama placed each dish before me and announced the ingredient. He seemed unconcerned by the rituals of transference that can encumber a more formal sushi bar. He was fun to speak with.

The sushi kept coming: beautiful slices of shiitake tasting pleasantly of the forest; abalone that was both salty and crunchy; sea urchin, almost luridly unctuous, yet breathtakingly fresh; briny and sweet sea eel; a red clam roll; and then Kobe beef with lime and salt, as tender and rich as the toro, which it surprisingly resembled.

I asked Mr. Takayama whether it was a slow night, and he shrugged, saying two parties were coming the next night. The assistant asked me about my favorite sushi bars in New York.

Still more: maguro, which Mr. Takayama indicated was to be dipped, and a dried shrimp stuffed with sweetened egg. "I think

I'm almost full," I said. "Good, because this is the last dish," Mr. Takayama replied, placing a toro-shiso leaf roll that was almost beefy in its rich intensity.

I leaned back, sipping the last of my sake, and the assistant put before me a small goblet with chilled, minced grapefruit sections, as sweet as sorbet, yet more refreshing. And I was done.

Except the check: $250, plus $20 for the sake. "Not $300?" I asked. "Only for blowfish season, November to March," Mr. Takayama said. With tax and tip, it was $352.28.

Was it worth it? I could have spent the money on a sport coat, round-trip airfare to London, a half-dozen New York parking citations, maybe two tickets to a Knicks game. Or, as a friend dourly suggested, "you could have fed a lot of hungry people with that money."

Later, I tracked down the Snukals, Robert and Sheila, whose chairs I had borrowed. They have been regulars since Ginza first opened, 16 years ago, at another site.

"It's probably one of the few places we go—it kind of spoils you," said Ms. Snukal, who lives in Brentwood and is in the health care business with her husband. "It's so sublime that in terms of justifying it, I don't have a psychiatrist: this is our therapy. This replaces trips to France. It replaces 10 meals somewhere else. Masa is amongst the greats—he really is."

I do know that the meal was superb, singular and memorable. And as I left, past the bathrooms, down the elevator and out to the garage, I had one more surprise before me: parking, the smiling attendant told me, was free.

—*Ginza Sushiko is at Two Rodeo, second floor, 218 North Rodeo Drive, Beverly Hills; 310/247-8939.*

The Past on a Plate

by Jane and Michael Stern

from *Gourmet*

In pursuit of culinary Americana, husband-and-wife team Jane and Michael Stern have eaten their way in and out of countless roadside diners, lunch counters, and storefront restaurants. On a visit to Chicago, they zeroed in on four classic restaurants and two dishes that have long defined "fine dining" in Chicago.

Chicago's liveliest culinary sport is rating city specialties. Food journalists and freelance eaters are forever debating whose Red Hots, deep-dish pizzas, Italian beef, and rib racks are the best. From street vendors to four-star dining rooms, untold numbers of food purveyors unblushingly tout their fare as Chicago's best. Curiously, despite this patent gastronomic pride, two of the most beloved local specialties remain above the ratings game. Shrimp de Jonghe and chicken Vesuvio share an abundance of garlic but little else. They are served in old-time steak houses and fine neighborhood Italian restaurants as well as at dinner tables in homes of diverse ethnic backgrounds. They are as fundamental a part of Chicago food life as a flaming dinner in the Pump Room or a Maxwell Street Polish sausage, yet so basic to the city's taste that they fly below the ratings radar.

Many of us who grew up along Lake Michigan's southwest shore take them for granted, and they may even fade from our memories if we move away to eat through other towns and new cuisines. But to inhale the sweet Sherry-garlic aroma of a shrimp de Jonghe casserole or the starchy warmth of crisp-crusted potatoes in a well-prepared plate of chicken Vesuvio is like sniffing the perfume of a long-lost love.

And so, to ex-Chicagoans as well as to visitors who want a true Chicago meal, we are delighted to report that both dishes remain a staple in dining rooms that are bastions of the old ways; they also appear on menus of newer restaurants where chefs respect tradition.

The Vesuvio way of doing things is a passion at **Harry Caray's,** which was opened in 1987 by the late sportscaster who was known as the voice of the Chicago Cubs (it boasts a phone number honoring his most famous exclamation: 773/HOLYCOW). In this festive, brick-walled dining hall—patronized by Windy City glitterati, sports stars, tourists, and devotees of prime beef—you can get any steak in the house served Vesuvio style, as well as archetypal chicken Vesuvio and the less soulful boneless white-meat Vesuvio. The menu warns that the old-time version takes 30 minutes to prepare, and when you apply silverware to it, you understand why. The chicken, sautéed and then baked, is encased in a dark, red-gold crust of lush skin that slides from the meat as the meat slides off the bone. Piled among the chicken pieces are wedges of potato, long cooked in a bath of white wine, garlic, olive oil, and oregano until they are soft as mashed inside but develop luscious crunchy edges. Spilled across this powerfully seasoned mountain of food is a handful of green peas, more for color than for taste. Steaks Vesuvio are grilled to order in a traditional manner, then smothered with potatoes and peas that have been given the white wine, herb, and garlic treatment.

It will come as no surprise to epicures who know Chicago that superb versions of both chicken Vesuvio and shrimp de Jonghe are on the menu at the restaurant that also happens to serve the city's best steak, the venerable **Gene & Georgetti.** Here we are reminded that chicken Vesuvio was supposedly named not only for its eruption of flavors but also because it really looks like a great volcano—a lofty jumble of crusty potatoes and glistening sections of chicken rising up from a pool of the garlic-tinged white wine in which they have been cooked. The skin, plastered with herbs and permeated with the savor of chicken fat, looks like strips of crisp-fried bacon.

Shrimp de Jonghe at Gene & Georgetti is unusual. Traditionally, the dish is cooked at a high temperature so that the garlicky crumbs form a crust around the edge of the ramekin, and is served oven-hot. Scraping off sizzling crust is part of the pleasure of great shrimp de Jonghe. However, you'll do no scraping at Gene & Georgetti, for its version is not just a baked casserole. It is a broad, deep platter that holds melted herbed garlic butter laced with crumbs so soft they have become supple specks of flavor. You can cut the huge pink shrimp into bite-size pieces with a knife and fork, but you also need a spoon, or plenty of Gene & Georgetti's stout Italian bread for mopping all that garlic butter. If you are willing to spend almost twice the price of a two-pound porterhouse steak, the lobster de Jonghe is a veritable seascape of plump white hunks of sweet tail meat in a luminous pool of butter. This dish is so rich it is dizzying.

In the fine old **Cape Cod Room** of the Drake Hotel, we witness a shrimp de Jonghe epiphany that reminds us that food culture is a reflection not only of social history but of personal history, too. Ensconced in the dimly lit, Down East–decorated dining room with its red-checked curtains and anachronistic menu of Thermidors and Newburgs and wonderful Dover sole, we eavesdrop on the adjacent booth as a man says, "I don't know how it happened. I just don't know. I must be the luckiest man in Chicago." Glasses clink, and he toasts his wife on the occasion of their 49th anniversary. At this moment, the aroma of Sherry and garlic begins to fill the air as two casseroles arrive at their table. "Shrimp de Jonghe!" the man exclaims tenderly, as if greeting a beloved grandparent, explaining to the waiter that this has been their anniversary meal since the day he and his wife were married in 1950.

In fact, shrimp de Jonghe tastes as if it goes back far earlier than 1950, back to the heyday of the chafing dish and shrimp wiggle. Historians have been unable to convincingly document its exact origins, but according to Pierre de Jonghe's granddaughter Nancy Buckley, Pierre and his siblings opened de Jonghe's restaurant at the 1893 Columbian Exposition and later moved to Monroe Street in downtown Chicago. It was at their restaurant that shrimp de Jonghe was created, by Pierre or perhaps by Pierre and his employee Emil Zehr. Zehr's son, a professional accordionist, wrote us several years ago to say he was quite certain it was his father who invented it, a possibility Buckley allows.

Our happiest moment in the hunt for shrimp de Jonghe and chicken Vesuvio comes at **Eli's,** an urbane Gold Coast steak house with a Jewish accent. It is just the sort of mature place we'd expect to find Chicago's signature dishes in their glory. Sure enough, when we call to inquire, a hostess attests that shrimp de Jonghe is on the dinner menu every night. And chicken Vesuvio?

"Ohhhh, dear, no," she says with a voice full of genuine woe. "We used to make it. I am so sorry, so, so sorry."

Seated at a white-linen–clad table in Eli's small, privileged dining room (hey, there's *Chicago Sun-Times* columnist Irv Kupcinet at a table near the door!), we ask the waiter about chicken Vesuvio, explaining that we are from out of town and yearn to try this true Chicago meal.

"I regret to say we don't have it," says the young man, also distressed at having to give a negative answer in this accommodating place. "We used to make it," he recalls, then says, "Wait, wait right here," and disappears. We scarcely have time to spread a slice of fresh pumpernickel with chopped liver, crumbled egg, and onion before he returns. He is exultant. "We will make chicken Vesuvio!" he announces loud enough for diners at the next table to look up from their plates of calf's liver.

Eli's shrimp de Jonghe is expert—large, snapping-fresh shrimp sheathed in a red-gold coat of moist Sherry- and garlic-infused crumbs, served in a hot gratin dish. And the custom-made Vesuvio is nothing short of wondrous. Piled onto a big round plate is nearly a whole chicken, cut in pieces, cooked in white wine, garlic, and herbs until falling-apart tender, its skin roasted to savory ambrosia. The meat is intertwined with large segments of potato, also spangled with herbs. Some lengths of spud are so supple that they seem to pour along the pile of chicken like rivulets of molten lava and must be gathered with a fork and knife; others are cooked so brittle-crisp you can pick them up like steak fries. The dining room captain, other waiters, and a handful of knowing diners all watch the arrival of the chicken Vesuvio with awe, and they beam when we cannot contain our exclamations of pleasure as we begin to work our way through this magnificent meal.

After we finish supper and walk toward the door, Irv Kupcinet raises a glass to salute us. At the door, the maître d' asks if we found the dish satisfactory.

"Perfect!" we answer. "It was the chicken Vesuvio of our dreams."

"I made sure of that," he says with pride. "I was in the kitchen, watching."

Harry Caray's Restaurant
33 West Kinzie Street
Tel. 312/828-0966

Gene & Georgetti
500 North Franklin Street
Tel. 312/527-3718

Cape Cod Room
140 East Walton Street
(in the Drake Hotel)
Tel. 312/787-2200

Eli's The Place For Steak
215 East Chicago Avenue
Tel. 312/642-1393

Hot on the Barbecue Trail

by Vince Staten
from *Bon Appetit*

Journalism professor Vince Staten, in the interests of fairness, set aside his native Tennessee prejudices and ventured across America, ready to judge regional barbecue with an open mind and palate. After logging many miles (and wiping a lot of sauce from his chin), he weighed in with this assessment in *Bon Appetit*'s annual barbecue issue.

B arbecue is nothing if not versatile, adapting itself at each stop to local customs and local cuisine. So today *barbecue* means different things to different folks. In Texas, it means beef; in Tennessee, pork; in Kansas City, both. Ask for barbecue in Raleigh, North Carolina, and you'll get pork meat pulled from a whole hog, chopped finely and soaked in a thin, vinegary sauce. In Owensboro, Kentucky, you'll get grilled mutton covered with a Worcestershire sauce–type dressing that's called "black dip."

Which is best? They're all terrific. To get a taste, won't you join me on an expedition in search of great barbecue?

There are barbecue meccas—Memphis, Kansas City, the state of Texas—and then there is Lexington, North Carolina. *Mecca* doesn't begin to describe this town's love of barbecue. Lexington (population: 16,581) is home to 13 barbecue joints, and I'm talking full-time restaurants, not weekend-only places.

Picking a favorite is like asking for a whipping. The worst joint in town is wonderful. I lean toward **Lexington Barbecue,** also known as Lexington No. 1. Owner Wayne Monk says tradition is the reason his town is so barbecue-crazy. "We've been eating barbecue so long that we just know what's good."

In Lexington, that means tender pork plucked from slow-roasted shoulders, chopped and drizzled with a thin, tart, tomato-based sauce. It's topped with red slaw—coleslaw made with ketchup—so you get your entrée and your side dish all in one.

Head a hundred miles south to Columbia, South Carolina, and you'll think you're in a different country. When it comes to barbecue, you are. This state capital is home to a kind of barbecue sauce you won't find anywhere else: mustard sauce, a tradition that survives only within a fifty-mile radius of the city.

My family and I were driving from our home in Louisville, Kentucky, to Myrtle Beach, South Carolina, last year when I insisted on a detour to **Maurice Bessinger's Piggie Park** in West Columbia. The place looks like a fifties drive-in, which it is. I wanted my family to try Maurice's mustard sauce—yellow lava that looks nuclear when you first see it on pulled pork.

We were devouring the stuff when I spotted my cousin Herb from Burlington, North Carolina, coming through the door. I hadn't seen him in two years. That's how popular Maurice's is. You're apt to see folks there whom you haven't seen in ages. In fact the only person I haven't met at Maurice's is my cousin Pat, who actually lives in West Columbia.

From Piggie Park it's a long drive to the **Dreamland Drive Inn Bar-B-Q** in Tuscaloosa, Alabama. The place sits on a hill overlooking the city, and in the evening mist it looks like an Elks' club in heaven. But open the door, and it's celebration central, with enough boarding-house tables to house a large frat party.

Pork ribs are the thing here—white bread and beer are considered the side dishes—and have been since John "Big Daddy" Bishop set up shop four decades ago. Bishop has since gone on to that great pit in the sky, but the Dreamland is still in the family, run by John junior. He says his goal is to make the ribs so succulent that you can take your dentures out to eat the meat. They are, and you can.

From here we head north, as southerners have for years, to Memphis, the mecca of the mid-South.

People in Memphis argue about barbecue more than people anywhere else do. That's because the "wets" (folks who want their barbecue sauced) eat side by side every day with their rivals, the "drys" (folks who prefer a dry rub on their barbecue). They're not separated by geography, which tends to put a crimp in the feuding.

There's a new place in town—well, new by barbecue standards, which allow a twenty-year-old joint to be new—that has captured the hearts of wets and drys alike. **Corky's Bar-B-Q Restaurant** was established in 1984, and within two years it had overtaken such longtime local favorites as Gridley's and The Rendezvous in popularity. It has won *Memphis Magazine's* Best Barbecue poll thirteen years running—not bad in a city that sports more than a hundred barbecue spots.

The secret to Corky's success? Fine pork barbecue, wet or dry. The sauce is a near-chocolate color, rich but not sweet. Of course, if you're one of the drys, you don't care anyway. Whichever side you're on, you win at Corky's. Don't miss the beans (they're made from navy beans—they only look red because of the barbecue sauce) or Miss Linda's Pecan Pie, packed with so much Karo, syrup and so many pecans that even the rich call it rich.

The next stop is Kentucky's capital, Frankfort, where barbecue was Newton Vance's destiny. He grew up with it—"I started tending the pit as soon as I was tall enough to reach in," Vance says. When he went away to the University of Kentucky, he worked at Billy's Barbecue in Lexington. So it was part of the natural order of things that he would have a place of his own.

Come 1987, he opened **Capital BBQ** in a tiny cabin that he and his father built on Frankfort's west side. It wasn't much to look at, but who was looking? Folks came to eat.

A dozen years later Vance is still tending the pit himself—still pulling the pork shoulder meat and chopping it by hand. Oh, he has a helper, Wilma, who comes in to mix up his "world-famous" potato salad. But Vance makes all the sandwiches himself, and they truly are works of art, produced by a singular barbecue artist.

And like many an artist, Vance is a bit of an iconoclast. Capital BBQ is generally open Tuesday through Saturday for lunch only and is usually closed the months of January and February. Some years Vance has been known to stay in Key West until mid-March. And he keeps his own hours. "If the horses are running at Keeneland or UK's basketball team is playing," Vance says, "I have to slip out a little early." That means you might have to slip in a little early. Rearrange your schedule to coincide with Vance's. The experience is worth it.

Our expedition winds up in the place my friend Greg Johnson calls Barbecue Ground Zero: Kansas City, Missouri. All barbecue traditions come together here.

It has been more than twenty years since Calvin Trillin wrote in *The New Yorker* that **Arthur Bryant's Barbeque** in K.C. was "the single best restaurant in the world." Food mavens from around the globe heeded Trillin's call and rushed to this row house decorated in a style that is best described as "early dinette." To a person, they came away impressed. This was a place that took as much pride in its french fries and its burned ends as most restaurants did in their main courses.

But Bryant died in 1982, leaving many to search for a new

king of Kansas City barbecue. Consensus kept shifting, but for my money, the mantle never left the joint on Brooklyn Avenue. Arthur Bryant's barbecue was tops when Trillin let the world in on his secret in the seventies, it was tops in the eighties, and it's still the best in Kansas City. A new millennium won't change the barbecue equation there, either.

The reason is simple. Bryant may have died, and his heirs may have sold out to a couple of local businessmen. But one thing—the most important thing—remains unchanged: The same people still work in the kitchen. And you can see that they are the same people because the pit is in plain view of the dining room.

Sauce is rarely the secret to first-rate barbecue. The trick is usually the meat, and make no mistake—Bryant's thinly sliced beef brisket is tops. But what elevates this barbecue is a thick, gritty, tangy sauce so loaded with spices that if you let it sit for a while, the peppers will separate. It's as good on fries as it is on meat—well, almost.

That's my Hot Half Dozen Barbecue joints list. But it's not my be-all and end-all list. On another day it might be different. And there may be some terrific spots that I've never heard of. Because great barbecue is where you find it. If you happen to be one street over and looking the wrong way, you might not see the smoke of a new place. Yes, as I write this, some guy is building a pit and lettering a sign that says "Bar-B-Q." And his just might be the next best joint.

The Belly of Paris

by Megan Wetherall
from *Saveur*

The term "bistro" is so over-worked these days, it's refreshing to take this journey to Paris with Megan Wetherall, prowling untouristed neighborhoods in search of the real deal. She shows us that it's not just the food that makes an authentic bistro authentic.

At seven o'clock in the morning, eight butchers, who have been working all night preparing meat for scores of Parisian restaurants, are sitting—still in their overalls—around a table that bears all the signs of a heartily relished meal: the dregs of three bottles of brouilly, decanted straight from a barrel precariously perched on the bar; crusts of baguettes; smeared mustard pots; a plate with the remains of a half-dozen cheeses so pungent their rinds seem to smolder. One of the butchers pushes back his chair, disappears into the kitchen, and returns with a platter of golden pommes frites; another tucks into a plate of tête de veau—calf's head, brain, tongue, and skin, garnished with parsley and sauce ravigote. *"On mange bien, eh, les gars?"* one of them clucks approvingly—"We eat well, don't we, guys?"—as he mops up the last of his sauce and reaches for a cigarette.

Les Halles, the centuries-old central Parisian food market, was banished from the city to the suburb of Rungis in the late 1960s and early '70s, its beautiful old iron pavilions pulled down; a soulless modern shopping mall later took its place. But here at Á la Tour de Montlhéry—which regulars (like me) call Chez Denise, in honor of its proprietor, Denise Benariac—and at a handful of other genuine old style bistros that remain, and thrive, in the old Les Halles quarter, something of the market's golden age lives on.

When the first half of Les Halles was shut down and relocated 31 years ago this March (the rest followed in 1973), the bistros of the quarter were struck hard; their livelihood depended almost exclusively on the business generated by the market community. Located in the first arrondissement of Paris—its very heart—Les Halles was alive 20 hours a day, 365 days a year, for most of its existence. Until the market's dismantlement, the streets around Les Halles boasted what was undoubtedly the densest concentration of bistros in France—literally hundreds of them, catering to the hunger, thirst, and temperaments of the thousands of people involved in this sprawling marketplace. When Zola described Les Halles as *le ventre*—"the belly"—of Paris, he could have been talking about its bistros as much as its market stalls.

Of those hundreds of bistros, only a few survive today, and ever since I worked in my first basement kitchen in Paris at the age of 18, I have been irrepressibly curious about the myths and legends surrounding the old market. I've wondered at the outrage and nostalgia, the fierce pride, sentimentality, and melancholy that surround its memory—and I've always approached the heroic remnants of this quarter as an impressionable and slightly intimidated outsider. Revisiting some of the old surviving bistros of Les Halles recently, though, after having been away from Paris for a year, I found myself overwhelmed by the power of the stories locked within their walls, and decided to try to find the spirit (and the food) of the old Les Halles in the few bistros that have managed, against the odds, to hold on.

The Bistro as an institution emerged in the 19th century as an eating and drinking place accessible to the working man—unlike more formal restaurants or even cafés, which tended to cater to the intellectual set. The cooking was simple but flavorful, the portions copious, the wine modest but abundant—and the customers and waiters were on a first-name basis.

The origins of Les Halles can be traced to the 12th century—but it was not until 1890, under Napoléon III, that Victor Baltard's extraordinary pavilions of steel and glass, which came to symbolize the market, were erected to group various foodstuffs under separate roofs: poultry and game, tripe and other offal, fish and shellfish, meat, B.O.F. (for beurre-oeuf-fromage—butter, eggs, and cheese), fruit and vegetables, and flowers. The employees of each pavilion tended to frequent the cluster of bistros nearest them, and thus a distinct fishiness would perfume one place, an astringent leekiness another. (This was often literally true: The poorer workers were paid partly in the raw materials they sold or prepared, and they'd bring them along to their bistros—where the chefs, in return for a portion of the goods, would cook them up; the workers paid only for their wine.)

The idea of moving Les Halles out of Paris had been under discussion since the early 1950s (among other things, there were questions of hygiene—the market had a daunting rat population—and of the fearful traffic that swirled around the place), but it was nevertheless a terrible shock to the quarter when the first pavilions were actually emptied early on the morning of March 1, 1969. At the time, Claude Cornut was a young man working in his father's bistro, Chez Clovis, on the rue Berger in the heart of the market area. "Les Halles was a village inside a city," he tells me, "and the ambience was extraordinary. When I was growing up, my friends were all from one of the three pavilions closest to us—poultry, tripe, and fish—and you'd see them anywhere from three to maybe 15 times a day, which meant that you ended up knowing them as if they were family."

Cornut remembers standing with his father in the middle of a deserted Les Halles at 3 a.m.—usually the busiest time of the day—two nights after the market move began, and looking around at the emptiness in disbelief. "We had 20 people working for us," he says, "and the next day we had to let all but one of them go. Without Les Halles, we had no customers. That was when the bistros started to close their doors, one by one. As for my father, he never recovered, and for months would come downstairs at midnight to turn on all the coffee percolators and throw open the doors. Then he would sit and wait in silence for the familiar noise and bustle to begin."

I'll never forget the first time I walked into Chez Clovis—and walked into the past. The bistro still glows, still looks the way it has for years: Its walls are covered with black-and-white photographs of life in the old Les Halles—portraits of legendary characters like Bébé the butcher (who, legend has it, froze to death in his own meat locker) and scenes of rollicking crowds pressed up against the bistro's bar. Charcuterie from the Clovis family's native Auvergne swings from the ceiling, and comforting smells waft up from the downstairs kitchen—slowly braising beef stews, browning shallots, reducing sauces.

The flavors of the food at Chez Clovis are earthy and satisfying, and the abundance of the servings indicates the generous bistro spirit that characterizes the place. This is authentic Les Halles fare: saucisson lyonnais gently cooked with lentils and served in a steaming, seemingly bottomless black cast-iron pot— or combined with meaty potatoes and greens into a hearty salad; beef slowly braised with carrots; heaps of the thick-cut french fries called pommes Pont Neuf; pot-au-feu. It was at Chez Clovis, in fact, that I was awakened to the ultimate pot-au-feu experience, spooning wobbly mounds of beef marrow onto a crust of baguette, sprinkling it with rough, gray sea salt, and then eating the results with eyes screwed tight to enjoy so delectable a moment undisturbed.

Two doors down from Chez Clovis is the aforementioned Chez Denise (À la Tour de Montlhéry). Its proprietor, Denise Benariac, also lived through the death of Les Halles (she took over the place in 1966 with her late companion, Jack Paul). "To run a bistro," she says, her face trembling with all that she has seen and remembered, "you have to be in a good mood and agreeable to your customers every day, which . . ." She finishes the sentence with an utterly expressive French shrug and a purse of her rigorously painted lips. When Les Halles closed, À la Tour de Montlhéry—named for the town just southwest of Paris which was traditionally the source of the first spring vegetables to reach the city each year—survived by staying open all night anyway, creating a niche for itself as a colorful remnant of the old times.

Some years ago, when I was working in a Parisian wine bar, my night-owl friends and I would sometimes head to the place at two or three in the morning for steak tartare—its onions, capers, and Tabasco dance a jig on your tongue—and homemade frites, liters of brouilly, and merriment all around, topped off eventually with plenty of vieille prune or poire (purely for medicinal purposes, of course). There was always a regular restaurant crowd here—waiters, yes, but chefs too, sometimes from grand places, men who felt at home here and seemed to need this kind of change of pace to unwind. Michel Anffray, the night chef, knows how each man likes his steak tartare—remembering that one prefers onions to shallots, that another likes his roughly chopped and with very little ketchup.

Lots of people felt at home here: Bernard Noël, who has relieved Anffray as day chef for 27 years, recalls that at 5 a.m.

the late Jack Paul would offer garbage collectors a glass of white wine—with the same grace with which he welcomed the president of France, Jacques Chirac, who celebrated his birthday here three years ago.

There are three levels of wine cellars in the damp 16th-century foundations beneath Chez Denise, and once as I walked downstairs through cobwebs, feeling lost in time, I stumbled across a pile of mossy old skulls near the champagne racks. "Oh, those," Noël remarked casually when I jumped. "They're from the cemetery. Jack would invite his closest friends down to drink champagne from them." This bistro world, I was finding out, was a subculture unto itself—where people worked hard and lived their days to the fullest, with food, drink, and a Rabelaisian bawdiness.

The waiters at Chez Denise, many of whom have worked here for 30 years or more, are of the old school—real characters who pretend to be gruff and won't stand for any nonsense, like people ordering just a salad or refusing wine. One night I made the mistake of calling one of them "Monsieur"—to which he loudly retorted, "'Monsieur?' 'Monsieur?' I am Pascal!" I was eventually forgiven, but only after I had polished off every last bit of my haricot de mouton—a bread-crumb-topped casserole of tender lamb and succulent white beans (one of the regular plats du jour, along with tête de veau, blanquette de veau, and pot-au-feu, all served in the gargantuan portions emblematic of the bistros of Les Halles).

Claude Gousset has dinner at lunchtime every weekday at Aux Tonneaux des Halles, a bistro situated just behind the church of St. Eustache on the cobbled old market street of rue Montorgueil. Gousset, a meat cutter at Rungis who started his career in the butcher's trade at Les Halles, buys meat for the bistro every day. He has also lived next door to Aux Tonneaux since his Les Halles days, and has had his own table at the bistro for forty-odd years. "You know," he tells me one afternoon, nodding sagely, "it is only the most courageous and passionate bistro owners that have persevered through the really difficult years." He speaks highly and fondly of both Chez Clovis and Chez Denise in this regard, and then tells me about Aux Tonneaux: The original owners, he says, had let the place sink into sad decline, when Patrick Fabre—a 27-year veteran of other old bistros in the area—took it over in 1991. Fabre has revivified the place, keeping old customers like Gousset happy, but developing a new, younger clientele as well—by not only cooking bistro standards like entrecôte bordelaise, served with its marrow; rump steak with a creamy roquefort sauce; and andouillette (tripe sausage) with a mustard sauce; but also dishes like a simple melon de Cavaillon in summer; a deliciously light filet of salmon with leeks; and a hearty cod steak with baby spinach.

Gousset speaks passionately about the differences between the modern wholesale markets at Rungis and the old Les Halles, too. "Even though my job at Les Halles, which lasted every morning from 1 a.m. till 11, was extremely physical and demanding," he tells me, "the atmosphere made it all worthwhile. When the meat came in, we would start prepping, then go for our first coffee at three. Then the big meal would be eaten at about five—usually the best-quality entrecôtes or grillades, which we brought to the bistros to cook for us. At Rungis there have never been little bistros like that, so a lot of people are obliged to bring their own lunch already cooked. Another difference is in the customers. Our clients in the old meat pavilion were mostly butchers from all over Paris, with whom we got on famously, and they were always joining us for champagne or a meal. Nowadays, the butchers who come to Rungis are in a hurry and just want to get the business done. At Rungis there is none of the old camaraderie, the human warmth. When my generation retires, the last link is going to be cut."

It's a balmy June evening and I am sitting happily at a trestle table under the trees in the gardens of Les Halles, at a party put

together by the Commune Libre des Halles—an organization created in 1992 to help keep the history of the community alive.
After a parade led by the old *forts* des Halles—"strong men" who
used to be the porters—we sit down to rillettes, assorted pâtés
and terrines, cheese, and raspberry tarts, all prepared by Chez
Denise and Chez Clovis and washed down with brouilly decanted
from a Chez Denise barrel into plastic Volvic water bottles.

At dusk the dancing begins and I am mesmerized by the zest
and sprightliness of a small woman in her eighties, a local character, who is positively leaping about; last year, I am told, she
turned up in a red dress, brandishing maracas. There is something
surreal about a celebration so rustic and old-fashioned in the very
center of Paris, and the Parisian friends that I have dragged along
are both incredulous and enchanted. At one point, Claude Cornut
from Chez Clovis comes over and tells me that Michel Caldaguès,
the mayor of the 1st arrondissement, would like me to join him
and *madame le maire* at their table to toast Les Halles over a glass
of champagne. I am inordinately delighted and touched when the
mayor stands to welcome me as I approach, and I return the
smiles of all these now-familiar faces—realizing that, somehow,
I have been accepted into this small merry band, here in the
belly of Paris.

The Waiting Game

by Ruth Reichl
from *Gourmet*

Author of the wonderful culinary memoir *Tender at the Bone*, former *New York Times* restaurant reviewer Ruth Reichl has given up the daily paper grind to become editor-in-chief of *Gourmet*. Those of us who miss her weekly restaurant reviews must content ourselves with her monthly editor's columns—richly detailed musings on a life of food.

R ules don't much interest me. They never have. Still, I do have one that I *never* break. When I see a line in front of some one selling food, I join in. No matter where, no matter when.

That is how I happened to find myself standing behind a group of burly workmen in Palermo's Vucciria Market last month, wondering what I would find when I made my way to the head of the line. It could have been anything, for the Vucciria is one of the more remarkable markets of the world, a raucous display sprawling across several blocks near the city's center.

On one street a man stood in front of a huge swordfish, singing his customers in. *"Bello, bello,"* he caroled in a deep tenor as he sliced great steaks from the fish. Nearby a weather-beaten man proudly displayed baskets of wild vegetables he had gathered on the mountains early that morning: frail asparagus with tiny heads balanced on slender purple stalks and leafy fennel as fragile as lace. One stand featured eight varieties of shrimp and another had baby goats, still in their fur.

The customers were fascinating, too. Mostly male, they were a hungry crowd drifting from one stand to another, eating constantly. Some munched on rich rolls stuffed with fresh ricotta and warm spleen, while others stood in the center of the piazza devouring pieces of just-boiled octopus. An impeccably dressed man in an elegant tan suit leaned over as he ate slices of squid, careful not to spatter his baby-blue shirt. When he straightened up, I saw why he was being so cautious: A ring of squid ink circled his mouth.

But the largest group was gathered in front of a cart in the corner of the market watching an elderly gentleman concoct sandwiches. He carefully wrapped each one in paper before handing it over, so I couldn't see what was inside. I hoped it wouldn't turn out to be too strange, but I was prepared for anything.

The line inched forward. The crowd was so dense that I could not see what I had been waiting for until I was actually in front of the sandwich man.

Working with the concentration of a great chef, he selected a crusty roll. Balancing it in one hand, he swooshed a knife through, cutting it in half. Putting the knife down, he reached into an enormous can of oil-coated tuna and with his fingers scattered the fish across the roll. Closing the roll, he squeezed it, hard, over a tray of salad, extracting excess oil. Opening the roll, he delicately selected leaves of lettuce, slices of tomato, and shards of purple onion to add to the sandwich. He tossed in a hefty pinch of coarse sea salt. Then he drizzled some olive oil on top, wrapped it all in a sheet of paper, and handed his masterpiece over.

The entire crowd watched as I took a bite. The crunch of the roll against the softness of the fish, the sweetness of the tomatoes, the snap of the onion, and the tang of the olive oil made it one of the best things I've ever tasted. I instantly asked for another. The tuna man smiled and with the same deliberation began creating a second little masterpiece.

I had many meals in Sicily that week, and all of them were good. I remember homemade pasta topped with sea urchins, thinly sliced steamed swordfish, and gorgeous salads made of blood oranges and onions. I remember white wines with the delicate aroma of almonds and whole grilled prawns the size of baby lobsters. But nothing I had was better than those tuna sandwiches, and I don't think any chef was ever prouder of his creations than the tuna man in the Vucciria market.

To me, it was an eloquent reminder that a big part of cooking is choosing the ingredients. And that a big part of serving is doing it with pride.

Spamming the Globe

by Jonathan Gold
from *L.A. Weekly*

Writing *L.A. Weekly*'s "Counter Intelligence" column, Jonathan Gold scouted around Los Angeles for great ethnic eateries and hole-in-the-walls. His agile prose and refined taste buds won him a prestigious slot as *Gourmet*'s Manhattan restaurant critic, but what shines out here is his zesty enjoyment of a decidedly unglamorous local specialty.

We can be proud of many things, we Americans, from the Declaration of Independence to Elliot Carter's string quartets, from quantum physics to the interstate highway system, from Martha Stewart to the . . . Spamburger. Which is to say, an inch-thick slab of Spam, seared on a hot griddle and slid into a toasted hamburger bun with ketchup, mustard, tomatoes, lettuce—the whole nine yards. A Spamburger is sort of crisp, the Spam part of it anyway, which is abundantly speckled with those crunchy black bits, and sort of sweet—actually, very sweet, a corrosive, penetrating sweetness that lingers on your palate for about the same length of time as the faded pomegranate notes in a great, old Côte Rotie. You've heard of those nuanced lunch-counter hamburgers where each ingredient lends its own layer of crunch and the scorched meat patty acts more as a condiment than as, well, the meat of the sandwich? This isn't that, baby . . . a Spamburger is all about the Spam, its cloying, porky essence, the overgenerous nature of salty, fatty food manufactured for and revered by folks for whom salty, fatty food is, or used to be, the ultimate in unobtainable luxury. Spam is what this country is all about, a pig in every can and two cars in every garage. (In some parts of the Pacific, the average consumption is something like a can per day per person.) Spam tastes like America.

Spamburgers with sliced avocado and teriyaki sauce taste even more like America, or certain parts of it anyway, at least as served at **Mago's,** the Culver City hamburger stand that is to Westside Japanese-Americans what El Tepeyac is to Eastsiders and a Pancho's enchilada plate is to people who grew up in the South Bay. Mago's tastes like Culver City. I used to go to Mago's a fair amount in the late '70s, when I was dating a woman who lived a few blocks away, and even then I was astonished by the diversity of the burger stand's menu. You could get a million different kinds of shakes back then, and every variety of fast food prepared in every possible way and described with Magic Marker on paper plates Scotch-taped to the windows. I swear I once had a sashimi burrito at Mago's, with beans and onions and everything, although nobody will bear me out on that one. I also had such oddities as fried calamari tacos, teriyaki sticks threaded with avocado, taquitos with soy-laced guacamole and a cherry soda so good that I can still conjure up the particular tingle of it today. (None of which are on the menu anymore, although you can still get regular teri sticks, taquitos and [awful] fried won-ton. Mix 'em up yourself.)

Mago's may have been chopped and channeled, outfitted with an indoor seating area and a beer-and-wine license, acres of bright Formica and an array of smiling cat totems, but it really hasn't changed much if you discount the fact that nothing about the place really seems that weird anymore. There are a whole lot of Hawaiians on the Westside now, so the existence of classic teriyaki plate lunches—one scoop mac, two scoops rice—is less than an oddity, even if the restaurant is pretty explicitly Japanese-American.

The neighborhood (and the staff) leans Chicano—across the street from Mago's is a classic, East L.A. taco stand—so the street-level fusion, the tricultural incorporation of Asian ingredients into Mexican structures with American flavors, seems almost natural. Witness the delicious tacos stuffed with slippery chunks of ripe avocado and slices of sweet, red-rimmed chashu, barbecued pork. Note the fat burritos swelling with grilled strips of teriyaki-greased beef, avocado and cheese, or the hamburgers composed of chashu and avocado, or really, the resplendent Spamburger. Which, as we've previously noted, tastes like America. Don't miss the banana shakes.

Mago's 4500 S. Centinela Ave., Culver City, 800/900-MAGO. Open Mon–Sat for lunch and dinner. Beer and wine. Takeout. Lot parking. Lunch for two, food only, $12–15. AE, DC, DISC, MC, V. Recommended dishes: Spamburger, chashu avocado taco, teriyaki burger with avocado, banana shake.

Recipes for Dummies

by Jim Quinn
from *Philadelphia Magazine*

Every city has a handful of long-established restaurants with "signature dishes," the treats every regular swears by. Philadelphia's prime dining-scene insider, Jim Quinn, wondered if he could persuade the chefs to share their formulas. What he discovered may be one of the restaurant business's best-kept dirty little secrets.

H ow about getting a recipe for me?" says a friend. "That's what I envy most about food writers. Chefs tell them all their secrets. And this is one of the most famous secrets in the City of Philadelphia—the salsa at Pamplona. How do they make it taste so good, even in the winter, when tomatoes are lousy?"

Well, in my experience, chefs will give anybody their recipes. Half the secrets come down to the advice you might get if you asked Venus Williams how to imitate her tennis serve: "I hit the ball real hard." Anybody who can hit as hard as Venus doesn't need advice. The other secrets are so simple that anybody could do them. So hardly anybody dares to.

Amateur cooks like you and me tend to think of recipes in terms of complications—and the more of them, the better. Measurements should come in 16th-tablespoonfuls. Taboos should be exclamatory: "Add slowly! Stirring constantly! In one direction only!" Nothing counts as a real recipe to us unless you need a book in front of you as you cook, to be checked and rechecked constantly for expert advice: "If the sauce curdles, throw it out and start again."

Professionals think differently.

"I look at a recipe, and if it's complicated, my impulse is, forget it," says Dmitri Chimes, owner of Pamplona, at 225 South Locust Street, Philadelphia, and also of Dmitri's and Stix. "If a recipe's simple, I'll try it. Because simple recipes are about food, not fuss. But to tell you the truth, even for me, our salsa recipe is . . . embarrassing, it's so easy."

Here's the secret salsa of Pamplona, plus secrets of three other chefs. Five recipes in all, only two of which require any complicated kitchen skills. (By complicated skills, I mean boiling water or heating oil in a frying pan.) All these recipes are so good that your friends will beg you for the secret—and probably refuse to believe you when you tell them what it is.

Pamplona's famous salsa

> One can good Italian-style plum tomatoes
> Chopped cherry peppers in vinegar
> Chopped cilantro

Open the can. Drain the tomatoes. Mash them with a fork, or squeeze them in your hands. Pamplona uses Pastene brand chopped cherry peppers. "You can get them in supermarkets in

South Philly," Dmitri says. "I think it's the same thing they have in the condiment jar at Pat's Steaks. We like the touch of vinegar. Anything hot, even a hot sauce, would do, though." Mix tomatoes, chopped cherry peppers and chopped cilantro. Serve.

"Our salsa recipe's so old, I don't even know where it came from. We serve it with everything from softshells to brisket," says Dmitri. "When I eat in Pamplona, I always try the salsa. Every time I taste it, I think, There's something that really worked out."

Need measurements? Dmitri says, "You're just shading the taste of the tomatoes—good tomatoes, remember—with heat and cilantro. Unless you like more heat or more cilantro." Start with a tablespoon each of peppers and cilantro; add more of each till you find the secret combination you like.

Varallo's famous potato recipe

Rosa Varallo works days waiting on customers at Varallo Brothers bakery (1639 South 10th Street), where her husband, Michele, and their sons bake fancy pastries, pies, cakes and bread. Nights, she is executive chef at La Cucina Varallo, the family restaurant next door (1635 South 10th). Cucina Varallo is a restaurant at once authentically Italian and resolutely South Philly. There are real brick-oven pizzas, big plates of pasta and seafood, pastries from the bakery and, to start your meal, an unusual freebie. "You want my mother's potato recipe?" says Rosa. "It's so easy. Anna, her name was, Anna Gregorio. I grew up on a farm outside Avellino, near Naples. My mother made these potatoes all the time. We give them to the people in the restaurant just for a little something, you know? To eat while you wait. It's easy to make, it's cheap, and it gets you in the mood for food. Besides, I think of my mother when people tell me how much they like it."

This potato salad is so delicious and so simple that it reminds me by opposites of the traditional picnic potato salads of my childhood. Every kid's mom had a different complicated recipe, though all turned out to be slathered with mayonnaise and full of tasteless chef d'oeuvres of heart-attack cuisine like hard-boiled eggs, suppurating and changing from yellow to dark orange in the heat. American Don't-Know-How has never produced a worse and more unhealthy foodstuff, except perhaps those cheesecakes that stick to the roof of your mouth like peanut butter and have names like Sex on the Beach or Boilermaker, after the cocktails they're artificially flavored to taste like.

If you still make anything like traditional potato salad, try this instead:

Potatoes
Celery
Fresh tomatoes
Onions
Salt, pepper and "a little oregano if you like it"
Extra-virgin olive oil

"The kind of potato doesn't matter," says Rosa. Boil potatoes, unpeeled, till they're tender enough to be pierced easily with a fork. Peel potatoes. I ask Rosa how about leaving the skin on. "Are you kidding?" she says. "An Italian woman would never serve potatoes to her family without peeling them first!" This is the only exclamatory taboo in any of these recipes. But I break it, and luckily, nobody complains. Peel potatoes or not, and cut into cubes. Size? "Any size you want." Mix in a little celery and onion cut in small pieces. Dice tomatoes and squeeze them dry; add tomatoes. Add salt and pepper to taste and as much oregano as you like. I don't use oregano unless I can find fresh. Add enough olive oil to make a salad.

Measurements: To a pound of potatoes, add one small tomato, one small onion and one rib of celery cut in quarter-inch bits.

"No garlic? " I ask.

"No, you have the onion for sharpness. Italians don't eat garlic in everything, you know. My mother always served this at room temperature," says Rosa. "That's the way I like it. You can taste the potatoes and the raw vegetables best that way."

God's cherry unjam

"Most of the time, good cooking is just a matter of buying fresh ingredients and then getting out of God's way," says Jack McDavid, owner-chef of Jack's Firehouse (1130 Fairmount Avenue) and the Down Home Diner. "I don't even have to buy the cherries I serve. They grow on a tree in my backyard. We start everybody off at the Firehouse with complimentary homemade bread and biscuits, and a bowl of cherries instead of jam. We serve a lot of it. Sometimes I think we could make more money giving away the dinner free and charging for those cherries. But whenever I think I'll start charging for cherries, in comes a couple with a fussy baby. Now, I'll tell you what, there's never been a baby born, at least never one come into the Firehouse, who won't stop fussing if you stick a cherry in its face."

This recipe makes cherries that can be simply mashed into, or balanced atop, a chunk of biscuit. Or served with whipped cream or yogurt. Or eaten with fingers right out of the bowl. And it's so easy that, as Jack says, "There's nothing to it at all!"

> Fresh cherries
> A cherry-pitter
> Sugar

Jack has a sour-cherry tree. Sour cherries are incomparably better than the bing cherries available in stores. But bing cherries are extremely good. If you have your own tree, just give each cherry a squeeze as you pick it, and the stone will drop out.

If you buy cherries, you will need a cherry-pitter. This little chrome invention looks something like a dental tool and something like a debraining forceps. I got mine at Fante's. They cost around $11. A beginner with no skills or small-motor graces to speak of can pit three or four pounds of cherries in about 15 minutes.

Pit cherries. Put them in a bowl. Add about one-eighth cup of sugar per pound of cherries—less if the cherries are very sweet. Toss gently with your hands until cherries are coated. Cover, and refrigerate overnight. The cherries will give up a sweet, lightly syrupy liquid. Serve cold if you like, though they taste better at room temperature.

In season, I buy cherries at Giordano's in the Italian Market. Commercial cherries have been coated with oil and even lacquer to keep them from going bad, so they don't give up quite as much liquid as fresh-picked. But they still taste good. My intended and I have cherries at every meal whenever we can find them.

Can't find cherries? Try this sugar method with any fresh berry or soft fruit. "Just cut it up and give it a dry sugar rub," says Jack. "You could cook your fruit up and make jam out of it. But why? Enjoy fresh fruit raw while you can. Winter will be back again, when even God needs help with flavors."

If you like, pour off the fruit liquid, boil it to reduce, let cool, and add back to the fruit. It makes things sweeter and stickier.

Desanka's breads

"You want to make a panne mollo? It's the best food you can eat when the tomatoes are ripe. Don't do it unless you grow the tomatoes, or buy them very fresh from somebody you know who is trustworthy. Never buy tomatoes from a stranger!"

Desanka Giampaolo was born in Yugoslavia and went to Italy with her husband at age 16. She has spent her life as a cook for her family and as a chef in restaurants she and her husband have owned in Milan and Philadelphia. She retired as a chef years ago but is not able to stay out of the kitchen. "I need to cook," she says. "No sitting in front of the television! I go crazy! "

Desanka now runs a cafe, called Desanka's, down near the south end of the Italian Market (1165 South 9th Street), where she sells exquisite cannoli and pastries, makes occasional dinners for private parties on order, gives cooking lessons, and provides free-wheeling advice about food to her many friends who stop by.

Her recipes are, after years of work, reduced to a delicious minimum of efficient labor. All start out the same way: "Get good ingredients! You can't make good food out of bad! " Here's a sample, before we even get to panne mollo, of a bread recipe that is cooked—but only minimally.

Desanka's bruschetta

There are many recipes for bruschetta, toasted Italian bread brushed with garlic. To me, none is as good or as easy as Desanka's.

> Italian bread
> Olive oil
> Garlic

Peel the garlic cloves. Cut in half lengthwise. Cut the bread into one- or two-inch slices. Put approximately one-eighth inch of olive oil in a heavy frying pan, and heat. Put slices in pan. When they are dark brown on one side, remove them. Give sliced garlic cloves to each person. Tell each to brush the clove against the toasted side of the bread. Eat. This delicious appetizer can be made even better topped with a mix of chopped fresh tomatoes, red peppers and olive oil. Or top with Pamplona's salsa. When Desanka first gave me this recipe, I asked if I should toast both sides of the bread. "Why?" she said. "You will only brush one side with the garlic. Let the bread taste like bread."

Panne mollo

This is one of the simplest and most delicious of all traditional Italian recipes. Once again, Desanka's version is the best to me.

> One loaf of good Italian bread

Fresh, ripe, juicy beefsteak tomatoes
Fresh basil
Garlic
Salt and pepper
Extra-virgin olive oil
Fresh mozzarella "if you want to be fancy"

Pull the bread into pieces and let it sit until stale. Start with all ingredients at room temperature. Tomatoes that most Americans think of as overripe are best. Dice them, then put them and their juice into a large bowl. Cut basil and garlic small, or use a food processor. Soak the bread in filtered water till it gets soft again. Squeeze the bread dry. "Squeeze hard!" says Desanka. Mix the damp bread, garlic, tomatoes, basil, salt and pepper together. Toss with forks or your hands. Dice fresh mozzarella, made that day, and scatter atop the mix. Pour olive oil over—enough to get the extra-virgin flavor. When in doubt, add a little more. Mix again and serve. Panne mollo makes a fine lunch

In Italy, people even eat it for dinner.

Personal
Tastes

A Tale
of Two
Chowhounds

by Jim Leff
from chowhound.com

Jim Leff, jazz trombonist and trencherman extraordinaire, has been led by his love of food to write *The Eclectic Gourmet Guide to Greater New York City* and to set up a website— www.chowhound.com—where passionate eaters share their food finds. But what should this food-loving fraternity call themselves? Leff defines for us the term he's chosen.

F or crying out loud, just get the 42, willya?!?"
I'd made the salesman MESHUGA with my waffling between two overcoats. Howard Turkell, 60-ish and a garment center veteran, had tried to be polite with the weirdo hipster kid who'd turned up at his third-floor shop that fateful morning, but patience had finally worn thin.

"The 40's too tight, you don't wanna tight coat. You wanna 42 or not?!?" I wanted, I wanted. Howard wrote up the bill on a pad that might still retain pen impressions from the 1949 sale of your uncle's prom suit, and, though he was anxious to get rid of me, we plunged into the rigamarole. Licking ballpoint, Howard asked my address. As he copied down the information, an eyebrow suddenly cocked. "That near Steinway Bakeshop?" "Yeah," I replied, "but they've gone downhill. So I get bread at Parisi's, and pastries at Lefkos Piergos." Howard's attention had been caught. "Parisi's I could see, but . . . Lefkos Piergos?!? That's Greek! You won't find the German stuff like they got at Steinway!" "Steinway? German? Listen, I don't know when you were there, but nowadys it's middle of the road French. I'll take a bogatsa at Lefkos anyday." "Maybe so. Haven't been out there in ages. But what the hell's a bogatsa?!?" Howard had put down his pen. I was late for an appointment, but, sensing free alterations in my future, kicked into a twenty minute food shmooze. Once again, I'd bumped up against the mysterious brotherhood of chowhounds, an invisible network running through our city.

Months later, I get an email from some guy in Brooklyn:

"Got your address from your article. Like your stuff. Here's pizza. Old guy makes everything by hand; thin crust and good sauce. 1424 Ave J. Larry."

I'm picturing a nerdy teen. I get lots of email. I jot back "Thanks, Larry! I'll put it on my list! Keep in touch!"

Then, a few days later, it's . . . Larry again.

"Did you try the pizza? Here's another: Randazzo's Clam Bar, Emmons Avenue. Fried calamari. Larry."

The messages are unsettlingly flat. But I sense a devoted chow obsessive, and go try the pizza. It's good.

"Very nice, Larry! You're a heckuva pizza scout! Thanks so much. See you around, now!"

But Larry writes back with more suggestions, always asking whether I've checked the previous ones. Larry seems a tad sheltered—I wonder if he gets out much. Then one day, this:

"I had an op-ed piece published in the paper. Do you wanna see it? Larry."

"Sure, Larry! Why not! Send away!"

The article is wonderful. Assured, funny writing—this is no

sheltered kid. He's written an autobiographical account of a chowhound ("I eat to live. I live to eat. I eat to eat"). I'm flabbergasted, jealous. It all fits together when I read his bio blurb, revealing that Larry's actually an acclaimed screenwriter. But food is his true love, and I am a food writer, and—more importantly—a respected chowhound. Cassavetes on line two? I'll call him back, I've got Jim on the phone, and we're talking french toast.

Every few weeks, I'd find myself awakened at ungodly hours by Howard's voice blasting from my answering machine. "Jim, this is Howard Turkell!" Always the last name, as if I have legions of 63-year-old Bronx-accented guys named Howard calling me at 7 in the morning. "I have something VERY IMPORTANT to speak with you about. Please return my call at your EARLIEST CONVENIENCE." I'd call back the store, and Howard would shoo away customers and fabric salesmen and recount his latest Polish and Italian discoveries; the "Balducci's of Brooklyn" he'd found in Greenpoint, the good $4 Chinese dinner in midtown. I'd scrawl the tips in my notebook, as did he while I recounted my finds.

Howard's chowhound friends had all moved away, leaving him a lone hound; he was delighted with the opportunity to compare notes. The striking thing was that although Howard could go on and on about matzoh balls and pastrami, he was also familiar with dozens of other cuisines.

A chowhound can be any age. He might be any nationality— one of the savviest I ever met was a young, street-tough Yemeni cab driver next to whom I once slurped soup in a hole-in-the-wall Egyptian luncheonette. The guy, clutching obligatory pull-out radio with his non-spooning hand, spoke knowledgably (though in broken English) about Thai, Italian, and South American restaurants all over town. A chowhound's collar can be blue or white—it's recognizable above all by the gravy stains.

I've met a few women chowhounds, but they're not the same. They never have decaying french fries under the seats of their cars. When really desperately hungry, they always seem to. . .

just go somewhere and eat. True chowhounds use their last adrenal reserves to trek crosstown for a slightly better muffin. Snapple won't do; it's got to be After the Falls, and we'll dehydrate like two day-old carrot peelings before giving up the search.

I must admit, though, that the most heroic display of chowhound valor I've ever been privileged to witness was performed by a woman. She had just bitten into a burning-hot chunk of something right out of the oven, and began waving hands frantically in front of her mouth, bobbing up and down in her chair with crimson-cheeked urgency, pained gutteral barks issuing from deep in her throat. I offered water. "No! No!" she gestured, "NO WATER!!" Waving/barking/bobbing continued for a good 30 seconds while I watched helplessly. Later, asked why in her blistering pain she'd refused a drink, our heroine replied: "To have diluted the incredible flavor would have been a sin." That's the spirit.

We are not foodies. They are a recent phenomenon, an avatar of that early 1960's archetype, The Gourmet. A foodie, setting out to make a hamburger, buys ground venison (ultra lean, though it's fat that makes a burger toothsome) then grills it in his top-o'-the-line Weber over mesquite and hickory, serving it with brie and vidalia onions on a sourdough Portuguese roll. By contrast, a chowhound fries chuck in a (well-seasoned cast iron) pan, and munches it while running out the door to satisfy his sudden dessert craving for Pepperidge Farm Sausalito cookies, which he'll warm briefly over the radiator to make the chocolate gooey. Barbarians may eat and the civilized may dine, but chowhounds feed. Mind you, it's not a class thing; chowhounds with bucks do go to Lespinasse. But, unlike foodies, they have not the slightest compunction about stopping for a slice on the way home.

Larry is late getting a script out to the coast, but he's set aside an hour for Chinese suckling pig. We're in Chinatown, and he's rising above his anxieties, all attention on restaurant windows rushing past, eyes scanning for new places, new treasure.

Finally we enter the little shop, and—showing no perceptible joy, just bristling excitation, like a skater about to perform her routine—grab takeout bags and rush them with clinical urgency to shelter for The Feeding. Talk is not about the beautiful fall day or Bette Midler's reaction to the last story proposal. We talk about the food, in microscopic detail. Analogies are made, theories posited, hidden flavors probed. We one-up each other's praise while pillaging the porcine bounty: "Unbelievable" "Does life get better than this?" "This isn't life. I'm dead and in heaven" "Are you allowed to eat pork in heaven?!?"

A year ago, Howard had a stroke, and had to quit his job. He still calls me sometimes, but he can't remember numbers or names of things, and it takes him forever to write stuff down. I tell him about new discoveries—very slowly and patiently; he notes them as faithfully as ever. Howard doesn't get out much anymore, but he tells me about food articles I've missed, and asks about restaurants that have caught his eye while thumbing through Zagat (while foodies consider the Zagat Guide a bible, only a convalescent chowhound would be caught reading one—Howard and Larry both found places ages ago that won't show up in the book for years to come). Sometimes Howard gets frustrated, and has to call his wife to the phone to help write down an address. I find him restaurants in his neighborhood—ones that deliver—but he insists on hearing about the GOOD joints, the latest Georgian in Brighton Beach, Malaysian in Flushing. He won't ever get to try them, I'm afraid. After little trips out, he calls excitedly: "Jim? This is Howard TURKELL . . ." I can picture the business cards and takeout menus fanned out in front of him, better to keep all the information straight for his report. And his tips are still right on the money. If, heaven forbid, Howard should have another stroke and be confined to a hospital bed, he'll undoubtedly be bribing orderlies to search for cinnamon buns in expanding circles from the building. And I'd bet my last bogatsa he'll find GREAT ones.

The Reluctant Gourmet

by Mark Kurlansky
from *Food & Wine*

Author of the acclaimed cookbook *Cod*, Mark Kurlansky has also puzzled over how to describe his place in the culinary world. Like most good writers, he is sensitive to the connotations of words—and terms like "gourmet" and "foodie" carry so much weight these days. Kurlansky not only tells us why, he shows us.

No one ever knows when they are well off. Whenever I was called a gourmet, I suspected that I was being accused of something at least slightly unpleasant. But that was before I heard the term *foodie*. I am still not sure that a gourmet is a good thing to be, but it must be better than a foodie.

I may not know what a gourmet is, but like Justice Stewart said about pornography, I know it when I see it. I am contemplating the meaning of the word *gourmet* because I am clearly in the company of a couple of them. Two gourmets have invited me to lunch in a rural Basque restaurant in the green mountains of

Vizcaya province: the small, red-faced and energetic author of a popular Spanish food guide and an enormously round man of unclear profession whose business card labels him a gastronomic adviser.

The enthusiastic author rates all his food from one to ten, and he wants the well-fed gastronomic adviser and me to do the same. He gives the *lomo,* a thinly sliced, burgundy-colored prime cut of cured pork, only an eight. The gastronomic advisor has ventured a nine, and so they turn to me, the Hamlet of our group, who can't make up his mind and requests clearer definitions of eight and nine.

A *gourmet,* according to one dictionary definition, is a judge of choice foods. The term comes from an Old French word for a winetasting servant. *Gourmand,* on the other hand, comes from an Old French word for glutton. From this it appears that medieval Frenchmen knew the difference between a judge, who is guided by intelligence, and a glutton, who is guided by appetite. But Americans, I've observed, always get *gourmet* and *gourmand* confused. Indeed, being called a gourmet in the States is as likely to be an accusation as a compliment.

In French, by the way, the two words are still distinct. I used to write about food for a French-staffed publication and the accountant who processed my expenses would take enormous delight in pointedly calling me Monsieur Gourmand.

Can it be a lingering puritanism that makes Americans dislike gourmets? In 1901, Picasso depicted a little girl reaching up to a table to scrape the last bits of food from a bowl. The painting is usually labeled by its French title, *Le Gourmet*. But at a recent show in the United States, the name was translated into English as *The Greedy Child*. Is a gourmet greedy? Is all that judging and analyzing really just an excuse to eat as much as possible? Picasso's little girl did finish off the contents of her bowl.

My gourmets are discussing the lobster. The red-faced author has given it a 10 and is trying to get me to concede that these tough little clawed creatures from northern Europe are far better than the lobster from what he does not realize is my native New England, which in fact they are not.

Plato would not have thought much of my lunch companions. He mistrusted any interest in food. In the *Republic* he writes that the enjoyment of food is not a true pleasure because the purpose of eating is to relieve a kind of pain—hunger. And in *Gorgias* he indirectly compares cooking to "a form of flattery . . . a mischievous, deceitful, mean and ignoble activity, which cheats us by shapes and colors, by smoothing and draping. . . ."

A 1996 novel, *The Debt to Pleasure* by John Lanchester, plays on our aversion to gourmets. The narrator is a man who applauds "the application of intelligence to pleasure." In telling the story of his life he rambles on about soups, stocks, curry, the perfect vinaigrette, the perfect martini. The reader instinctively dislikes this pompous dilettante. And just as we are growing angry with his smugness, we begin to see that there is something truly abnormal about him. His interest in food is not about a shared human experience; it's about setting himself apart. Finally we realize that he is deranged, that he is, in fact, a psychopath.

My tablemates don't like the monkfish, and give it a five.

What should a gourmet look like? I'm afraid most Chinese would not consider the fat gastronomic adviser to be a gourmet. A true gourmet, they would say, has the wisdom to know when to stop eating. From Confucius to Mao, most Chinese philosophers have contended that excess is unnatural, wasteful and alien to proper dining. Chinese food writing emphasizes the healthfulness of gourmets and their choices.

Karl Friedrich von Rumohr, an early 19th-century *Feinschmecker* (literally "a fine taster"), concurred. He wrote in 1822 that "dullwitted, brooding people love to stuff themselves with quantities of heavy food, just like animals for fattening. Bubbly intellectual people love foods that stimulate the taste buds without overloading the belly. Profound, meditative people prefer neutral foods, which do not have an assertive flavor and are not difficult to digest, and therefore do not demand too much attention."

Jean Anthelme Brillat-Savarin, the 19th-century French lawyer, politician, food writer and self-declared gourmet, also insisted that a true gourmet was health conscious. But, curiously, Brillat-Savarin rejected any distinction between *gourmet* and *gourmand*, denying that gourmandism had anything to do with gluttony. Still, plump men were of little appeal to him, and so he denounced overeating by men while stating in his book, *The Physiology of Taste,* that "gourmandism is far from unbecoming to the ladies."

My companions order an imposing, garnet-colored Rioja as a thick *chuleta* (a rare, salted grilled steak) arrives at our table. After polishing off his portion and giving it a 10, the enthusiastic author places the bone on my plate. "Take that," he says. "It's the best part, but you have to pick it up with your hands and gnaw on it."

I take the bone in my hands.

A gourmet knows that the best food is not always the most expensive food. Although poor people can be gourmets, able to discern a good potato from a bad one, judging foods without regard for cost is a rich man's game. Only the wealthy can follow a thick aged steak with a black-sauced peasant stew, as my lunch companions do. The stew earns a double-digit rating as well.

Dessert arrives, a white mousse with berry sauce, and my two friends engage in lively discourse about whether or not it contains *queso de Filadelfia,* which leads into competing eulogies in praise of cream cheese.

Isn't anyone who spends all his time talking about food in need of a doctor? In 1997, the American Academy of Neurology announced the discovery of a syndrome in which sufferers suddenly become compulsively addicted to thinking about and eating fine foods. In a study of 723 patients with brain lesions, 36 became gourmets, and of those, 34 were found to have lesions in the right anterior part of the brain. A businessman who suffered a brain hemorrhage "couldn't stop talking or writing about food." One patient had been a political journalist until a brain hemorrhage led him to become a food writer. Maybe I should go to a clinic now for my scan.

But maybe not. Being called a gourmet, I've decided, isn't necessarily a bad thing; it's the same kind of compliment-insult as being called an intellectual. I have to learn something about the prejudices of the person who is using the label before I can decide how I feel about wearing it.

Things are getting worse at the table. Over brandy and Cuban cigars, my companions turn from praising cream cheese to rating Cuban versus Brazilian women. I notice by the physical descriptions offered to bolster their arguments that they both like their women the same way Brillat-Savarin did—well fed. That must be what gourmets like. Or is it gourmands? As I listen to my tablemates, I don't feel much inclined to be either.

Sundays with Ravioli

by Alex Witchel
from *The New York Times*

Proust had his madeleines, *New York Times* feature writer Alex Witchel has meat ravioli, a favorite childhood food that proved surprisingly hard to find in the year 2000. With a natural reporter's curiosity, Witchel set off to track it down, and to uncover how one generation's staple dish can fall off the culinary radar.

It may have been my first love—before Clark Gable, before Bobby Sherman, even before Jonathan Mink in the second grade.

Meat ravioli.

My fixation began with a prototype more appropriate to a Jewish girl, meat kreplach, which my grandmother fried and served with applesauce. But growing up in the era of checkered-tablecloth Italian restaurants, I soon established a pattern of gluttony by ordering—and finishing—two portions of meat ravioli from the children's menu. By the time I was in first grade, my parents figured it was cheaper to pretend I was 21.

The last time I remember ordering meat ravioli was in the mid-80's at La Bohème in Greenwich Village. It was delicious, with its tomato and meat sauce and thin topping of toasty mozzarella, like ravioli and pizza in one.

I haven't seen it since.

"Have you noticed that no one serves meat ravioli anymore?" my friend, Suzanne, asked recently. A native Tennessean who moved to New York in the 60's and immediately fell in love with all things ethnic, she was the only one who shared my fixation, except for a Jewish friend whose parents took him for Italian on the rare Sunday nights they skipped Chinese.

I assured her I had noticed (it's been off the menu at La Bohème for years) and decided it was time to take action. I asked two Italian-American friends for recommendations, both of whom said they had grown up with cheese ravioli and looked askance at the notion of meat.

But meat's what I remember most vividly. We used to go out to dinner every Sunday, my mother's weekly emancipation, and when we went for Italian, we drove to one of a few places near where we lived in Passaic, N.J., either Bob's or Pompeii or Giuliano's. The last was a dark restaurant where my mother would order a cocktail, delivered from the even darker bar in the next room, while my brother and I each had Cokes (only one!) which we had to make last. My father drank wine and gave us a sip, but who wanted that when you could have Coke?

Then, as the adults started in on plates of antipasto filled with stinky anchovies and slimy peppers, they gave us quarters so we could each pick songs from the jukebox (Pompeii's was the coolest, boasting selections like "Pretty Woman"), and when we were done fighting over whose songs went first and got back to the table and still didn't drink our Cokes, my ravioli would finally appear. It came nestled in its individual silver pan, casserole style, and I would cut through the steaming layers with a fork, which felt like opening 10 presents at once.

There was no mozzarella on top then, just Parmesan cheese, if you wanted it, which I never did. It smelled awful, which was why I never ordered cheese ravioli, convinced it would smell the same. And anyway, I didn't want anything to interfere with the way the meat inside the pasta tasted different from the meat in the tomato sauce, and I made sure each bite had some of both, until, alas, the pan was empty.

And what that really meant was that the weekend was over and there was school the next day. And even though we got pennies to throw in the wishing well at Giuliano's, that was it. Finished. The meal, the weekend, all of it. We had no choice but to face the doom of school.

With the taste of those Sundays in my mouth, I sat down and called 52 Italian restaurants in Manhattan, looking for meat ravioli. Eight had it. Eight! Almost every restaurant had cheese ravioli. Some had pumpkin. Or butternut squash, shiitake mushroom or smoked salmon. I even found rabbit and venison ravioli in truffle broth. But old-fashioned meat ravioli in a tomato-based meat sauce? Sorry, Signora, no.

Not one of the eight restaurants was in Little Italy. I called every one I could find, with no luck. At Il Palazzo, a waiter told me that no one carries it anymore. "People don't trust meat filling as much as they did," he said. "Most restaurants buy it frozen, so I wouldn't order it unless it's a special. Cheese you can whip up quickly. Meat takes longer."

Andrew Raffetto, president of the Raffetto Corporation, a family-owned business in SoHo that supplies restaurants and stores with ravioli, said: "Everyone now wants pumpkin and lobster. We still make meat for our store on Houston Street, with my grandfather's recipe from Genoa. We sell a nice little amount, and around Christmas and Easter we sell 10 times as much. But it ain't what it used to be. Grandma passed away, the kids moved to the suburbs, and over the years we've sold less and less."

But I ate my meat ravioli in the suburbs. Where did it go?

I asked a few Italian chefs, who told me that meat ravioli, like other stuffed pastas, was originally a labor-intensive feast-day dish in certain regions of Northern Italy. First the stuffing is made, then the pasta, then the individual pieces are filled and cooked, and mixed with the sauce—cooked separately—that accompanies the dish.

But in America this tradition, like so many, changed to fit the immigrants' new circumstances, which meant a drastic shift in ingredients. Lidia Bastianich, who with her son, Joe, owns Felidia and Becco in New York and Lidia in Kansas City, is at work on a series about Italian-American cooking for PBS. She makes the point that, as with meatballs, which were not cooked with sauce in Italy, but began to be here to improve the flavor of lackluster tomatoes, ravioli was also transformed, from the festive to the ordinary.

"I think with ravioli, the idea of it sort of got switched here through commercialization," she said. Certainly, most Americans learned to think of meat ravioli as nothing more complicated than opening a can of Chef Boyardee.

In some Italian households, though, the dish became a way to use up odds and ends. As Mario Batali, the chef at Babbo and Po, said: "The classic meat ravioli of our childhood was based on the economics of the kitchen, using leftovers. That was how Grandma stretched the meat." Though Mr. Batali does not make a traditional meat ravioli at Babbo, he makes something called Angel's Pyramids, a larger variation that is filled with either braised lamb, pork shoulder or brisket, and served in butter and sage. "After braising it for days, I don't want to mask the nuance of the stuffing with a tomato sauce," he said.

I see his point, though I also agree with Tony May, the owner of San Domenico and Gemelli, when he says: "A standard recipe is no longer of interest. A chef who cooks ravioli standing on his head, that's of interest." (For the record, neither of his places serves meat ravioli, either.)

I began my search at Gino on Lexington Avenue at 60th Street, a restaurant I love. Michael Miele, the chef, assured me that meat ravioli was on the menu, though I'd never noticed it before. There it was, Homemade Ravioli, which I had always assumed was cheese. It was served on a plate, not in a pan, and I found it only ordinary. I spent most of the meal snitching the excellent sausage and peppers from my husband's plate, instead.

Next, I tried Gene's on West 11th Street, with dismal results. The ravioli were undercooked and had the consistency of cardboard, one step up from a school cafeteria.

Maybe this quest was hopeless, I thought, trudging back to the subway with heartburn. Here I am, trying to recreate a phantom taste from childhood with food my mouth might no longer crave. After all, everyone's tastes change. Maybe even the best meat ravioli wouldn't thrill me now.

But that night I went to Pietro's, the Italian steakhouse on East 43rd Street. Meat ravioli is available as an appetizer or entree, and it was quite good. The winy-tasting Bolognese sauce was more sophisticated than what I remember, but the dish was satisfying enough to order again.

My spirits rose. Until I went to Da Tommaso, on Eighth Avenue at 53rd Street. Ravioli there is made with a sauce of sundried tomatoes, peppers and white wine. Sun-dried tomatoes and meat ravioli? For heaven's sake! The ravioli themselves were tasteless, the entire enterprise misconceived and depressing. I quit halfway through.

My luck was not much better at Via Oreto, on First Avenue at 61st Street, or Nanni's on East 46th Street. Via Oreto made the ravioli to order after I called ahead, and it was adequate, though salty. Nanni's serves meat ravioli as a lunch special every Wednesday, but when I sat down at 1 p.m., I was told that all 20 portions had sold out by 12:15. I wasn't sure I believed it, and with flashbacks of sun-dried tomatoes, wasn't sure I cared.

At Villa Mosconi, on Macdougal Street at West Houston, the veal parmigiana was very good, and the staff couldn't have been nicer. My friend, Suzanne, couldn't have either. She came with me and hid her disappointment when the ravioli tasted like paste.

So I was relieved that she agreed to try again the following night when I discovered meat ravioli nirvana at Bravo Gianni on East 63rd Street. When I had called, the chef, Gianni Garavelli, answered the phone. I had asked my standard question, "Do you have meat ravioli on your menu?" and he said: "I am making once in a while on Sundays. I can make if you want."

I wanted. "The ravioli has a very particular taste," he said. "It's been distorted in the United States, where the press has encouraged people to sell invented dishes as authentic food. In Italy I learn the authentic way. I make for my family, but it's a very laborious dish."

That Sunday, Mr. Garavelli sat down at the table with us. "I learned this from my sister Clementina, who lives near Genoa," he said. "In the meat sauce there is also spinach, borage and Swiss chard, and you cook that with beef, veal, chicken gizzard, sausage, sweetbreads and brains."

He saw the look on my face.

"Knowing that might take away the poetry for many people, but that's the way it's supposed to be done," he continued. "And the dough is very thin. The beauty of ravioli is the most fine pasta, because the edge is double. The meat sauce with it is a ragu. Are you ready?"

It was too late to back out now. I smiled bravely. Bring on the brains.

The minute he presented a copper pan filled with ravioli, my bliss began. The smell was heavenly. The pasta was supple, almost springy, the filling divine. I didn't care what was in there; it was light and tasty, and I only wanted more. The sauce was old-fashioned enough to qualify as what I remembered, while revealing a complexity I could appreciate only after decades of eating and cooking. I suddenly couldn't remember the other taste; there was only this taste, the only one that had ever mattered. It was the romance novel of meat ravioli, the true love that had eluded me for so long.

Mr. Garavelli looked at us from across the room, and I saw him smile. This man had accomplished what I had assumed was impossible: the perfect adult rendering of a childhood memory, Cokes and wishing wells not required. When I realized I didn't have to go to school the next day, I thought I might cry.

After unabashedly stuffing myself, I took the scant leftovers home. The next morning, I woke up and devoured them before I even made coffee. I looked at the empty container for about two seconds before picking up the phone to make another reservation.

"Do you want to come into the kitchen before and see how I make?" Mr. Garavelli asked.

I considered it. "No, I don't think so," I said, finally. "But have you ever thought about getting a jukebox?"

Indian Takeout

by Jhumpa Lahiri
from *Food & Wine*

Winner of the Pulitzer Prize for fiction for *Interpreter of Maladies*, Jhumpa Lahiri in this essay touches on so much—the power of childhood sense memories, an emigrant's hunger for the homeland, and an assimilated child's distance from exotic immigrant customs. Yet with precise and sinuous prose, she brings it all vividly to life.

I am the daughter of former pirates, of a kind. Our loot included gold, silver, even a few precious gems. Mainly though, it was food, so much that throughout my childhood I was convinced my parents were running the modern equivalent of the ancient spice trade. They didn't exactly plunder this food; they bought it in the bazaars of Calcutta, where my mother was born and to which we returned as a family every couple of years. The destination was Rhode Island, where we lived, and where, back in the Seventies, Indian groceries were next to impossible to come by.

Our treasure chest, something we called the Food Suitcase, was an elegant relic from the Fifties with white stitching and brass latches that fastened shut with satisfying clicks. The inside was lined in peach-colored satin, had shirred lingerie pockets on three sides and was large enough to house a wardrobe for a long journey. Leave it to my parents to convert a vintage portmanteau into a portable pantry. They bought it one Saturday morning at a yard sale in the neighborhood, and I think it's safe to say that it had never been to India before.

Trips to Calcutta let my parents eat again, eat the food of their childhood, the food they had been deprived of as adults. As soon as he hit Indian soil, my father began devouring two or three yellow-skinned mangoes a day, sucking the pits lovingly smooth. My mother breakfasted shamelessly on sticky orange sweets called *jelebis*. It was easy to succumb. I insisted on accompanying each of my meals with the yogurt sold at confectioners in red clay cups, their lids made of paper, and my sister formed an addiction to *Moghlai parathas*, flatbread folded, omelet-style, over mincemeat and egg.

As the end of each visit neared, our focus shifted from eating to shopping. My parents created lists on endless sheets of paper, and my father spent days in the bazaars, haggling and buying by the kilo. He always insisted on packing the goods himself, with the aura of a man possessed: bare-chested, seated cross-legged on the floor, determined, above all, to make everything fit. He bound the Food Suitcase with enough rope to baffle Houdini and locked it up with a little padlock, a scheme that succeeded in intimidating the most assiduous customs inspectors. Into the suitcase went an arsenal of lentils and every conceivable spice, wrapped in layers of cloth ripped from an old sari and stitched into individual packets. In went white poppy seeds, and resin made from date syrup, and as many tins of Ganesh mustard oil as possible. In went Lapchu tea, to be brewed only on special occasions, and sacks of black-skinned Gobindovog rice, so named, it is said, because it's fit for offering to the god Govinda. In went six kinds of *dalmoot,* a salty, crunchy snack mix bought from big glass jars in a tiny store at the corner of Vivekananda Road and Cornwallis Street. In, on occasion, went something fresh, and therefore flagrantly illegal: a bumpy, bright green bitter melon, or bay leaves from my uncle's garden. My parents weren't the only ones willing to flout the law. One year my grandmother secretly tucked *parvals,* a vaguely squashlike vegetable, into the Food Suitcase. My mother wept when she found them.

My parents also bought utensils: bowl-shaped iron *karhais,* which my mother still prefers to ordinary pots and pans, and the areca-nut cracker that's now somewhere in the back of the silverware drawer, and even a *boti,* a large curved blade that sits on the floor in Bengali kitchens and is used instead of handheld knives. The most sensational gadget we ever transported was a *sil-nora,* an ancient food processor of sorts, which consists of a massive clublike pestle and a slab the size, shape and weight of a headstone. Bewildered relatives shook their heads, and airport workers in both hemispheres must have cursed us. For a while my mother actually used it, pounding garlic cloves by hand instead of pressing a button on the Osterizer. Then it turned into a decorative device, propped up on the kitchen counter. It's in the basement now.

The suitcase was full during the trip from Rhode Island to Calcutta too, with gifts for family. People there seldom asked for any food from America; instead they requested the stuff of duty-free, Dunhills or Johnnie Walker. We brought them Corning Ware plates and bowls, which, in their eyes, were exotic alternatives to the broad, gleaming stainless steel dishes they normally used. The only food we packed for ourselves was a big jar of Tang, which my father carried with him at all times and stirred obsessively into the bitter purified water.

In spite of everything we managed to haul back, the first meal we ate after returning from India was always a modest affair. My mother prepared the simplest of things: rice, some quartered potatoes, eggs if she was motivated, all boiled together in a single pot. That first meal was never an occasion to celebrate but rather to mourn for the people and the city we had, once again, left behind. And so my mother made food to mirror our mood, food for the weary and melancholy. I remember thinking how strangely foreign our own kitchen felt that first night back, with its giant, matching appliances, water we could safely drink straight from the tap and rice which bore no stray stones. Just before we ate, my mother would ask my father to untie the ropes and unlock the suitcase. A few pappadams quickly fried and a drop of mustard oil drizzled over the potatoes would convert our survivalist meal into a delicacy. It was enough, that first lonely evening, not only to satisfy our hunger but to make Calcutta seem not so very far away.

My parents returned last August from their 13th visit to India in their 30-odd years abroad. When I asked my mother what foods they'd brought back she replied, with some sadness, "Nothing, really." My father observed matter-of-factly that most everything was sold here these days. It's true. Saffron and cardamom grace supermarket shelves, even in the small towns of Rhode Island. The world, the culinary world in particular, has shrunk considerably. Still, when my cousin's mother recently visited New York City, she packed several pieces of fried *ruhi,* the everyday fish of Bengal, into her bags. Of course, the Indian markets of Jackson Heights, Queens, were only a subway ride away, but the fish had been sliced, salted and fried in Calcutta. This was what mattered.

Today the Food Suitcase sits in our basement, neglected, smelling of cumin. When I opened it on my last trip home, a few stray lentils rolled around in one corner. Yet the signs were still visible, in the cupboards and the refrigerator, that my parents have not abandoned their pirating ways. You would know as much, were you to visit them yourself, by the six kinds of *dal-moot* my mother would set out with tea and the mustard oil she would offer to drizzle on your potatoes at dinner.

P.C. and Proud of It

by James Villas
from Gourmet

Pimento cheese may not be a gourmet delicacy, but to born-and-bred Southerners—like former *Town and Country* food and wine editor James Villas—it is a prized foodstuff worth fighting over. In case y'all have never tried it, he gives us his momma's recipe, too, which is right neighborly.

"Son," Mother would say while feeding chunks of sharp Cheddar and strips of sweet pimento into the meat grinder as I turned the handle and picked at the mixture collecting in a bowl, "if you keep eating that, I'm not going to have one iota left to make your or anybody else's sandwich. Now stop it this minute and just grind."

She would then carefully examine the mixture and maybe, if the blend didn't look exactly right to her expert eye, drop a little more cheese or pimento into the grinder. Taking the bowl from our kitchen table to the counter, she next casually added a few globs of homemade mayonnaise, a quick squeeze of fresh lemon juice, a dash of Worcestershire, and a sprinkling of cayenne, then mashed everything with a fork till the concoction was as smooth as silk and ready for her to sample. "Here, honey, taste this," she'd then direct proudly, handing me the other half of a cracker topped with the tangy spread. "If I say so myself, that's pretty good pimento cheese."

Although time has a cruel way of dissipating childhood memories, one that remains crystal clear is helping Mother make pimento cheese for the delectable sandwiches she routinely packed into my bright red-and-white school lunch box when I was growing up in North Carolina. Also included might have been a fried chicken drumstick or zesty country-ham biscuit, carrot sticks, a fat juicy pear, and a few homemade cookies. But what I really loved and never, ever tired of were her soft, pungent pimento cheese sandwiches on whole-wheat bread with just enough of the luscious spread oozing from the edges onto the wax-paper wrapping to make for a good initial lick.

Pimento cheese? When I mention the name to most non-southerners, I usually get little more than a puzzled stare. But utter those two words in front of anyone from Dixie, and the same enlightened, ecstatic smile will twinkle as when the subject of buttermilk biscuits or chopped-pork barbecue or peach cobbler is broached. Long before the term *politically correct* was conceived, P.C. generally connoted only one thing in the South: the simple, piquant utterly addictive combination of grated Cheddar cheese, diced pimentos, cayenne pepper, and mayonnaise that is spread on crackers and sandwiches, stuffed into celery stalks and cherry tomatoes, incorporated in salads, turned into dips and festive balls, and used as a topping on grilled burgers and various breads.

You can search food dictionaries till you're blue in the face and never find a reference to pimento cheese. But in the South, nobody in his or her right mind would spell pimento with an extra *i*, and the correct pronunciation of the spread is "pa-*men*-uh" cheese.

It's been quaintly called southern pâté, and just about the only cookbooks that include recipes for the stuff are those written by southerners. When, where, and how pimento cheese originated remains a total mystery, but then, nobody in the South really cares. All that matters is that a day never passes without a jar or crock of fresh P.C. in the refrigerator to dip into when the urge strikes or when folks show up unexpectedly or when there's a quick lunch or picnic to prepare.

Of course, arguments do become heated when the question of what constitutes great pimento cheese is raised. There does seem to be common agreement among the wise that the cheese must be the finest sharp or extra-sharp Cheddar available and the mayonnaise, top-grade (which means only Duke's or Hellmann's or fresh), but there all civility stops. To attain the best texture, for example, should the cheese be finely grated, coarsely shredded, or run through a meat grinder the way my mother still does? Must the spread be mixed and mashed with a fork the old-fashioned way, or can an electric mixer or a food processor yield comparable results? What are the ideal proportions of cheese to pimentos to mayo? Are roasted red bell peppers a viable substitute for canned pimentos? And does pale pimento cheese, made with white Cheddar instead of traditional orange-dyed, really look like classic pimento cheese?

These are cardinal considerations, to be sure, but the fur really begins to fly when optional ingredients are debated: chopped celery, onions, hard-boiled eggs, garlic, jalapeños, parsley, and herbs; lemon juice, Worcestershire sauce, and Tabasco; additional cheeses such as Parmesan, cottage, and cream. There's one lady down in Nashville who adds Durkee's dressing and Dijon mustard to her pimento cheese; another at Lake Wylie, South Carolina, who's convinced that evaporated milk gives her mixture exceptional smoothness; and Ruth Fales, co-owner of the Pinckney Cafe & Espresso in Charleston, South Carolina, who couldn't imagine making P.C. without a few chopped green olives. For these and hundreds of other serious enthusiasts, homemade pimento cheese is a very emotional topic, though not quite as emotional as the horrifying alternative of using any one of the many prepared versions available in small tubs at all southern supermarkets. The least said about commercial pimento cheese, the better. None other than the renowned North Carolina author Reynolds Price summed it up best when he likened these products to "congealed insecticides."

Over the years, I've made pimento cheese every way conceivable, and while I'd never be so reckless as to dictate a strict formula for a spread that lends itself to endless interpretation and experiment, I do have my own strong convictions and prejudices. First of all, since the marriage of Cheddar and pimentos is blessed from on high and must therefore be treated with respect, never should any other ingredient be allowed to alter or nullify these primary flavors. This is why I personally disapprove of adding garlic, sugar, vinegar, bulb onions, and horseradish or inordinate amounts of chile peppers, crumbled bacon, assertive mustard, Worcestershire, or Tabasco. Nor do I ever salt a basic spread, because of the salty nature of the cheese and mayonnaise—not to mention olives, bacon, and mustard. Today I use only Hellmann's mayonnaise, being careful—as with any other ingredient—not to overwhelm the cheese and pimentos.

I'm obsessed with Cheddar intended for P.C. and am forever in search of premium styles. When I was a child, Mother's butcher shop always had enormous wheels of sharp, gloriously mellow country Cheddar we called "rat cheese" (and it was my duty at home to set mousetraps in the basement with tiny morsels), but those days are long gone. Well-aged (at least 12 months) extra-sharp Cheddar found in some supermarkets is respectable enough (A&P's Master Choice New York State brand is my favorite), but what I really seek out are exceptional artisanal products: Vermont's Cabot, Crowley, Shelburne, and white Grafton; Oregon's Colby, white Tillamook, and Monterey Jack; any all-natural Canadian Cheddar; and, noblest of all, a real, cream-colored English farmhouse Cheddar or feisty Cheshire. Anybody who would try to make pimento cheese with that appalling processed American cheese or Velveeta needs serious psychiatric help.

I'm equally touchy about using genuine pimentos versus ordinary roasted red bell peppers, not only because of the superior flavor but also because the canning liquid is ideal for thinning overly dense pimento cheese. Contrary to certain confusing etymological implications, the large, red, heart-shaped pimento pepper (indigenous to the Americas and taken back to Spain by Columbus) is not the same as its humbler cousin and can make all the difference between extraordinary and mediocre pimento cheese. Although pimento production and packing is done in the South, canned whole, sliced, and diced pimentos are available at supermarkets nationwide in four and sometimes seven-ounce jars. I'm almost as adamant about using plenty of pimentos in my P.C. as about mixing the spread to a slightly coarse consistency with a fork, and I even toss pimentos into certain doughs and batters to produce such savory marvels as pimento-cheese straws, cocktail biscuits, and muffins.

Obviously, I consider myself as much a P.C. aficionado as the next Reb, but the sad irony is that I've still never quite succeeded at creating what I perceive to be the ideal spread. I'm not alone, for if you challenge any honest southerner to augur once and for all a definition of the world's perfect pimento cheese, the elusive and frustrating response remains the same: Mom's.

Mother's Everyday Pimento Cheese

> Makes about 3 cups
> Active time: 25 minutes
> Start to finish: 2 ½ hours

If you really want to make this pimento cheese the way my mother does, and you happen to own a hand-crank meat grinder, run the two cheeses once through the fine blade of the grinder into a mixing bowl. Mother simply used to grind the pimentos with the cheeses, but now she prefers to mash them with a heavy fork on a plate until they break up into tiny pieces. She uses homemade mayonnaise but also endorses Hellmann's (a.k.a. Best Foods).

> ½ lb extra-sharp Vermont white Cheddar
> ½ lb extra-sharp New York (orange) Cheddar
> 1 (7-oz) jar pimentos, drained and finely chopped
> ½ teaspoon black pepper
> cayenne to taste
> ⅔ cup mayonnaise

Finely grate cheeses into a large bowl. Stir in pimentos, black pepper, cayenne, and salt to taste with a fork. Then stir in mayonnaise, mashing mixture with fork until relatively smooth. (It should be flecked with small pieces of pimento.)

Scrape pimento into a crock or jar and chill, covered, at least 2 hours to allow flavors to develop.

Serve pimento cheese with crackers or use as a filling for finger sandwiches.

Cooks' note: Pimento cheese keeps, tightly covered and chilled, 4 days.

The Chinese Kitchen

by Eileen Yin-Fei Lo
from *The Chinese Kitchen*

Esteemed cooking teacher and cookbook writer Eileen Yin-Fei Lo is a woman with a mission: to teach Westerners that Chinese food isn't just nutrition, isn't just fuel, isn't just about pleasing the palate, but is an expression of an entire ancient culture. In assured, uncluttered prose, she passes on the tradition like a carefully guarded treasure.

I was brought up to believe in the long, rolling swell of greater Chinese history, even though at times I, and my family, have been hurt by some of its excesses. I am devoted to China's foodways. I preach them and their purity, and I despair when this purity is compromised. Food in China is a living continuum, and I believe in, and partake of, the religion, folk tales, and mythology that we eat and in the long culinary tradition that is always with us.

What we Chinese eat to nourish ourselves we also eat to contribute to our interior balance and well-being. Food in China is to a great degree medicine. One food will bring us heat, necessary in the winter months or to balance what is cool within our bodies. Other foods will provide coolness, necessary in the summer, necessary for balance. . . .

. . . Food is not only life-giving but also a source of familial or societal leanings. Our food is inextricably linked with manners, with form, with tradition, with history. I grew up with these beliefs. I remember my father, Lo Pak Wan, my first cooking teacher, telling me that we must eat our food first with our eyes, then with our minds, then with our noses, and finally with our mouths. He believed this. He taught this to my brother and me.

He would say, only partly joking, that fine vegetables should be chosen with as much care as one would a son-in-law. He would show me the correct way to prepare rice, telling me that if our rice was old then perhaps more water than customary might be needed to give our congee its fine and silky finish. "Keep an open mind," he would say. "Cook the way it has been written, but keep an open mind. If you keep walking only in a straight line, you will go into a wall. You must learn to make a turn if necessary. Do not be narrow." Or he would tell me, *"Tau mei haw yan tiu, mo mei haw yan tiu,"* an aphorism that translates as "If you don't have a tail, you cannot imitate the monkey; if you do have a tail, then do not imitate the monkey." By this he was telling me to follow the classical manner but not to be a simple, mindless imitator.

My mother, Lo Chan Miu Hau, encouraged me to cook as well. I recall her saying to me, "If you are wealthy and know how to cook, then servants cannot take advantage of you. If you are poor and know how to cook, you will be able to create wonderful meals with few resources." Cooking and its ramifications were that important to her, as well as to my father, when I was young and growing up in Sun Tak, a suburb of Canton, now Guangzhou.

They and my grandmother, my Ah Paw, my mother's mother, insisted that I be involved in our family table. Ah Paw, despite her houseful of servants, despite the presence of a family cook, made certain whenever I visited her, which was every opportunity I had, every school holiday, that I was in her kitchen.

My Ah Paw knew instinctively, without ever having had to personally put a spatula into a wok, how things ought to be cooked, what foods wedded in combination, and what clashed. I am tempted to suggest that she was a brilliant, instinctive kitchen chemist. I will say it. Brilliant she was indeed, her knowledge of foods was encyclopedic, and she was never wrong about cooking, then or now, in my memory. I spent much of the Lunar New Year at her house. I liked her home, I liked her kitchen, and she spoiled me. Except when it came to imparting cookery lessons.

When we ate raw fish, *yue sahng,* she taught, one had to prepare the fish in the proper manner. You hit the fish at the front of its head to stun it, then, when it was still nominally alive, you scaled it, gutted and cleaned it, then sliced it for eating. This special dish, which we ate on important birthdays and on the eves of family weddings, had to be prepared this way, only this way, Ah Paw said.

When we steamed a fish, she taught me to softly lay the fish atop a bed of rice at the precise moment that the rice was in the final state of its absorption of water. It would then be perfectly prepared.

Once I steamed a fish, quite well, I thought, and proudly carried it to her at the family table. She sniffed. I had forgotten to pour boiled peanut oil over it just before serving. "Take it back to the kitchen and add the oil," she ordered. My grandmother's kitchen always had a crock of boiled peanut oil near the stove. To pour it over fish was to give the fish fragrance and to dispel any unpleasant odors. It does, even if the oil is not warm.

She would eat no vegetables that were older than two hours out of the ground, which necessitated repeated trips to the markets by her servants, a lesson of the importance of freshness that was not lost on me.

She cautioned me to eat every kernel of rice in my bowl, for if I did not, she warned, the man I married would have a pockmarked face, one mark for each uneaten rice kernel, I did as she cautioned, and I must have eaten well, for my husband's face is clear.

Do not shout in the kitchen, Ah Paw would insist. Do not use improper words in the kitchen. Do not show shortness of temper in the kitchen by, for example, banging chopsticks on a wok. All of these would reflect badly on us as a family, she would say, when done in front of Jo Kwan, the Kitchen God, whose image hung on the wall over the oven. For just before the Lunar New Year the image of Jo Kwan, his lips smeared with honey, was always burned so that he would go up to heaven and report only nice things about our family.

Ah Paw would consult her *Tung Sing,* an astrological book, for propitious days on which to begin preparing the special dumplings we made and ate during the New Year festival. She would specify to the second the time to make the dough, heat the oven, add the oil, in what we called *"hoi yau wok,"* or, literally translated, "begin the oil in the wok." So admired was she for her knowledge that young married couples, not even of our family, would consult with her. A memory I have is of pumping the pedal of the iron and stone grinding mill in our town square, at her orders, to get the flour that we would use for our dumplings.

She was an observant Buddhist who declined to eat either fish or meat on the first and the fifteenth of each month and for the first fifteen days of the New Year, and our family ate similarly out of deference to her. She was happy that my mother always encouraged me to cook, happy that my father brought kitchen discipline to me as well. She nodded with pleasure, in support of my father, I remember—not in sympathy with me—when I complained how boring it was when my father gave me the task of snapping off the ends of individual mung bean sprouts. "If you wish to learn how to make spring rolls well, learn the beginning of the spring roll. It must be done," Ah Paw said.

We had no grinders. We chopped meats and fish and other seafood with the cleaver on a chopping board. "Clean it," Ah Paw would say when I was finished. "If you do not, the food you chop next will not stick together. It will fall apart. There will be no texture. If it falls apart, I will know that you did not listen."

All of this she conferred on me without ever setting foot in the kitchen of her house. As a further example of her vision I should note in passing that my Ah Paw, a most independent woman, as is evident, refused to have bound the feet of my mother, her daughter, much the practice of high-born women. This despite the fact that her own feet had been bound since babyhood and were no more than four inches long. This extraordinary woman, never more than seventy-five pounds, who could not totter more than one hundred feet and was usually carried by servants, brought my mother and then me into modern times in her own way. I wanted nothing more than to be with her, and I would listen, wide-eyed and receptive, to her talk about food and its meanings. . . .

. . . In her many and varied discourses on food, her advisories, Ah Paw would cite Confucius as she talked of techniques and the philosopher's opinions and dictates concerning food. He had been a simple man, she said of this most well known of Chinese philosophers, who lived and wrote in the fifth century B.C., who thought so much of food and its tastes and presentation that he would specify how foods ought to be cut up before cooking. Ah Paw told me that Confucius was a man satisfied to be paid for his teaching with a "small amount of dried meat" and that he was happy with "plain food to eat and pure water to drink."

It was as if she had learned by rote. Confucius, she said, desired rice to be at its whitest and meat to be finely chopped, but when food was overcooked he would not eat. When fish or meat had become tainted, or had lost its color, or had an odor he thought distasteful, he would not eat. He insisted that the food he ate be in season, not preserved, and sauce for it had to enhance it, and not change it. He drank wine, but not to excess. Nor did he overeat, she would say with a gesture of her finger, and "he would have no meal that did not have some ginger."

It was only later, as I grew up and studied, that I found that most of these dicta are included in Confucius's *Analects,* that collection of adages and dialogues Confucius wrote to, for, and with his followers. But for my Ah Paw they were valid and surely worth passing on to me, in particular her repetition of her favorite tale of Confucius, who, she told me, when asked for his opinions on war suggested that he knew more about meat preparation than about war. Good teaching. Though Ah Paw was an observant Buddhist, she did not reject some of the ways taught by Lao-Tzu, who wrote of the simple life, of direct, clean tastes, of foods prepared to reflect simplicity and honesty of flavor. In no other cuisine are the harmonies of color, appearance, tactile sensations, and textures so important. . . .

. . . Another patch in my personal quilt was another member of my family who helped mightily to make me a cook, my aunt, Pong Lo Siu Fong. That was her formal name, but we all called her Luk Gu Cheh, for "father's younger sister number six," which indeed she was. I often marketed with her, and she was known because she would have one of her servants follow her carrying an empty pail, the better to carry home a live fish. For her only that could be considered fresh.

She taught me how to kill and properly clean a fish. Another time I remember she asked, "Do you really want to cook?" and when I replied yes I did, she took me to the market to buy a live chicken. We brought it home. As she watched and instructed, I spread its wings back, bent its neck, and made a cut in its neck, draining the blood into a bowl of salted water, where it congealed. I then steamed it into a blood pudding, which Luk Gu Cheh taught me to stir-fry with broccoli, a dish her husband favored. Her husband, my uncle, was a senator, and she supervised many grand political and social dinners at her home, even cooking with her servants. At one of these she created her version of lemon chicken, wherein chicken is steamed with fresh lemons instead of the customary concoction in which the fowl is fried, then doused with a lemon sauce thick with cornstarch. It has become my recipe. She taught me the discipline of carefully cutting meats and vegetables for *ding* dishes, which means "little squares."

Is not all of this in direct descent from those early Chinese days? Luk Gu Cheh had nothing to do with my killing and dressing my first snake, at the age of nine. That was a matter of pride, done on a dare. One of my playmates, a boy, had caught a snake, a nonpoisonous, edible water snake. He teased me, saying, "Sure, you know how to kill a fish. Sure, you know how to kill a chicken. But can you kill a snake?" I never had, but I had watched. So I cut the skin around the base of its head, with a broken shard of glass, as was the custom, then stripped the skin downward completely from its body. It became my snake, and I raced home with it, proudly, to tell my mother, who applauded me, for snakes, then as now, are expensive, luxurious foods, particularly during winter. Moreover, it was filled with eggs, which made it an even worthier prize. I confess I have never done it since, nor, I expect, could I do it again, nor could I similarly prepare a live eel or a turtle. I simply cannot. Yet what I had done that afternoon was, in a small though real way, a continuation of Chinese history.

Why I Stopped Being a Vegetarian

by Laura Fraser

from *salon.com*

With vegetarianism scoring high on the trend-ometer at century's end, a backlash eventually had to surface. Here it is, in this deliciously wry on-line essay by Laura Fraser that tells the story of how a good vegetarian fell off the wagon—and why she's glad she did.

Until a few months ago, I had been a vegetarian for 15 years. Like most people who call themselves vegetarians (somewhere between 4 and 10 percent of us, depending on the definition; only 1 percent of Americans are vegans, eating no animal products at all), I wasn't strict about it. I ate dairy products and eggs, as well as fish. That made me a pesco-ovo-lacto-vegetarian, which isn't a category you can choose for special meals on airlines.

About a year ago, in Italy, it dawned on me that a little pancetta was really good in pasta, too. After failing to convince myself that pancetta was a vegetable, I became a pesco-ovo-lacto-pancetta-vegetarian, with a "Don't Ask, Don't Tell" policy about chicken broth. It was a slippery slope from there.

Nevertheless, for most of those 15 years, hardly a piece of animal flesh crossed my lips. Over the course of that time, many people asked me why I became a vegetarian. I came up with vague answers: my health, the environment, the impracticality and heartlessness of killing animals for food when we can survive perfectly well on soy burgers. It was political, it was emotional and it made me special, not to mention slightly morally superior to all those bloodthirsty carnivores out there.

The truth is, I became a vegetarian in college for two reasons. One was that meat was more expensive than lentils, and I was broke, or broke enough to choose to spend my limited budget on other classes of ingestibles. The other was that I was not a lesbian.

This is not to say that all lesbians are carnivores; in fact, there's probably a higher percentage of vegetarians among lesbians than most other groups. But there was a fair amount of political pressure to be something in those days. Since, as a privileged white girl from suburban Denver, I couldn't really identify with any oppressed minority group, I was faced with becoming a lesbian in order to prove my political mettle. I had to decide between meat and men, and for better or worse, I became a vegetarian.

The identity stuck, even though the political imperative for my label faded. It wasn't an identity that ever really fit: My friends thought it odd that such an otherwise hedonistic woman should have that one ascetic streak. It was against my nature, they said. But by then, I'd started to believe the other arguments about vegetarianism.

First was health. There's a lot of evidence that vegetarians live longer, have lower cholesterol levels and are thinner than meat-eaters. This is somewhat hard to believe, since for the first few years of not eating meat, I was basically a cheesetarian. Try leafing through some of those vegetarian recipe books from the early

'80s: You added three cups of grated cheddar to everything but the granola. Then vegetarianism went through that mathematical phase where you had to figure out which proteins you had to combine with which in order to get a complete protein. Since many nutritionists will tell you people don't need that much protein anyway, I gave up, going for days and days without so much as contemplating beans or tofu.

For whatever haphazard combination of proteins I ate, being a vegetarian did seem to have a stunning effect on my cholesterol level. This, of course, could be genetic. But when I had a very involved physical exam once at the Cooper Institute for Aerobic Fitness in Dallas, my total cholesterol level was a super-low 135, and my ratio of HDL (good) cholesterol to LDL (evil) was so impressive that the doctor drawled, "Even if you had heart disease, you would be reversing it." This good news, far from reassuring me that I could well afford a few barbecued ribs now and then, spurred me on in my vegetarianism, mainly because my cholesterol numbers effectively inoculated me against the doctor's advice that I also needed to lose 15 pounds.

"Why?" I asked. "Don't you lose weight to lower your cholesterol?"

He couldn't argue with that. Whether or not most vegetarians are leaner than carnivores, in my case I was happy to more than make up the calories with carbohydrates, which, perhaps not coincidentally, I always craved.

After the health rationale came the animal rights one. Like most vegetarians, I cracked Peter Singer's philosophical treatise on animal rights, and bought his utilitarian line that if you don't have to kill animals, and it potentially causes suffering, you shouldn't do it. (Singer, now at Princeton, has recently come under attack for saying that if a human being's incapacitated life causes more suffering than good, it is OK to kill him.)

It's hard to know where to stop with utilitarianism. Do I need a cashmere sweater more than those little shorn goats need to be warm themselves? Do animals really suffer if they have happy, frolicking lives before a quick and painless end? Won't free-range do?

My animal rights philosophy had a lot of holes from the start. First of all, I excluded fish from the animal kingdom—not only because fish taste delicious grilled with a little butter and garlic, but also because they make it a lot easier to be a vegetarian when you go out to restaurants. Now that's utilitarian. Besides, as soon as you start spending your time fretting about the arguments that crowd the inner pens of animal rights philosophy—do fish think?—then you know you're experiencing a real protein deficiency.

I rationalized the fish thing by telling myself I would eat anything I would kill myself. I had been fly-fishing with my dad and figured a few seconds of flopping around was outweighed by the merits of trout almondine. (Notice that I, not the fish, was doing the figuring.) But who was I kidding? If I were hungry enough, I'd kill a cow in a heartbeat. I'd practically kill a cow just for a great pair of shoes.

Which brings me to the leather exception. As long as other people are eating cow, I decided, I might as well recycle the byproducts and diminish the harm by wearing leather jackets and shoes. When everyone stopped eating meat, I'd stop buying leather jackets and shoes. In the meantime, better stock up.

Then there's the environmental rationale. There is no doubt, as Frances Moore Lappe first pointed out in her 1971 book *Food First*, that there is a huge loss of protein resources going from grain to meat, and that some animals, especially cattle and Americans, use up piggish amounts of water, grain and crop land.

But the problem really isn't meat, but too much meat—over-grazing, over-fishing and over-consumption. If Americans just ate less meat—like driving cars less often—the problem could be alleviated without giving up meat entirely. That approach has worked for centuries, and continues to work in Europe.

All my deep vegetarian questioning was silenced one day when a friend ordered roasted rosemary chicken for two. I thought I'd try "just a bite," and then I was ripping into it like a starving hyena. Roasted chicken, I realized, is wonderful. Meat is good.

From a culinary point of view, that's obvious. Consider that most vegetarians live in America and England, places tourists do not visit for the food. You don't find vegetarians in France, and rarely in Italy. Enough said.

As for health, if nutritionists are always telling you to "listen to your body," mine was definitely shouting for more meat. One roasted bird unleashed 15 years' worth of cravings. All of a sudden I felt like I had a bass note playing in my body to balance out all those soprano carbohydrates. Forget about winning the low-cholesterol Olympics. For the first time in a long time, I felt satisfied.

As a vegetarian, not only had I denied myself something I truly enjoyed, I had been anti-social. How many times had I made a hostess uncomfortable by refusing the main course at a dinner party, lamely saying I'd "eat around it"? How often did my vegetarianism cause other people to go to extra trouble to make something special for me to eat, and why did it never occur to me that that was selfish? How about the time, in a small town in Italy, when the chef had presented me with a plate of very special local sausage, since I was the American guest—and I had refused it, to the mortification of my Italian friends? Or when a then-boyfriend, standing in the meat section of the grocery store, forlornly told a friend, "If only I had a girlfriend who ate meat"? If eating is a socially conscious act, you have to be conscious of the society of your fellow homo sapiens along with the animals. And we humans, as it happens, are omnivores.

The Magic Bagel

by Calvin Trillin
from *The New Yorker*

In his life as a food writer (as opposed to his other careers as satirical poet, *Time* columnist, and *New Yorker* essayist), Calvin Trillin never shrinks from a food fixation. It usually begins innocently enough, but eventually rises to a shade of mild hysteria. In this case it's triggered by a search for the perfect New York bagel.

My wife and I came up with differing interpretations of a conversation I had with our older daughter, Abigail, not long ago after a dim-sum lunch in Chinatown. Abigail, who lives in San Francisco, was in New York to present a paper at a conference. As a group of us trooped back toward Greenwich Village, where she'd grown up and where my wife, Alice, and I still live, Abigail and I happened to be walking together. "Let's get this straight, Abigail," I said, after we'd finished off some topic and had gone along in silence for a few moments. "If I can find those gnarly little dark pumpernickel bagels that we used to get at Tanenbaum's, you'll move back to New York. Right?"

"Absolutely," Abigail said.

When I reported that exchange to Alice, she said that Abigail was speaking ironically. I found it difficult to believe that anybody could be ironic about those bagels. They were almost black. Misshapen. Oniony. Abigail adored them. Both of my daughters have always taken bagels seriously. My younger daughter, Sarah, also lives in California—she's in Los Angeles—and she often complains about the bagels there being below her standards. For a while, I brought along a dozen bagels for Sarah whenever I went to L.A., but I finally decided that this policy was counterproductive. "If a person prefers to live in California, which happens to be thousands of miles from her very own parents," I told her, "it seems to me appropriate that such a person eat California bagels. I understand that in some places out there if you buy a dozen wheat-germ bagels you get one bee-pollen bagel free."

Abigail, it should be noted, always had bagel standards at least as high as Sarah's. I have previously documented the moment when I realized that she was actually a New Yorker (until she was four or five, I had somehow thought of her as being from the same place I'm from, Kansas City): we were back in Missouri visiting my family, and she said, "Daddy, how come in Kansas City the bagels taste like just round bread?" In other words, she knew the difference between those bagel-shaped objects available in American supermarkets and the authentic New York item that had been hand-rolled and boiled in a vat and then carefully baked by a member in good standing of the Bakery and Confectionery Workers International Union. My sadness at the evidence that she wasn't actually from my home town was offset by my pride in the evidence that she was precocious.

Would Proust have been ironic about the madeleine, particularly if he had fetched up in a place where you couldn't get a decent madeleine if your life depended on it? When my daughters were children, bagels were not only their staple food but also the food of important rituals. On Sunday mornings, I often took them to Houston Street, on the Lower East Side. At Russ & Daughters, which is what New Yorkers call an appetizer store, we would buy Nova Scotia salmon—a transaction that took some time, since the daughters (of Joel Russ, the founder, who stared down at us from a splendid portrait on the wall) had to quit slicing fish now and then to tell me in glorious detail how adorable my girls were. Then we'd go next door to Ben's Dairy to get cream cheese and a delicacy known as baked farmer's cheese with scallions. Then we were at Tanenbaum's, a bakery that was probably best known for a large, dark loaf often referred to as Russian health bread. We were not there for Russian health bread.

"So you think she's just humoring her old dad?" I asked Alice, when we discussed the conversation I'd had with Abigail on the way back from Chinatown.

"I do."

Alice was probably right. I understood that. Abigail enjoys living in California, and she's got a job there that she loves. Children grow up and lead lives of their own. Parents are supposed to accept that. Still, I decided that I'd look around for those pumpernickel bagels. As my father used to say, "What could it hurt?"

It wasn't my first try. When the pumpernickel bagels disappeared, I immediately made serious inquiries. Without wanting to cast blame, I have to say that the disappearance occurred on Mutke's watch. Mutke's formal name is Hyman Perlmutter. In the early seventies, he bought Tanenbaum's Bakery and transformed it into the downtown branch of a bakery he ran eight or ten blocks away called Moishe's. For some time, Mutke carried Tanenbaum's full inventory. Then one day—I don't remember precisely when, but Abigail and Sarah were still living at home—the pumpernickel bagels were no longer there. Confronted with the facts, Mutke was sanguine. Those particular bagels weren't available anymore, he explained, but, as a special order, he could always provide me with a dozen or two just like them. Eventually, he did. I pulled one out of the bag. It was a smooth bagel, uniformly round. It was the color of cappuccino, heavy on the milk. It was a stranger to onions. It was not by any means Abigail's bagel.

I realize now, of course, that I gave up too easily. Sure, I stopped by to try the pumpernickel anytime I heard of a promising new bagel bakery—even if it was uptown, a part of the city I don't venture to unnecessarily. But I didn't make a systematic search. How was I to know that bagels can be instrumental in keeping families intact? This time, I was going to be thorough. I had read in Molly O'Neill's "New York Cook Book" about a place in Queens where bagels were made in the old-fashioned way. I figured that there must be similar places in Brooklyn neighborhoods with a large population of Orthodox Jews—Williamsburg maybe, or Borough Park. I was prepared to go to the outer boroughs. But I thought it made sense to start back on Houston Street.

The area where Abigail and Sarah and I used to make our Sunday rounds has seen some changes over the years. The old tenement streets used to seem grim. Now they sport patches of raffish chic. On Orchard Street, around the corner from our Sunday-morning purveyors, stores that have traditionally offered bargains on fabrics and women's clothing and leather goods are punctuated by the sort of clothing store that has a rack of design magazines and a coffee bar and such a spare display of garments that you might think you're in the studio apartment of someone who has bizarre taste in cocktail dresses and no closet to keep them in. These days, the Lower East Side is a late-night destination—both Orchard and Ludlow have bars too hip to require a sign—and a cool place to live. After spending years listening to customers tell him that he ought to move Russ & Daughters uptown, Mark Federman, the son of one of the daughters, is renovating the apartments above the store and expressing gratitude that his grandfather held on to the building.

Ben's Dairy has closed, and Moishe's Bakery has moved to a tiny place around the corner. But Russ & Daughters has been carefully preserved to look pretty much the way it did when the founder himself still had his arms deep in the herring barrel. I figured Mark might have some information I could use, and he was bound to be sympathetic to the project: his daughter, Niki, recently graduated from college and moved to San Francisco. "Do you think Niki might come back, too, if we found the bagels?" I asked, as Mark and I edged ourselves into the tiny office he shares with his wife, Maria.

"I don't think she'd come back for bagels," he said. "Maybe for an apartment upstairs."

Maria shook her head. "I already offered," she said.

Mark said that he knew precisely the bagel I was talking about, but that he had no idea where to find it. He phoned his mother, who's retired, in Florida. "Do you remember when Tanenbaum next door used to have this sort of gnarly" he began, and then started to laugh. "Not an old woman," he said. "I'm asking about bagels." Apparently, his mother remembered the gnarly old woman quite well. Not the bagels.

Although Russ & Daughters carries bagels these days, Mark insisted that he didn't have the expertise to be much help in tracing a particular baker; locating an obscure source of belly lox would have been more his line of country. Still, he made a couple of calls, including one to Mosha's Bread, a wholesale operation in Williamsburg, which has been turning out pumpernickel since the late nineteenth century (Mosha's Bread, it almost goes without saying, has no connection with Moishe's Bakery.) As I was about to leave Russ's, the boss of Mosha's, who turned out to be a woman named Cecile Erde Farkas, returned Mark's call. Mark introduced himself, and before he could explain my quest he began to sound like someone on the receiving end of a sales pitch. "To tell you the truth, I don't sell much bread," I heard him say, and then, "Here's what I could use—a good babka. I could sell the hell out of a good babka . . . plain, yeah, and chocolate."

• • •

There was a message on my answering machine that evening from Mark. He had reached a friend of his named Danny Scheinin, who ran Kossar's, a distinguished purveyor of bialys, for decades before selling out a year or two ago. "Danny says he thinks Tanenbaum got that bagel from somebody named Poznanski," Mark said, when I got back to him. "Also, he says it wasn't a real bagel."

"Not a real bagel!"

"I don't know exactly what he means," Mark said. "Talk to him."

When I reached Scheinin, I found out that what he'd meant was this: In the old days, there was a sharp split between bagel bakeries and bread bakeries. The bagel bakers had their own local, No. 338. They didn't bake bread and bread bakers didn't make bagels.

Originally, of course, bagels were made only with white flour. But some bread bakers who trafficked in pumpernickel would twist some bread dough into bagel shapes and bake them. By not going through the intermediate boiling that is part of the process of making an authentic bagel, they stayed out of another local's jurisdiction. Scheinin was confident that Abigail's bagel had been made that way for Tanenbaum's by a bread baker named Sam Poznanski, in Williamsburg, who died some years ago. As far as Scheinin knew, the bakery still existed, under the management of Poznanski's wife. He gave me the number. "Tell her Danny from the bialys said to call," he told me.

Mrs. Poznanski, I have to say, did not seem terribly engaged by my quest. The longest answer she gave was when I asked her if Poznanski's had quit making the pumpernickel bagel when her husband died, and she said, "No. Before." Still, she confirmed that the object of Abigail's adoration was from Poznanski's and that it was not boiled. This was hard news to take. It sounded perilously close to saying that the bagel we were searching for was just round bread. But what bread!

The bread/bagel split was confirmed by Herb Bostick, a business agent of Local 3 of the Bakery and Confectionery Workers International Union, which by now has absorbed No. 338 into a local that mixes bagel bakers and bread bakers and cake bakers together the way someone faced with baking a pie at the last minute might mix in bits of whatever kinds of flour happened to be in the cupboard. What Bostick said was in line with what I'd learned from Cecile Farkas, of Mosha's, with whom I'd arranged a meeting after her babka pitch to Mark. She'd told me that for years her late father offered pumpernickel bagels that were baked without being boiled first. "Then they weren't real bagels?" I'd said.

"If my daddy called them bagels they were bagels," Mrs. Farkas said.

I hadn't had to journey to the outer boroughs to see Cecile Farkas. By chance, she was doing a bread promotion at a store on Twenty-third Street. She turned out to be a chatty woman in her sixties, who told me that she had joined Mosha's only when her father became elderly; she'd been trained as an electrical engineer. That didn't surprise me. Mark Federman had been a lawyer. A family business is no respecter of degrees. Mrs. Farkas told me that her own daughter, having earned her master's in career counseling, plans to launch Mosha's West. Would Mosha's West be a few blocks closer to Manhattan than the original Mosha's? No. Her daughter lives in San Francisco. Cecile Farkas said that, with only a few hours' notice, Mosha's could duplicate the sort of bagel Abigail craves. "It would be my pleasure," she said.

"If that happens and Abigail moves back to New York, you would have done a mitzvah," I said. "It would be written next to your name in the Book of Life."

Mrs. Farkas shrugged off any thought of reward. "It would be my pleasure," she repeated. I had recognized her as a person of character the moment she'd told me that whatever her daddy said was a bagel was a bagel.

I tried to present the situation to Alice in an objective way: "I

suppose you think that if Mosha's really did succeed in dupli-
cating the bagel and I told Abigail that it was readily available in
the neighborhood and I didn't trouble her with the really quite
arcane information that it's not, technically speaking, a bagel, I
would be acting completely contrary to everything we tried to
teach her about honesty and integrity."

"Yes," Alice said.

"I thought you might."

She's right, of course. I know that. Lately, though, it has
occurred to me that there were areas I left unexplored in my conversation with Mrs. Poznanski. It's true that she expressed no
interest whatsoever in bagels, but what if I got Mark Federman
to agree to carry those little pumpernickel numbers—not instead
of Mrs. Farkas's babkas, I hasten to say, but in addition to Mrs.
Farkas's babkas. Would the Russ & Daughters account be
enough to propel Poznanski's back into the bagel business? This
is assuming, of course, that Sam Poznanski's recipe still exists.
All in all, it's a long shot. Still, I'm thinking of making a trip to
Williamsburg. What could it hurt?

My Dragon-Dancing Years

by Fae Myenne Ng

from *Gourmet*

For many second-generation immigrants, assimilation means resolutely turning your back on the ways of the old country. It took a very special friend to lead novelist Fae Myenne Ng back to the Chinese comfort food her mother cooked so well.

My first food rebellion was about rice. The day our elementary school started serving lunch, Veda Qwan and I stared at the mounds on our plates and wondered, Could we really be that ice-cream lucky? When Lily Chan tried to pick it up, her fingers disappeared in the white.

"No smell," I reported.

Veda held her braids back, leaned over her plate, and licked. "Nope. It's warm and it's salty!"

Then we all tried. First taste, it was strange-soft on the tongue, then smeary like paste, but grainy and tastier. Best part, no chewing. Easy, easy. Just swallow. We three nodded, a gulp race. Better than baby *congee!*

That night I told my mother I didn't want rice anymore. I wanted mashed potatoes.

The rebellion comes and goes but is always a full-size battle whenever I visit San Francisco. My mother has always believed food is the key to immortality, and she's fought hard to keep my yin and yang balanced. A body's beauty is about its emanation of energy, and she had me diagnosed before she'd even got me in the house. She'd brought a lively kid into the world, so who is this sallow dullard with the wet cough, the white palms, the limp hair?

Home. The whole trip is about rejuvenation. Mine. One time I find a live tortoise in the bathtub, its markings squares inside squares like a puzzle, and at night its clawing keeps me fitful. When I wake to that telltale aroma, I run screaming into the bathroom, "Where's that turtle?!"

"*Boo* for you." My mother hands me the brew; the layer of fat that rims the bowl is greenish. "*Boo* for breath."

Boo. A protecting word to mean treasured, Supreme Nurturance.

I don't ask what's in it. I don't want to know. I've learned that it's not really important what the twigs and grass and shells of bugs are in my soup, or how come that curly, crunchy stuff is elasticky, or why that brew gives me a buzz. Because my energy does improve. I do feel brighter. I breathe deeper, and I face the world with a lot more punch.

Moving to New York, I was the happiest immigrant. I ate irre-sponsibly and with joy. All yang food one week (crab), all yin (salads) all summer. Awake during yin, asleep during yang, I flipped everything inside out, and I looked it. Mom called it a *wuloong* lifestyle—a hand in everything, a foothold nowhere, the heart aflutter.

"You're dragon-dancing. Chasing the immortal pearl."

But in this chaos, I forged an immortal friendship with Moira Dryer, a young Scotch-Irish Canadian painter. She built stage sets and broke plates as an art assistant to Julian Schnabel. Her work studio was in Times Square. At her 1993 MoMA retrospective, several paintings depicted her daily walk through its peep-show, combat-circus craziness. I was writing, and bartended lunch and hostessed evenings at two un-Chinese uptown places as well as teaching English at Berlitz.

Moira and I knew what we wanted, so everything else was just stuff. After intense work periods, we shopped and giggled and did all the girl things. But, most fun, we ate well together.

Then one day she asked me to accompany her to Chinatown. She was shopping for a stage-set project—was it for Sting? But I was hopeless. I had no contacts, no negotiation skills, and so after we spent a few humiliating hours wandering around, being treated like tourists, she said, "How about some roast duck?"

I made a face. "So bad for you, so fatty."

But it was Moira who introduced me to Big Wong's. Walking in, she waved to the fattest of the front-line guys, the smiley one with the giant tweezers who was plucking the half-singed hairs off the duck butts. Quick away, her favorite waiter came with tea, barking hello, hello! and already knowing her order. When the duck and *congee* arrived, she showed me how to scrape the fatty layer off with a fork.

As she ladled a spoonful of *congee*, I told her I hadn't eaten it in ages; that I'd grown up on the baby *congee* my mother brewed in tiny clay pots. Moira laughed when I told her I had looked like a bird. My mother nicknamed me Mouth Always Open, said I ate as if just released from Famine China. I told Moira my mother's obsession was hunger because she'd spent her childhood hungry and running. First she'd run from the Invading Japanese and then from the Retreating Nationalists and then from Mao's Advancing Men. Good guy, bad guy. A game of tag, and everybody was it.

During one run, my mother had carried a half-cooked pot of rice into the mountains. Then, a good meal was a bowl of rice, and the best side dish was salt, wok-fired. She'd dip her chopsticks into the salt treasure before lifting her bowl to take her first big bite. Today she still prefers a nutty crunch to her rice.

"Your mother's still around?" Moira stared at me, surprised, "You've never talked about her before."

I looked up. She was right, it was true.

After Moira got ill, after it got bad and the repeat treatments grew treacherous, nourishment and comfort became the project, and often it was *congee* she wanted. So I got in good with the big brothers at Big Wong's. I'd call in my order. Twenty minutes from Brooklyn and I'd pull up to Mott Street, zap the window down, and Fatty Wong would slip that famous sun-yellow bag onto the front seat, filling the car with perfume and heat. On to Moira's apartment, the *congee* at perfect slurping temperature. We ate right out of the tubs, construction workers us.

"Here," she'd fly me a magazine. "Have a *Vogue* place mat."

When Moira wanted to try a medicinal tea, I knew I had to talk to Mom. And when I finally made the call home, Mom immediately offered to help. She contacted relations, who then called cousins, and I went to Chinatown with an introduction. How un-American, how un-independent, how I hated that clannish stuff, but now I knew Moira would get the best ingredients. With Mom's connection, I bought 30 packets, as much as I could carry, absolutely sure they were filled with magic. Its brewed pungency and raw, tree-twiggy breeziness seeped into everything.

Moira wanted to know more about the herbs, so I called home again. Mom kept trying to tell me how to make good, nutritious *congee*—about free-range, fresh-killed chickens, ginkgo nuts. "Tell me what the herbs mean! Tell me what she needs! What else?!"

But something happened. Mom was quiet in a way that made me stop. Behind the quiet, I heard a breath. And then my diaphragm bloomed and I felt my own breath reach deeper. My words came out softer. I was calling to my mother like when I was a child, afraid.

Answering, my mother's voice was firm but kind. She said two Chinese words. The first word meant peace, I didn't know the meaning of the next, so I asked.

"Hold. Embrace. Protect. Nurture. Soothe."

Comfort.

The first time I made *congee* for Moira, she asked about the herbal prescription. I could only repeat what Mom had said, *"Oon-wei."*

Moira was quiet. "That sounds like 'one way.'"

We laughed softly. When the *congee* was cooked, I took it out to her in her favorite green bowl.

Moira's last day, we all knew. Moira had a peaceful night, and I went home to walk my dog, Idaho. Strangely buoyed by exhaustion and fear and expectation. I wandered, walking from the Village toward the east past the apartment she shared with her husband on Eleventh Street, then down First Avenue. Then I was in Chinatown, then at Big Wong's

I heard my order repeated in one word: "Walking."

And I walked for Moira, revisiting all her places of meaning, where she married, where she had her first show, where she painted, I walked to my apartment. I barely greeted Idaho but went straight into the kitchen, laid out the food on the kitchen counter, foil tin next to plastic tub.

Then I ate. I ate to feed my departing friend.

I ate the duck with my fingers, bit into the dark, rich breast. I sucked the crispy joint on the wing, the aged soy and the drum. I spooned mouthful after mouthful of smooth *congee*. I remember the textures, crisp and moist, the warm swallow of *congee*. I ate with an urgency to feed the body, not out of hunger but for farewell, the ritual need of the living.

Assault and Battery

by Betty Fussell
from *My Kitchen Wars*

Late-bloomer Betty Fussell traces her evolution from accomplished home cook to acclaimed food writer in her wonderful memoir. Spanning some fifty years, it reveals a woman finding her voice as a writer amidst America's culinary coming-of-age. This opening chapter sets the scene—with a stove, of course, at center stage.

Come in, come in. I've just made coffee and it smells, as good coffee should, of bitter chocolate.

Don't mind the mess. It's always this way, because a kitchen is in the middle of things, in the middle of life, as I'm living it now, this moment, the detritus of the past heaped like a midden everywhere you look. That squat brown bean pot we got in 1949 for our first kitchen, in a Boston slum, when I didn't know beans about cooking. That tarnished copper bowl I bought at Dehillerin in Paris in 1960, used heavily for soufflés during my Julia decade, which I haven't used since for anything at all.

I like food because it's in the middle of the mess. I like thinking about what I ate yesterday, what I'll eat tonight, what we're eating now—this hot crumbly shortbread full of butter and toasted pecans. So delicious. So tangible, sensuous, real. I can hold it in my hand, in my mouth, on my tongue. I can turn it over in my mind. I can count on it. The next bite will bring the same intense pleasure the last bite did, and the same pleasure tomorrow, if there are any bites left.

Do you take milk, and would you like it frothed? This little glass jar has a plunger fitted with a wire-mesh screen, and when I pump it up and down, the hot milk thickens into a blanket of foam. It's the little things that count, and everything in my kitchen counts heavily. Look at this olive pitter that I use maybe twice a year, this shrimp deveiner which removes that telltale line of gut in a trice, this avocado skinner, ingeniously fiddle-shaped to allow me to separate soft flesh from shell in a single motion. When I try to explain to my grown children, to friends, to myself, why I still live a kitchen life, I begin with the naming of kitchen parts. Well-made implements, well chosen and well used, turn labor into art, routine into joy.

And yet the French got it right when they christened the kitchen arsenal the *batterie de cuisine*. Hunger, like lust in action, is savage, extreme, rude, cruel. To satisfy it is to do battle, deploying a full range of artillery—crushers, scrapers, beaters, roasters, gougers, grinders, to name but a few of the thousand and two implements that line my walls and cram my drawers—in the daily struggle to turn ingredients into edibles for devouring mouths. Life eats life, and if we are to live, others must die—just as if we are to love, we must die a little ourselves.

I've spent most of my life doing kitchen battle, feeding others and myself, torn between the desire to escape and the impulse to entrench myself further. When social revolutions hustled women out of the kitchen and into the boardroom, I seemed to be caught *in flagrante,* with a pot holder in my hand. I knew that the position of women like myself was of strategic importance in the war between the sexes. But if you could stand the heat, did you have to get out of the kitchen? For even as I chafed at kitchen confinement, cooking had begun its long conquest of me. Food had infiltrated my heart, seduced my brain, and ravished my senses. Peeling the layers of an onion, spooning out the marrow of a beef bone, laying bare the skeleton of a salmon were acts very like the act of sex, ecstatically fusing body and mind.

While cooking is a brutal business, in which knives cut, whisks whip, forks prick, mortars mash, and stoves burn, still it is our most civilized act. Within its cardinal points—pots, a fan, a sink, a stove—my kitchen encompasses earth, air, water, and fire. These are the elements of nature that cooking transforms to make the raw materials of food, and the murderous acts of cooking and eating it, human. Cooking connects every hearth fire to the sun and smokes out whatever gods there be—along with the ghosts of all our kitchens past, and all the people who have fed us with love and hate and fear and comfort, and whom we in turn have fed. A kitchen condenses the universe.

Food, far more than sex, is the great leveler. Just as every king, prophet, warrior, and saint has a mother, so every Napoleon, every Einstein, every Jesus has to eat. Eating is an in-body experience, a lowest common denominator, by nature funny, like the banana peel or the pie-in-the-face of slapstick. The subversive comedy of food is incremental. Little laughs add up to big ones, big enough to poke a hole in our delusions of starwars domination and bring us down to earth. The gut, like the bum, makes the whole world one.

That's why I write about food. It keeps me grounded in small pleasures that add up to big ones, that kill time by savoring it, in memory and anticipation. Food conjugates my past and future and keeps me centered in the present, in my body, my animal self. It keeps my gut and brain connected to each other as well as to the realities of the world outside, to all those other forms of being—animal, vegetable, mineral—of which I am a part. Food keeps me humble and reminds me that I'm as kin to a cabbage or a clam as to a Bengal tiger on the prowl.

That's why I decline the epic view from the battlements in favor of the view from my kitchen window, fogged by steam from the soup in the pot. When I chop onions and carrots, crush garlic, and hunt out meaty bones for my soup, I'm doing what I've done for decades and what women before me have done from the beginning of time, when they used stones instead of knives and ashes instead of pots. There's comfort in this, in the need, in the craft, in the communion of hands and of hungers. A wooden spoon links me to my grandmother in her apron and to the woman who taught Jacob to stir a mess of pottage. History can turn on a spoon, on a soup.

And so of arms and the woman I sing, while we drink our coffee, you and I. The singer is an "old stove," as they say in San Francisco of a woman who's done time at the burners. But the songs of an old stove, no matter how darkly they glitter, are gay.

acknowledgements

We gratefully acknowledge all those who gave permission for written material to appear in this book. We have made every effort to trace and contact copyright holders. If an error or omission is brought to our notice we will be pleased to remedy the situation in future editions of this book. For further information, please contact the publisher.

Excerpt from *The Cook and the Gardener* by Amanda Hesser. Copyright © 1999 by Amanda Hesser. Used by permission of W.W. Norton & Company. ❖ "The Smoky Trail to a Great Bacon" by R.W. Apple, Jr. Copyright © 2000 by The New York Times Company. Used by permission. ❖ "Corn in the U.S.A." by Warren Schultz. Copyright © 1999 by World Publications. Used by permission of *Saveur* magazine. Originally appeared in *Saveur*, September/October 1999. ❖ "Pasta Meets the Tomato" from *The Italian Country Table* by Lynne Rosetto Kasper. Text copyright © 1999 by Lynne Rosetto Kasper. Reprinted by permission of Scribner, a Division of Simon & Schuster. ❖ "It Takes a Village to Kill a Pig" by Jeffrey Steingarten. Copyright © 1999 by Jeffrey Steingarten. Used by permission of the author. Originally appeared in *Vogue* as "On the Spit," October 1999. ❖ "The Flavor of Autumn" by Lori Zimring De Mori. Copyright © 1999 by World Publications. Used by permission of *Saveur* magazine. Originally appeared in *Saveur*, September/October 1999. ❖ "Getting Sauced" by Michael Hood. Copyright © 1999 by Michael Hood. Used by permission of the author. Originally appeared in *Seattle Weekly*, Fall 1999. ❖ "Nothing Is Better than Butter" by Al Martinez. Copyright © 2000 by Al Martinez. Used by permission of the author. Originally appeared in *Bon Appétit*, January 2000. ❖
"Smell the Coffee" by Dara Moskowitz. Used by permission of

City Pages, Minnesota. Originally appeared in *City Pages*, October 27, 1999. ✤ "Food Court" by Nancy Harmon Jenkins. Used by permission of the author and *Food and Wine* magazine, August © 1999 American Express Publishing. All rights reserved. ✤ Excerpt from *The Primal Feast* by Susan Allport. Copyright © 2000 by Susan Allport. Reprinted by permission of Harmony Books, a division of Random House, Inc. ✤ Excerpt from *The Best Thing I Ever Tasted: The Secret of Food.* Copyright © 2000 by Sallie Tisdale. Used by permission of Riverhead Books, a division of Penguin Putnam. ✤ "One Knife, One Pot" by John Thorne. Copyright © 1999 by John Thorne. Used by permission of the author and The Robert Cornfield Literary Agency. Originally appeared in *Gourmet*, September 1999. ✤ "Bottom-Drawer Blues" by Kim Severson. Copyright © 1999 *The San Francisco Chronicle*. Reprinted with permission. Originally appeared in *The San Francisco Chronicle*, November 24, 1999. ✤ "Herbs at the Kitchen Door" from *Herbfarm Cookbook: A Guide to the Vivid Flavors of Fresh Herbs* by Jerry Traunfeld. Copyright © 2000 by Jerry Traunfeld. Reprinted by permission of Scribner, a Division of Simon & Schuster. ✤ "Eggs" from *Madhur Jaffrey's World Vegetarian* by Madhur Jaffrey. Copyright © 1999 by Madhur Jaffrey. Reprinted by permission of Clarkson Potter/Publishers, a division of Random House, Inc. ✤ Excerpt from *One Bite Won't Kill You* by Ann Hodgman. Copyright © 1999 by Ann Hodgman. Reprinted by permission of Houghton Mifflin Company. All rights reserved. ✤ "Vegetarian Turkey" from *Bread and Chocolate* by Fran Gage. Copyright © 1999 by Fran Gage. Used by permission of Sasquatch Books. ✤ "Dinner for 7: What Could Be Easier?" by William Grimes. Copyright © 2000 The New York Times Company. Used by permission. ✤ "The Breath of a Wok" from *The Wisdom of the Chinese Kitchen: Classic Family Recipes for Celebration and Healing* by Grace Young. Copyright © 1999 by Grace Young. Used by permission of Simon & Schuster. ✤ "The Cook, Her Son, and a Secret" by Maya Angelou. Copyright © 2000 by Maya Angelou. Reprinted by permission of The Helen Brann Agency, Inc. Originally appeared in *Gourmet*, October 1999. ✧ "Weekend Lunch" from *How to Eat: The Pleasures and Principles of Good Food* by Nigella Lawson. Copyright © 2000 by Nigella Lawson. Used by permission of John Wiley & Sons. ✧ "Bragging Rites" by Rick Bragg. Copyright © 1999 by Rick Bragg. Reprinted with permission from *Food & Wine*, November © 1999 American Express Publishing Corporation. All rights reserved. ✧ "The Chef Challenge" by Tom Sietsema. Copyright © 1999 by Tom Sietsema. Reprinted with permission of the *Washington Post*. Originally appeared in the *Washington Post*, November 10, 1999. ✧ "The Objects of Our Culinary Affections" by Greg Atkinson. Copyright © 2000 Seattle Times Company. Used with permission. Originally appeared in the *Seattle Times*, October 13, 2000. ✧ "A Day in the Life" from *Kitchen Confidential: Adventures in the Culinary Underbelly* by Anthony Bourdain. Copyright © 2000 Anthony Bourdain. Used by permission of the author. First published by Bloomsbury. ✧ "The Chef of the Future" by Phyllis C. Richman. Copyright © 2000 Phyllis C. Richman. Used by permission of the author. First appeared in *Gourmet*, October 1999. ✧ "Natural-Born Keller" by Michael Ruhlman. Copyright © 1999 by Michael Ruhlman. Reprinted by permission of Ellen Levine Literary Agency, Inc. First appeared in *Gourmet*, October 1999. ✧ "On Burgundian Tables" from *From My Château Kitchen* by Anne Willan. Copyright © 2000 by Anne Willan, Inc. Reprinted by permission of Clarkson Potter/Publishers, a division of Random House, Inc. ✧ "Jacques Pépin's Safari" by Kate Sekules. Used by permission of *Food & Wine*. Originally appeared in *Food & Wine*, November 1999. ✧ "Rice: From Ripe Lips to 'The Ultimate Act of Love in the Kitchen'" from *Ripe Enough?* by Cherry Ripe. Copyright © 1999 by Cherry Ripe. Used by permission of the author. ✧ "The Risotto Lesson" by Dorothy Kalins. Copyright © 1999 by World Publications. Used by permission of *Saveur* magazine. First appeared in *Saveur*, November 1999. ✧ "Should Chefs Write Cookbooks?" by Anne Mendelson. Copyright ©

1999 Anne Mendelson. Used by permission with the author. First appeared in *Gourmet*, October 1999. ❖ "Restaurant Baby" by Karen Stabiner. Copyright © 2000 by World Publications. Used by permission of *Saveur* magazine. First appeared in *Saveur*, March 2000. ❖ "...And $300 Fed a Crowd?" by Eric Asimov. Copyright © 2000 by The New York Times Company. Used by permission. ❖ "The Past on a Plate" by Jane and Michael Stern. Copyright © 2000 Jane and Michael Stern. Used by permission of the authors. First appeared in *Gourmet*, April 2000. ❖ "Hot on the Barbecue Trail" by Vince Staten. Copyright © 1999 Vince Staten. Used by permission of the author. First appeared in *Bon Appètit*, July 1999. ❖ "The Belly of Paris" by Megan Wetherall. Copyright © 2000 by World Publications. Used by permission of *Saveur* magazine. First appeared in *Saveur*, March 2000. ❖ "The Waiting Game" by Ruth Reichl. Copyright © 2000. Used by permission of *Gourmet* magazine, a division of Condé Nast Publications. First appeared in *Gourmet*, June 2000. ❖ "Spamming the Globe" by Jonathan Gold. Copyright © 1999 by Jonathan Gold. Used by permission of St.Martin's Press. Originally appeared in *L.A. Weekly,* October 29–November 4, 1999. ❖ "Recipes for Dummies" by Jim Quinn. Copyright © 1999 by Jim Quinn. Used by permission of the author. First appeared in *Philadelphia Magazine*, September 1999. ❖ "A Tale of Two Chowhounds" by Jim Leff. Copyright © 1999 by Jim Leff. Used by permission of the author. ❖ "The Reluctant Gourmet" by Mark Kurlansky. Copyright © 1999 by Mark Kurlansky. Used by permission of the author. First appeared in *Food & Wine*, October 1999. ❖ "Sundays with Ravioli" by Alex Witchel. Copyright © 2000 by The New York Times Company. Used by permission. ❖ "Indian Takeout" by Jhumpa Lahiri. Copyright © 2000 by Jhumpa Lahiri. Used by permission of the author. First appeared in *Food & Wine*, April 2000. ❖ "P.C. and Proud of It" by James Villas. Copyright © 1999 by James Villas. Reprinted by permission of the author. First appeared in *Gourmet*, November 1999. ❖ Excerpt from *The Chinese Kitchen* by Eileen Yin-Fei Lo. Copyright © 1999 by Eileen Yin-Fei Lo. Reprinted by permission of William Morrow & Company, a division of HarperCollins Publishers. ❖ "Why I Stopped Being a Vegetarian" by Laura Fraser. Copyright © 2000 by Laura Fraser. All rights reserved. First reprinted in Salon.com. ❖ "The Magic Bagel" by Calvin Trillin. Copyright © 2000 by Calvin Trillin. Originally appeared in *The New Yorker*. This usage granted by permission of Lescher & Lescher, Ltd. ❖ "My Dragon-Dancing Years" by Fae Myenne Ng. Copyright © 2000 by Fae Myenne Ng. Reprinted by permission of Donadio & Olson. First appeared in *Gourmet*, February 2000. ❖ "Assault and Battery" from *My Kitchen Wars* by Betty Fussell. Copyright © 1999 by Betty Fussell. Reprinted by permission of North Point Press, a division of Farrar, Straus & Giroux, LLC.

Alice Waters is the founder and proprietress of Chez Panisse Restaurant and Café and Café Fanny in Berkeley, California. Her several books include *Chez Panisse Café Cookbook*, *Fanny at Chez Panisse* and *Chez Panisse Vegetables*.

In addition to numerous other honors, Alice and Chez Panisse have, respectively, been awarded the Best Chef in America and Best Restaurant in America by the James Beard Foundation.

Alice is also actively involved in the development of an edible garden and kitchen classroom at Berkeley's Martin Luther King, Jr., Middle School. This project, known as the Edible Schoolyard, involves children directly in planting, gardening, harvesting, cooking, and eating and has been conceived as a pilot project that will serve as a model for schools across the country.

Alice is currently working on her next book, *Chez Panisse Fruits*.

Holly Hughes is a writer, the former executive editor of Fodor's Travel Publications and author of *New York City with Kids*.

Submissions for
Best Food Writing 2001

Submissions and nominations for *Best Food Writing 2001* should be forwarded no later than June 1, 2001 to *Best Food Writing 2001,* c/o Balliett & Fitzgerald Inc., 66 West Broadway, Suite 602, New York, NY 10007, or e-mailed to nate@balliett andfitzgerald.com.